The Internet of Things

Connected into the Digital Transformation

Opportunities and Risks of Connected Computer Systems for the Global Economy

At this point I would like to thank all those who have accompanied me in the context of this publication. In particular, I would like to thank **Friederike Weismann** and **Nenad Prelic**, who accompanied me with excellent professional and personal support. I would also like to thank **Katja Steinert, Andrea Schultheiß, Tina Heinz** and **Bianca Fuchs** for correcting some spelling or grammatical mistakes. Last but not least, a big thank you to my family and friends who have continuously improved this book through numerous suggestions.

Christian Werner

The author

Christian Werner

Dipl.-Wirtsch.-Inf. (FH)

http://xing.to/wernerchristian

http://linkedin.com/in/christian-werner

http://facebook.com/dasinternetderdinge

Translated from German to English by the Author.

Please excuse any translation errors.

Third edition, November 2019

Contact: mail@christianwerner.eu

Content

I. List of abbreviations

Abbreviation	Meaning
2FA	two-factor authentication
3D	Three dimensional
5G	fifth mobile generation
A2P	Application-to-Person
BDSG	Federal Data Protection Act
BI	Business Intelligence
BSI	Federal Office for Security in IT
CDO	Chief Digital Officer
CEO	Chief Executive Officer
CERN	Conseil Européen pour la Recherche Nucléaire
CoAP	Constrained Application Protocoll
CPS	Cyber Physical Systems
CRM	Customer Relationship Management
DIN	German industrial standard
DNA	Deoxyribonucleic Acid

EDGE	Enhanced Data Rates for GSM Evolution
EFI	Expert Commission Research and Innovation
ETSI	European Institute for Telecommunications Standards
FinTech	Financial Technology
GPRS	General Packet Radio Service
GPS	Global Positioning System
GSM	Global System for Mobile Communication
HSPA	High Speed Packet Access
HTML	Hyper Text Markup Language
HTTP	Hyper Text Transfer Protocoll
IaaS	Infrastructure as a Service
ICE	Inter City Express
IEEE	Institute of Electrical and Electronical Engineers
IETF	Internet Engineering Task Force
IIC	Industrial Internet Consortium
IIS	Institute for Integrated Circuits

IoT	Internet of Things
BI	Business Intelligence
IP	Internet Protocol
IPv4	Internet Protocol Version 4
IPv6	Internet Protocol Version 6
ISO	International Organization for Standardization
IT	Information Technology
ANN	Artificial Neural Networks
LiFi	Light Fidelity
LoRaWAN	Long Range Wide Area Network
LPWA	Low Power Wide Area
LTE	Long Term Evolution
M2M	Machine-to-Machine
MIT	Massachusetts Institute of Technology
MQTT	Message Queue Telemetry Transport
MWC	Mobile World Congress
NFC	Near Field Communication

NFV	Network Functions Virtualization
Ngena	Next Generation Enterprise Network Alliance
OCF	Open Connectivity Foundation
OIC	Open Interconnect Consortium
OTT	Over-the-Top
P2P	Person-to-Person
PaaS	Plattform as a Service
PIN	Personal identification number
QR	Quick Response
RCSe	Rich Communcation Suite enhanced
RFID	Radio-Frequency Identification
SaaS	Software as a Service
SDN	Software-Defined-Network
SIG	Special Interest Group
SIM	Subscriber Identity Module
SMS	Short Message Service
TAN	Transaction number
UMTS	Universal Mobile Telecommunications System

VPN	Virtual Private Network
W-LAN	Wireless Location Area Network
WiFi	Wireless Fidelity
WWAN	Wireless Wide Area Network
XaaS	Anything as a Service

1 Introduction

As an interested reader on the topic, you have probably read many times that there will be several billions of connected devices in the next years. Well, this figure varies between 50 to 100 billion connected devices until the end of 2030, depending on which consulting company you ask. The fact is, however, that there will be a hyper-connection of small devices. Every human being will own five to ten connected devices. This could be in the form of a smartphone, a wristwatch, headphones, an implanted blood glucose meter or an electronic contact lens or glasses. A figure from the year 2019 indicates that by the year 2025 up to 76 billion devices worldwide will be connected to the Internet.[1] This is almost five times more than in 2015. This all-encompassing networking of visible and invisible devices leads to a connection between the physical and the virtual world: the *Internet of Things*. This massive network of devices also increases the amount of data collected. Intelligent computing systems ensure that this mass data is converted into information, which is the basis of

---

[1] Vgl. Evans 2011, S. 3.; https://www.statista.com/statistics/471264/iot-number-of-connected-devices-worldwide/

knowledge. And knowledge is of enormous value especially for the optimization of business processes. You can say that it is not necessarily the data, but the knowledge gained from it, which can be described as the new gold in the digital age.

The increasing penetration of digital technologies in business and society is referred to as digital transformation. It forces companies in all industries to realign their business models. However, the focus here is not only on adapting to these new events, but also on the maximum benefit that can be derived from these innovations.[2] In order to remain competitive in the digital age, companies must respond to market changes in real time. Once global companies such as *Nokia, Kodak, Blackberry* or entire industries such as the music industry or the taxi industry have recognized this too late. These traditional companies and industries, some of which are well over 100 years old, have been driven out of the market by disruptive and digital business models within a very short time or have suffered very large financial losses.

---

[2] Vgl. Cole, Digitale Transformation: Warum die deutsche Wirtschaft gerade die digitale Zukunft verschläft und was jetzt getan werden muss! 2015, S. 35.

Objects from the real world such as credit cards, money, tickets or keys are increasingly dematerialized and replaced by software.

Intelligent and globally connected machines are not only taking over work steps in the manufacturing industry, but increasingly also tasks with particularly high cognitive requirements. This has a massive impact on value creation in companies and on large sections of society.

Technologies that were called fiction just a few years ago are becoming reality. It is already possible today to draw conclusions about future crimes or imminent machine failures by evaluating mass data. With the help of this mass data, intelligent computer systems are in a position to provide precise medical therapy recommendations or to carry out an extensive analysis of existing and potential customers. However, the comprehensive collection of data also entails risks and raises questions. To whom does this often personal data belong? How is it used and does the collection affect informational self-determination?

1.1 Objective of this book

The objective of this book is to examine the technical, economic and social aspects of digital transformation and to highlight the opportunities and risks associated with it. The impact of digitization on industry, the labour market, data protection aspects and current and future business models will be presented. In particular, the hypothesis that telecommunications providers will not be able to develop their own innovative business models.

Accordingly, the following questions will be addressed:

- How does the *Internet of Things* work?
- What effects does the digital transformation have on companies, business models and the labour market?
- What role does data protection play in the processing of mass data?
- Which economic potentials and perspectives result from these results for European telecommunication providers?

4

1.2 Chapter Description and Procedure

The present publication aims at a deductive approach based on a comprehensive literature work. In a meta-analysis, a large number of studies and reference books on the same topic are evaluated in a result-oriented manner. However, care should be taken to ensure that a few of these studies were prepared by business consultants and system manufacturers who themselves generate profit from the digital transformation. An intensive exchange with experts also took place in the run-up to the study.

After in the first chapter the objective, the procedure and the classification into the scientific context takes place, in the second chapter first the technical bases of the *Internet of Things* are explained, in order to equip the reader with a basic knowledge to the functionalities of the techniques involved. Current and future data transmission technologies and communication protocols will be discussed. Finally, the importance of the standardization of such technologies, which consortia participate in a common world standard and which problems arise will be described.

The third chapter introduces the reader to the importance of mass data. Building on this, the possibilities and risks arising from cognitive computing systems and data cloud technologies are explained. The last part describes the necessity and importance of high information quality.

The fourth chapter begins with an introduction to the so-called privacy paradox to inform the reader about the paradoxical handling of personal data. Building on this, the reader is made aware of the unavoidability of maximum information security on the *Internet of Things* and in public and hybrid data clouds. In addition, the business and life-threatening effects of inadequately protected cyberphysical systems are explained. Finally, a legal evaluation of the handling of the data collected by cyberphysical systems is carried out.

The fifth chapter deals intensively with the economic potential of globally connected and fully automated industrial plants and describes the role Germany's small and medium-sized enterprises play in the digitization of industrial processes.

The sixth chapter presents business models resulting from the technologies described. A distinction is made between disruptive and innovative models. Numerous practical examples are used to illustrate the economic and socio-political potentials and dangers that arise when dealing with hyper-connected or virtualised technologies.

Chapter Seven explains the impact of the Digital Revolution on the world of work. The connection between the construction of the Berlin Wall and the invention of the steam engine serves as an illustration. On the basis of this comparison, conclusions are drawn regarding the consequences of the fourth industrial revolution on today's society. The study is used to make study-based forecasts for the next five to 20 years.

The eighth chapter is about the hypothesis that European telecommunications providers will in future act exclusively as network providers for so-called data-driven over-the-top services and will not be able to earn money with their own innovative business models. The focus is on innovative business models that result from the digital transformation and have the potential to transform telecommunications providers into full-service providers for IT and communications services.

The ninth chapter summarizes the results.

1.3 Definition and Demarcation

This book describes the impact of digitisation on existing business models and on large parts of the international economy. The reader is then able to deduce these effects on his own company. Explicitly no detailed economic statements are made about all existing business forms or geographical economic areas. There is no further in-depth presentation of the technical material, as it does not lead to the desired results. Furthermore, a description and evaluation of technologies that lie far in the future, such as artificial super intelligence and the resulting topics such as trans- and posthumanism, will not be given. These would not provide any added value when working on the objective. There is no binding legal advice. The comments on data protection and information law merely serve to clarify the questions and complexity for legal framework conditions. This paper mainly deals with publications and technical developments until mid 2019.

2 Technical basics

2.1 The Internet of Things

The idea of the *Internet of Things* was first described by the US-American computer scientist MARC WEISER.[3] In his early 1990s published article called *"The Computer for the 21st Century"*[4] he describes his vision of so-called "ubiquitous computing". Accordingly, visible computers will disappear as individual devices and be replaced by "intelligent objects". These objects ("things") are intended to support people imperceptibly without distracting them or even attracting attention.[5] The term *Internet of Things* is derived from this vision. It characterizes the combination of numerous technologies from different areas into a complete system.[6]

> *„The most profound technologies are those that disappear.*
> *They weave themselves into the fabric of everyday life until*
> *they are indistinguishable from it. "*[7]
>
> — MARC WEISER

---

[3] Vgl. Kern 2015.
[4] Vgl. Weiser 1991.
[5] Vgl. Kern 2015.
[6] Vgl. Abicht und Spöttl 2012, S. 28 f.
[7] Vgl. Keil-Slawik und Kerres 2005, S. 316

The rapid development of communication technologies in recent years, such as smartphones, the ubiquitous Internet or the miniaturization of powerful computer systems, are major steps towards realizing WEISER's vision.

The terms machine-to-machine communication (M2M) and *Internet of Things* are often used synonymously. Both terms are subject to different histories. The term M2M stands for the automated exchange of information between two machines. The information is exchanged over the Internet either by cable or increasingly with the help of mobile radio technology.[8] This is a primarily closed system, as no other machines participate in the exchange of information.[9] One scenario in this context is the remote monitoring or remote maintenance of machines and equipment, such as vending machines, which automatically inform a central computer when they have to be refilled.[10]

2.2 *Mechatronic Systems*

In order for the computer systems participating in the *Internet of Things* to be able to exchange data with

---

[8] Vgl. Eppinger, Hölzle und Kamprath 2015, S. 487.

[9] Vgl. Research 2014, S. 3.

[10] Vgl. Mattern und Floerkemeier 2010, S. 6.

each other, standardized interfaces and technologies for interaction with the environment and for unambiguous identification are necessary. Sensors, actuators and tags form the digital interface between the physical and virtual world.[11]

If all three technologies are combined with a microcontroller in one module, this is referred to as a mechatronic system. In this system, the sensor measures the environmental variables (e.g. temperature, pressure, level), forwards them to the microcontroller for decision making on the basis of control algorithms and then sends the corresponding command to the actuator.[12] This can be, for example, a valve that should open or close automatically at a certain temperature. An acoustic signal could also be triggered when a set threshold value is exceeded.

In order to gain a better understanding of the relevance of the *Internet of Things* and of the complexity of the individual technologies, the following section describes how they work..

---

[11] Vgl. Höller, et al. 1. Auflage (2014), S. 23.
[12] Vgl. Bishop 2008, S. 17-1.

2.2.1 Sensors

Sensors (lat. sentire: to feel or sense) enable computer systems to perceive different environmental parameters from the physical world, such as temperature, pressure or brightness. The recorded data is then made available to a microcontroller for evaluation and control purposes and forms an elementary component of the *Internet of Things*.[13]

Examples of sensors are microphones, seismometers, barometers, humidity sensors, smoke detectors, gas sensors, thermometers, gyro stabilizers or motion detectors.

Due to the high mobility of sensors in the *Internet of Things*, the special challenge is to get by with as little energy as possible. The aim is to be able to operate sensors with just one battery for several years and read them wirelessly. Since the data in most sensor networks does not have to be read continuously, power consumption is low by nature.

Examples of this are temperature sensors or electricity meters, which only have to transmit one measured value per minute or per billing cycle. The power supply is more problematic. It puts

---

[13] Vgl. Krauße und Konrad 2014, S. 31 f.

manufacturers under great pressure to innovate. A particularly interesting option is so-called energy harvesting, i.e. harvesting energy from external sources such as temperature, vibration, light or air flow. Philips already offers a wireless light switch that is operated entirely without a battery and only by the kinetic energy of the mechanical keystroke. With Energy Harvesting, the running times of sensors are no longer limited to the battery, but to the durability of the material used, the mechanics or possibly the planned obsolescence.[14].

2.2.2 Tags

Tags offer the possibility of labelling things in order to identify them unambiguously and to recognize them mechanically and automatically. There are tags that are optically evaluated, such as bar codes or quick response codes. In addition, there are also tags that can be read and written to without visual contact, such as Radio Frequency Identification (RFID) or Near Field Communication (NFC).

---

[14] Vgl. Süddeutsche Zeitung 2013. Mitte Februar forderte das Umweltbundesamt eine Kennzeichnungspflicht für die voraussichtliche Lebensdauer von elektronischen Geräten (Vgl. Umweltbundesamt 2016).

The coding of the data contained in the barcode results exclusively from the sequence of white and black bars. This is a binary code that is read by optical reading devices such as barcode scanners or cameras and then processed electronically..[15]

RFID-Tags:

The technology better suited to the *Internet of Things* has its origins in military technology: Radio-Frequency Identification (RFID). These tags allow contactless identification without visual contact and are therefore playing an increasingly important role in the networking of machines. The technology was used for the first time in the Second World War. Aircraft and tanks were equipped with RFID tags to distinguish them from enemy units.[16]

The changeover from wired to wireless sensor networks that communicate with each other holds a high savings potential. The elimination of cabling not only reduces installation and maintenance costs, but also errors during installation. In addition, wirelessly communicating sensors and tags can also be mounted in places where no cables can otherwise be laid due to

---

[15] Vgl. Lechner 2008, S. 9.
[16] Vgl. Bundesamt für Sicherheit in der Informationstechnik 2005.

the structure of the building or inaccessibility.[17] Unlike the barcode or QR code, the data is not captured by optical readers, but by inductive coupling or electromagnetic waves..[18] Another advantage of RFID is that the tags are also used for reading and can be (re)written to with comparatively little effort. This capability enables the data of the tag to be written, changed and rewritten at any time and without visual contact. The data of a bar code or QR code, on the other hand, is irreversibly fixed by printing. Compared to a barcode, RFID tags have over 600 times more storage capacity.[19] RFID tags are considered a potential successor to bar codes due to their reprogramming capability and higher storage density.[20]

It can be said that the barcode is superior only in terms of acquisition costs, which is why many entrepreneurs are still waiting for the changeover. The cost of a barcode strip is approximately one cent. An RFID tag currently costs between 10 and 50 cents. This does not make installation on food packaging, for example, economical enough at present.[21] The use

---

[17] Vgl. Andelfinger und Hänisch 2015, S. 17 f.
[18] Vgl. Günther und Hompel 2010, S. 114.
[19] Vgl. Klimonczyk und Sebastian 2010, S. 29 f.. Bis zu 64 Kilobyte.
[20] Vgl. Klimonczyk und Sebastian 2010, S. 30.

of less expensive materials and mass production processes is expected to lead to a sharp drop in prices in the coming years.[22]

QR-Codes:

QR-Codes[23] are much more complex than the bar codes described above, but have elementary advantages. This code, which is arranged in a square matrix, requires only a tenth of the physical size for the same amount of stored information. Due to its structure, it has an error tolerance of up to 30 percent, which reduces the error frequency during reading and increases the processing speed.[24]

NFC:

Near Field Communication (NFC) is a short-range coupling method based on RFID technology.[25] While RFID tags can be read from a distance of up to five meters,[26] communication between NFC tags is limited to a distance of a few centimeters.[27] The special

---

[21] Vgl. Ebd., S. 31.
[22] Vgl. Bundesamt für Sicherheit und Informationstechnik 2005, S. 78.
[23] QR stands for Quick Response
[24] Ebd.
[25] Vgl. Langer und Roland 2010, S. 6 f.
[26] Vgl. Klimonczyk und Sebastian 2010, S. 30.
[27] Vgl. Fleisch und Mattern 2005, S. 49.

feature here is the separation into reader and transponder.[28]. While RFID technology always has one energized active and one de-energized passive component, an NFC device integrates both functions. This means that an NFC device can both emulate a contactless smart card and power other NFC devices. The ability of communication between two active devices is called active-active communication.[29] In contrast, RFID technology is only capable of active-passive communication, i.e. only sending information stored statically on the chip.

Due to the advancing miniaturization of communication technology, NFC tags are small enough to be attached to credit cards, identity cards or mobile phones.[30] Communication through physical proximity thus enables a new communication paradigm, as the exchange of data between devices seems to be effortless and intuitive for the end user. The short distance of only a few centimeters required for communication creates an important security feature.[31] For this reason, near-field communication

---

[28] Transponder is a suitcase word from the terms transmitter and responder. It accepts incoming signals and answers them or forwards them.

[29] Vgl. auch Peer-to-Peer (engl.) genannt; Vgl. Krauße und Konrad 2014, S. 118.

[30] Vgl. Kröll und Schnauber 1997, S. 62.

technology is particularly suitable for contactless payment functions with mobile phones or credit cards equipped with NFC tags: so-called mobile payment. This is discussed in more detail in Chapter 8.1.2.

Actuators

The actuators are also mentioned for completeness.[32] Actuators are mechatronic components[33] hat convert incoming electrical signals into energy or power [34],[35]. This enables actuators to actively influence their environment, such as closing or opening a valve. These transducers form the counterpart to the sensors described above.[36] They are also called the muscles of technology because they are responsible for the movement of technology.[37]

---

[31] Vgl. Fleisch und Mattern 2005, S. 50.
[32] In der Literatur werden Aktoren auch Aktuator oder Actuator (engl.) genannt.
[33] Vgl. Bishop 2008, S. 17-1.
[34] Vgl. Z. B. Licht, Bewegung oder Druck.
[35] Vgl. Janocha 2013, S. 1.
[36] Vgl. Krauße und Konrad 2014, S. 31 f.
[37] Vgl. Greiner, et al. 2011, S. 58; Bishop 2008, S. 17-1.

JANOCHA distinguishes in his work *„Unkonventionelle Aktoren: Eine Einführung"* between eleven types of actuators[38]. These include piezoelectric actuators (e.g. diesel injection in common rail systems) or actuators with electroactive polymers that change shape when voltage is applied. These are used, for example, in peristaltic pumps for pumping fluid in the human body.[39]

2.3 Data transmission

In order to connect as many devices as possible to the *Internet of Things*, a multitude of communication technologies are required. Already today there is a large variety of different technologies that are used. In order to realize the vision of a global network, the bridging of the last meters with modern radio technologies is of great importance.[40]

In the following, the advantages and disadvantages of data transmission technologies that are already established but also newer and specially developed for the *Internet of Things* will be briefly dealt with.

---

[38] Vgl. Janocha 2013, S. V.
[39] Vgl. Schlaak, Lotz und Matysek 2006.
[40] Vgl. Fleisch und Mattern 2005, S. 48.

2.3.1 Wireless Location Area Network

The Wireless Location Area Network (W-LAN or WiFi) is one of the best-known wireless data transmission technologies and is an indispensable part of our lives today. In 2013, more W-LAN-enabled devices were counted than there are people on earth. While approximately two billion units were sold in 2014, the number is expected to increase to more than 20 billion W-LAN-enabled devices by 2017 according to the forecast of the Association of the German Internet Industry.[41]

The W-LAN data transmission method, referred to as wireless local area network, is based on the IEEE 802.11 standard. IEEE is the abbreviation for the Institute of Electrical and Electronic Engineers.[42] Further details on the IEEE are described in chapter 2.5.

The big advantage of W-LAN is the high data throughput rate. This allows large data packets to be transmitted comparatively quickly. The IEEE-802.11g standard, which is currently most commonly used for private purposes, enables throughput rates of

---

[41] Vgl. Landefeld 2014, S. 2.
[42] Vgl. Spektrum Akademischer Verlag, Heidelberg 1998.

up to 54 megabits per second - equivalent to the transmission of over 200 high-resolution digital photos per minute..[43] In the standard IEEE-802.11ad, which launched end of 2016, up to seven gigabits per second should be possible. This corresponds to almost 25,000 digital photos per minute.[44]

A major disadvantage is the high transmission power and the energy-hungry modulation processes. However, these are prerequisites for high transfer rates in the W-LAN.[45] Current W-LAN standards are therefore not energy-saving enough to be used, for example, in sensor networks. Parts of these networks are only equipped with a single battery, which should work for several years. In addition, sensor networks rarely require high data throughput rates. Very small data packets of only a few bytes are sufficient to trigger an actuator or transmit meter readings.

Another disadvantage is the interference frequency. Since other radio technologies are also used at home and in industry, there is a danger that they will

---

[43] 54 megabits per second corresponds to 6.75 megabytes per second or 405 megabytes per minute. Assuming that a digital photo taken with an ordinary smartphone requires approx. 2 megabytes of storage space, this results in a total of about 202 photos per minute.

[44] Vgl. Yu 2013.

[45] Vgl. Belding-Royer, Agha und Pujolle 2005, S. 5.

interfere with each other. For example, current Bluetooth devices use the 2.4 gigahertz frequency band, which is also used by older W-LAN standards.

The advantages and disadvantages presented justify the statement that current W-LAN standards are particularly suitable for broadband application scenarios in which structural measures for cable laying are difficult or even impossible. The two biggest weaknesses are the high susceptibility to interference from external devices using the same frequency band and the comparatively high power consumption.

A special feature is the 802.11ah standard announced by the Wi-Fi Alliance in January 2016.[46] This was especially designed for applications in the Internet of Things. The standard, also known as Wifi HaLow, operates at a particularly low frequency of only 900 megahertz. This is intended to double the supply radius, work much more robustly and at the same time reduce power consumption. In addition, the integration and configuration of devices is to be made much easier and safer.[47] Data transfer rates are not

---

[46] Die Wi-Fi Alliance ist eine seit 1999 existierende Organisation, die Produkte verschiedener Hersteller auf Basis des IEEE 802.11-Standards zertifiziert um die Zusammenarbeit verschiedener Systeme und Techniken zu gewährleisten.

expected to be particularly high, which is not necessary for applications on the *Internet of Things* either.[48]. A major disadvantage of IEEE 802.11ah is that not all options of the standard have to be implemented. Possibly these are only those that are easy to implement. This would nip the potential for commercial success in the bud.

2.3.2 Light Fidelity

Light fidelity (Li-Fi) is a data transmission technology that does not correspond to the usual radio technology but is nevertheless very promising. This technology is an optical equivalent to W-LAN, which enables data rates of over ten gigabits per second.[49]. The carrier medium used is not radio waves, but light waves. The technology used is called Visible Light Communication (VLC) and was first demonstrated in 2003 by HARALD HAAS, a German computer science professor at the University of Edinburgh. The fact that data transmission is only possible with visual contact is both an opportunity and a risk. Attackers can only read if they have physical access to the light waves. This makes it impossible to connect devices

---

[47] Vgl. Wi-Fi Alliance 2016.

[48] Vgl. DeLisle 2015. Between 18 and 40 MBit/s are expected.

[49] Vgl. Kraus 2014.

through walls.[50] An application scenario is the connection of devices in a closed room, e.g. in an illuminated aircraft or living room.

2.3.3 Bluetooth

The Danish king Harald Blåtand (the English word for Blåtand is "Blue tooth") united hostile parts of Norway and Denmark in the 10th century. In the 1990s, the *Bluetooth Special Interest Group* (SIG) - named after him - had a similar goal: the unification of the computer- and communications industry.[51] Bluetooth provides a common and wireless interface that allows all devices such as desktop PCs, printers, mobile phones or headsets to communicate with each other wirelessly.[52] Even today, it is used to wirelessly connect external sensors, which, for example, monitor a person's bodily functions, to the wearer's mobile phone.[53] Bluetooth belongs to short-range radio technology, the so-called Wireless Personal Area Networks (WPANs).[54] The range is usually only a

---

[50] Vgl. Meusers 2015.

[51] Vgl. Bluetooth SIG, Inc o. J.

[52] Vgl. Sauter 2006, S. 297.

[53] Vgl. Parsad und Muñoz 2003, S. 207 f.

[54] Vgl. Parsad und Muñoz 2003, S. 20.

few metres, but can be up to 100 metres under optimum conditions.[55]

Due to technical reasons, current Bluetooth standards in version 3.x also harbour some risks for the *Internet of Things*. For example, they consume a relatively large amount of energy because they use a special frequency spread method, which leads to shorter battery life.[56] On the other hand there are complicated and relatively slow connections setups of up to 10 seconds.[57].

The standards specially designed for the *Internet of Things* from version 4.0 onwards should provide a remedy. The current Bluetooth Standard 4.2 was introduced in December 2014. It promises up to two and a half times higher data transfer rates than its predecessors, stricter security standards, faster connection times and a special low-energy-mode.[58] Bluetooth thus also qualifies as a radio standard in the *Internet of Things*. Not least because companies such as *Google* and *Apple* with their new navigation standards, the so-called beacons, are based on

---

[55] Vgl. Langer und Roland 2010, S. 226; Höller, et al. 1. Auflage (2014), S. 103.

[56] Vgl. Sauter 2006, S. 302.

[57] Ebd., S. 315.

[58] Vgl. Bluetooth SIG 2014.

Bluetooth technology.[59] [60] This should make it possible to offer navigation services even in closed rooms, to display personalised product information or to control the presence of students in a classroom.[61]

In August 2019 the vulnerability of Bluetooth was demonstrated at the security conference Usenix. The 20-year-old Bluetooth encryption technology was bypassed. This hack has become known under the name *Key Negotiation of Bluetooth* (KNOB) and allows a man-in-the-middle attack, which can execute code on any Bluetooth device. But even if the above described *Bluetooth Low Energy* Standard, which is used especially for devices in the *Internet of Things*, is not affected by KNOB, the vulnerability has also been successfully verified here. To sum it up: The Bluetooth security needs to be considered very seriously and security specifications should be followed to make Bluetooth devices more secure for the *Internet of Things*.[62]

---

[59] Beacons are small transmitting units. Google calls this technology Nearby, Apple calls it iBeacons.

[60] Vgl. Andelfinger und Hänisch 2015), S. 83 f.

[61] Vgl. Abram 2015.

[62] Vgl. HAKING – Practical Protection, VOL. 13, No. 6, Page 9 f.

2.3.4 ZigBee

At present, wireless sensor/actuator networks based on ZigBee are not yet widespread. Nevertheless, according to KRAUßE and KONRAD, ZigBee hides a high growth potential.[63] It is a communication standard whose specification is based on the IEEE 802.15.4 standard.[64] ZigBee also works in the short-distance range and offers the possibility to communicate several thousand devices at low power consumption in so-called meshed networks (Mesh-Network).[65] The transfer rates are relatively low. Depending on the channel selected, bandwidths between 20 kilobytes per second and 250 kilobytes per second can be achieved. This is sufficient for wireless sensor networks, since only a few bytes need to be transmitted in these networks after previously defined time intervals. In addition, the transmission time is very short due to the omission of unnecessary control information.

All in all, ZigBee is a serious protocol for the *Internet of Things* because of its very low power consumption, fast transmission time, low acquisition costs and low

---

[63] Vgl. Krauße und Konrad 2014, S. 2.
[64] Ebd, S. 5.
[65] Ebd, S. 32.

hardware requirements. These properties offer a wide variety of applications, such as medical and health data, building automation, warehouse management, early warning systems for natural disasters, merchandise management systems and toys.[66] [67]

Due to the announcement of Bluetooth 4.2 (IEEE-802.11ah) and its specifications, it remains to be seen which standard will prevail in the mass market in the future.[68] There are currently no well-founded forecasts for this. It was in November 2015 that it became known that ZigBee had a critical security gap in the encryption algorithm that could not be remedied by a firmware update.[69] This fact could weaken the growth potential for ZigBee.[70]

2.3.5 Mobile Radio (GSM, UMTS, LTE, 5G)

While the technologies described above such as W-LAN, LiFi, NFC, Bluetooth or ZigBee are exclusively suitable for short-distance operation from a few centimetres to several hundred metres, mobile radio networks offer the possibility of networking devices

---

[66] Z. B. Alarm systems, switches, temperature control, etc.

[67] Ebd, S. 6.

[68] Siehe vorhergehendes Kapitel, letzter Absatz.

[69] Vgl. Sokolov 2015.

[70] Vgl. Krauße und Konrad 2014, S. 2.

over very long distances. Mobile radio therefore belongs to the so-called Wireless Wide Area Networks (WWANs) and is the counterpart to the WPANs described in Chapter 2.3.3 or the WPANs described in Chapter 2.3.1.[71]. Mobile radio networks are characterised by a high degree of coverage and also have the ability of automatic connection handover.[72]. They currently represent the highest degree of mobility, as they enable the uninterrupted operation of Internet-bound devices over very long distances and do not require a separate local network connection.[73] [74] The A-network introduced in Germany in 1958 still had to be manually switched and was only capable of analogue voice communication. Some 34 years later, in 1992, the Global System for Mobile Communication (GSM) began operations in Germany.[75] Due to the digital transmission of information and the resulting high transmission quality, GSM became the worldwide standard in more than 200 countries.[76] Technological enhancements such as Global Packet Radio Service

---

[71] Vgl. Cisco Systems 2012.

[72] Vgl. Zarnekow, Wulf und Bornstaedt 2013, S. 98.

[73] Vgl. Eberspächer und Vögel 1997, S. 2.

[74] Vgl. Schnabel 2015.

[75] Vgl. Eberspächer und Vögel 1997., S. 5

[76] Vgl. Ebd., S. 5.

(GPRS) and Enhanced Data Rates for GSM Evolution (EDGE) enable data transmission rates of up to 14.4 kilobits per second (GPRS) to 230 kilobits per second (EDGE) in the GSM network, which is sufficient bandwidth for many current sensor networks on the *Internet of Things*.[77] The GSM network is still in operation today and, due to its worldwide availability and stability, still forms the basis for many machine-to-machine (M2M) applications.[78]

The exponentially increasing demand for more bandwidth for data transmission led to the development of the third generation of mobile communications: the Universal Mobile Telecommunications System (UMTS). Thanks to its expansion with High Speed Packet Access (HSPA), bandwidths of currently up to 42 megabits per second were now available.[79]

In 2011, the fourth generation of mobile phones was launched in Germany under the name Long-Term Evolution (LTE). This mobile network works completely packet-oriented on IP basis and was therefore initially only usable for data services. On 27

---

[77] Vgl. Ebd., S. 69.
[78] Vgl. Koeppen 2013.
[79] Vgl. Sauter 2006, S. 158.

May 2015, the Federal Network Agency additionally auctioned off the 700 megahertz band, which had previously been used for terrestrial television.[80] These frequency auctions set the course for the successful computerisation of industry and logistics as well as for the *Internet of Things*.[81] Thanks to the low frequencies, it is now also physically possible to allow high bandwidths to penetrate deeper into buildings and supply areas up to a radius of ten kilometers with just one base station. This is particularly relevant for sensor networks installed in cellars or sparsely populated regions..[82]

The main drivers for the future requirements of the next generation of mobile communications are the unbroken boom in smartphones and tablets, the operation of millions of SIM cards for M2M applications in logistics and industry, and the steadily increasing number of connected devices on the *Internet of Things*.[83] Future mobile phone generations must therefore not only be able to provide sufficient bandwidth for the exponentially increasing volume of

---

[80] Vgl. Bundesnetzagentur für Elektrizität, Gas, Telekommunikation, Post und Eisenbahnen 2015.

[81] Vgl. Weicksel, Kriegeskotte und Pentsi 2015.

[82] Vgl. Bundesnetzagentur für Elektrizität, Gas, Telekommunikation, Post und Eisenbahnen 2015.

[83] Vgl. Karcher 2015.

data, but also management mechanisms to cope with the predicted multiplication of SIM cards that have been booked in.

The following figure forecasts the extent to which the M2M data volume will change over the next years.

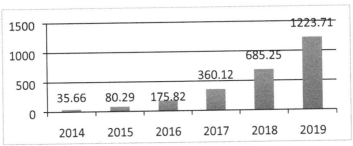

Figure 2 Forecast of worldwide mobile M2M traffic per petabyte per month..
Source: Cisco 2015, P. 36. (own revision)

Depending on the source, M2M traffic will grow to around 800 to 1000 petabytes per month in 2020. That's about 300 to 400 petabytes of growth per year.

In order to be able to process this enormous number of mobile radio connections, the first promising approaches are already available today. The fifth generation of mobile radio (5G) already promises data rates of guaranteed 50 megabits per second in the area up to one gigabit per second in the near range. And this with latency times of ten to less than one millisecond.[84] Whether such low latency times in the

5G network are actually feasible in applied practice due to the physical prerequisites can still be doubted at present.[85] In mid-February 2016, before the Mobile World Congress (MWC) in Barcelona, *Deutsche Telekom* and its partner Huawei presented the possibilities of increasing bandwidths in the 5G network to over 70 gigabits per second under laboratory conditions through the use of special antenna technology and frequency adjustments, while at the same time keeping latency times far below one millisecond. However, this technology is only intended as a local supplement to the normal 5G network.[86]

But not only bandwidth and latency are important prerequisites for the *Internet of Things*, but also efficient energy management. 5G promises up to ten times longer life for battery-powered devices.[87] The fact is that the 5G network represents one of the largest evolutionary steps in the development of mobile communications and is an important prerequisite for the establishment of conntected micro devices and computer systems. The European

---

[84] Vgl. Erfanian und Hattachi 2015, S. 26.

[85] Vgl. Warren und Dewar 2014., S. 12 f.

[86] Vgl. Kahle 2016.

[87] Vgl. Fallgren und Kusume 2015, S. 1.

Commission expects a market maturity of 5G for the European mass market in 2020.[88] In the US, the 5G network with up to 200 million interconnected devices is expected to be the most important and widely used mobile network by 2025. This corresponds to almost half of all interconnected devices in the US.

The software 17A announced on 6 January 2016 by the mobile phone supplier *Ericsson* could be described as bridge technology. With the help of this software, it should be possible to upgrade existing LTE / 4G network infrastructures for the *Internet of Things* on the basis of Low Power Wide Area (LPWA) technology. Once the software update has been installed in the base station, several million connections will be managed in a single mobile radio cell. In addition, a special power-saving function (LPWA) makes it possible to operate battery-powered devices for more than ten years.[89]

The fourth and fifth generations of the mobile network technology have outstanding features to ensure the operation of billions of devices that

---

[88] Vgl. Europäische Kommission 2014.
[89] Vgl. Ericsson Corporate Public & Media Relations 2016.

communicate and run on the Internet and batteries over long distances.

2.4 Communication Protocols

In addition to the classic communication protocols such as the Internet Protocol Version 4 (IPv4) and Version 6 (IPv6), the *Internet of Things* also requires specialized communication protocols. This is not only due to the special requirements these devices have to meet (small, cheap, energy-efficient), but also to the necessary interoperability. This means the cross-manufacturer exchange of information. Devices on the *Internet of Things* must also be able to work together with different components. A large number of specialized communication protocols already exist today. A small excerpt of promising protocols is described below.

2.4.1 IPv6 over low-power wireless area networks (6LoWPAN)

Since the Internet Protocol in versions 4 and 6 is not particularly suitable for administrative data due to its low effectiveness, the Internet Engineering Task Force (IETF) developed the 6LoWPAN protocol[90] [91]

---

[90] In technical jargon, administrative data is also called overhead.

Although this protocol is based on the IPv6 protocol, it offers a decisive advantage. The compression method used for the header data area makes it possible to reduce the usual 40 bytes in IPv6 to up to six bytes.[92] [93] [94]. This results in a much better relationship between the administrative data and the payload. As a result, less storage space and bandwidth is required using this protocol.[95]

2.4.2 Constrained Application Protocol (CoAP)

The Constrained Application Protocol is a web transmission protocol that is particularly used in wireless sensor networks with battery-powered devices.[96] CoAP was developed especially for M2M communication and for applications in the *Internet of Things*. It is based on the well-known hypertext transfer protocol (HTTP), but uses a binary header data area and is therefore particularly effective in handling bandwidth and memory requirements.

---

[91] Vgl. Mukhopadhyay 2014, S. 1 und S. 50.

[92] Vgl. Mukhopadhyay 2014, S. 56.

[93] In technical jargon, the header data area is also called "header".

[94] Vgl. Mukhopadhyay 2014, S. 57.

[95] Vgl. Minoli 2013, S. 126 ff.

[96] Ebd, S. 126.

2.4.3 Message Queue Telemetry Transport (MQTT)

Originally developed by IBM, the Message Queue Telemetry Transport protocol was developed specifically for telemetry data and is now one of the most important protocols on the *Internet of Things*. MQTT's history goes back to 1999, when *IBM* and *Arcom Control Systems* jointly developed a monitoring system for an oil pipeline.[97] Due to its lightweight design, this message protocol is particularly suitable for use in low-resource devices such as sensors, actuators or embedded systems, but also for use in fully developed computer systems.[98]

2.5 Efforts towards standardisation

The great added value of the *Internet of Things* is based on the joint exchange of information between different systems. Common standards therefore form the basis for communication between devices from different manufacturers. These so-called communication standards thus represent a common language, on the basis of which an intelligent connection of sensors and nodes to the Internet is possible.

---

[97] Vgl. Götz 2014.
[98] Vgl. OASIS 2013.

Many manufacturers currently use proprietary protocols that only allow communication between their own devices. Companies often work on individual solutions that look very different depending on the country and business model. The data generated in such individual solutions is stored in isolated silos and cannot be read or processed by systems from other manufacturers.[99] However, the basic idea of the *Internet of Things* is a global and manufacturer-independent exchange of information. In order to achieve a high level of interoperability, priority must therefore be given to uniform communication standards.[100] In the opinion of BULLINGER and HOMPEL, standardisation in some areas has been pushed aside for too long, which is why there is now an acute need to catch up.[101]

At present, it is particularly the German and European mechanical engineering companies and automation technology providers who create, promote and benefit from proprietary ecosystems due to their dominant market position.[102] Closed ecosystems are risky not

---

[99] Vgl. Bloching, et al. 2015, S. 14.

[100] Vgl. Kief, Roschiwal und Schwarz 2015, S. 679 und Schwarz 2015, S. 22 und Usländer, Pfrommer und Schleipen 2014.

[101] Vgl. Bullinger und Hompel 2007), S. 343.

[102] Vgl. Bloching, et al. 2015), S. 14.

only for the customer, but also for the companies themselves, not least because of the limited scope for adaptation. The extent to which a company can benefit from open standards is shown by the example of the American manufacturer of network devices, *Cisco Systems*. As early as the 1990s, the open Internet Protocol (IP) standard was used in this case, unlike most of its competitors. The result: Today, *Cisco Systems* is the world's leading manufacturer of network devices.[103] Competing telecommunications companies based on proprietary protocols disbanded or consolidated by competitors.[104]

A world standard for the *Internet of Things* has not yet been established. The reason for this is the very high complexity in industrial network infrastructures, from control systems to the sensors, actuators and robots described above. German and European engineers, companies and network operators, in particular, have proven with the development of the highly complex Global System for Mobile Communications (GSM) that they are very well able to constitute a world standard.[105]

---

[103] Vgl. Segal 1995.
[104] Vgl. Bloching, et al. 2015, S. 14.
[105] Vgl. Eberspächer und Vögel 1997, S. 5.

The Institute of Electrical and Electronics Engineerss (IEEE) has over 415,000 members from 150 countries worldwide working on standardization in the field of electrical engineering and information technology.[106] In addition, a large number of companies have joined together in different and non-profit consortia to promote the emergence of a common communication standard and to link the digital and real worlds together. Some of the most promising consortia will be presented below.

Founded in July 2014, the Open Interconnect Consortium (OIC) is a consortium of over 80 companies such as *Cisco, Samsung, Microsoft, General Electric and Intel*.[107] This organization develops solutions that, due to a mixture of open and proprietary industry specifications, are predominantly suitable for use in the corporate world.[108] At the end of February 2016, this consortium was renamed the Open Connectivity Foundation (OCF).[109] In the same month, the OCF showed at the Mobile World Congress in Barcelona how well German-American cooperation can work. Together with the European

---

[106] Vgl. Moesch 2012.
[107] Vgl. Open Interconnect Consortium 2015.
[108] Vgl. OIC 2015, Verge 2015.
[109] Vgl. Schindler 2016.

EEBus initiative, the partners presented a demonstrator that demonstrates the cross-industry interoperability of connected heating systems.[110]

The AllSeen Alliance is an alliance of well over 100 companies, including *Qualcomm, Microsoft, Philips, Sony* and *Canon*. Since December 2013, the focus of this organization has been on developing an open framework for object-oriented programming languages.[111] [112] A special focus is on the development of open communication standards for devices in private households. But not only the complete openness, but also the direct communication without the detour via external servers is considered groundbreaking.[113] Due to the fact that this open framework structure has been integrated into Windows 10, a development boost could be expected.[114]

The Industrial Internet Consortium (IIC) is an open group whose aim is to connect data, installations, organisations and companies in all industrial sectors. With the help of the IIC the way for a so-called Industrial Internet is to be cleared, which represents

---

[110] Vgl. Ludwig 2016.
[111] Die Rahmenstruktur (engl. Framework) heißt AllJoyn.
[112] Vgl. Isikdag 2015, S. 62.
[113] Vgl. Verge 2015.
[114] Vgl. Kaelin 2015.

the American counterpart to the German term "Industry 4.0". Its members include *AT&T, Cisco, General Electric, IBM, Intel* and *Siemens*.[115] In March 2016, the German-American cooperation with the German "Platform Industry 4.0" was announced in order to accelerate the development of a common standard. Further details on the "Platform Industry 4.0" are described in Chapter 5.[116]

The alliance founded by *Deutsche Telekom* is called *Qivicon* and is a merger of over 30 companies such as *BMW, Osram, EnBW, Sonos, Miele* and *Samsung*. The goal of this alliance is the development of manufacturer-independent solutions for connected building technology.[117]

All consortia are experiencing rapid membership growth, with some companies such as *Cisco Systems, Samsung* or *IBM* being members of several consortia as they often represent common interests. Paradoxically, all consortia seem to compete for the most "open" and "interoperable" standard. This carries the risk that there will be competing standards in the medium term and that the development of a

---

[115] Vgl. Heinze, Schleupner und Manzei 2016, S 138 f.
[116] Vgl. Reuters 2016.
[117] Vgl. Ohland 2013, S. 51 f.

unified world standard will be further delayed. The definition of this standard is currently difficult to predict due to the number of permanent foundations and consortia. True to the market rules, it is possible that it will not be the standard with the best characteristics that will prevail, but rather the consortium to which the most influential companies belong. For Europe's companies to play a role in the standardization debate, they must now bring their full weight to bear.[118] REINHARD CLEMENS, former Managing Director of T-Systems, also recognized this aptly when he said at the announcement of the new consortium [119]:

> *„We do not have to be afraid of standards from the US. We want Germany's voice to be heard on such an important issue. "*

> - REINHARD CLEMENS

---

[118] Vgl. Bloching, et al. 2015, S. 14.
[119] Vgl. DTAG 2015.

3 Processing of Information in Mass Data

„Big Data is not about the data!"

- GARY KING.[120]

3.1 Introduction

Two exabytes of information have been generated from the Earth's existence to the year 2000.[121] Today, this amount is produced in a single day. Every day, the sensors installed in machines generate several billion industrial measurement data. The shopping basket analysis of the American retail group *Walmart* generates more than 20 million transaction data every day. This corresponds to 24 terabytes per day. NASA's Earth Observing System produces 50 gigabytes of image data per second.[122] The front-runner in the generation of data is the multimedia level of the Internet: the World Wide Web (WWW). More than 1.35 petabytes of unstructured (images, videos) and structured data (texts, numbers) are

---

[120] Vgl. https://www.youtube.com/watch?v=mrb6tdVsVN0 [called 14.11.2019]

[121] Vgl. Becker und Knop 2015, S. 25.

[122] Vgl. Cleve 2014, S. 7.

generated *per minute* here.[123] For comparison: if these data are printed out on paper in A4 size, a 3.60 meter (11,8 feet) high wall could be built *every full hour* from Western to Eastern Europe (6,000 km or 3730 Miles).[124]

To understand the processing of mass data in the data cloud, it is necessary to make a distinction between data, information and knowledge. Data are values (e.g. characters or numbers) that are unrelated. If this data is put into context with the help of a table, for example, information is created. The initially meaningless character string "96515" can therefore be either a postal code or a PIN code. However, knowledge only arises when the human brain or an artificial neural network establishes relations between the information.[125] If the above character string is on an envelope, it is reasonable to assume that it must be a postal code. The knowledge is therefore only created by linking two data, which have a certain

---

[123] Vgl. Kroker 2014.

[124] Das Gewichtsäquivalent der Berliner Mauer in dichtbeschriebenen A4-Seiten beträgt 57 Terabyte (Vgl. Lewinski 2013, S. 5). Die Berliner Mauer war 3,60 Meter hoch und ca. 160 km lang.

[125] Der Vorteil bei der Entscheidungsfindung durch künstliche Intelligenz ist, dass diese nicht durch Emotionen oder charakteristischen Merkmalen geprägt ist. Der Nachteil ist die (noch) fehlende Kreativität von Maschinen. Die künstliche Intelligenz spielt auch eine große Rolle in der Entscheidungstheorie.

connection on the basis of experience. The quality of the knowledge depends on the correctness and completeness of the given information.[126] These processes are copied in approaches to artificial intelligence. The aim is not to collect as much data as possible, but to convert it into information and then into knowledge.

Knowledge is the basis of all decisions and today more than ever an essential success factor for companies, which must be treated just like raw materials, capital or labour from a business point of view. Growth and cost reduction potentials cannot be efficiently exploited solely through data or information, but only through knowledge. Knowledge is thus regarded as the driving force in the value creation and innovation process, while data is the underlying fuel of the digital economy.[127] [128] Chapter 6 examines the resulting business models in more detail.

The aim of this chapter is to generate an understanding of the concepts and the connection between data, information and knowledge and to

---

[126] Vgl. Knauer 2015, S. 2 f.

[127] Vgl. Warnecke, Bullinger und Westkämpfer 1996 und 2003, S. 362 f.

[128] Vgl. Abolhassan 2016.

bring the reader closer to the current state of development. The chapter ends with the realization that the business models and their successes that follow in the later chapters depend on the quality of the knowledge, on the correctness and completeness of the information given.

3.2 A defintion of Big Data

Since such amounts of data are hardly imaginable for the human mind, one generally speaks of Big Data. The origin as well as a generally valid definition of this term has not yet been clearly clarified.[129] It is also used inflationary in the media, politics and economy and has a very negative occupation not least since the secret service scandals uncovered by EDWARD SNOWDEN. [130] [131]

Another reason why the term Big Data is so difficult to grasp is the fact that it is not a singular technology, but the interaction of a number of innovations from different fields.[132]

---

[129] Vgl. Kalyvas und Overly 2015, S. 1.
[130] Vgl. Becker und Knop 2015, S. 139.
[131] Vgl. Reichert 2014, S. 117 f.
[132] Vgl. Bartel, et al. 2014, S. 12.

In order to define the term mass data more precisely, the following definition should be used:

> " It is always *Big Data* when a single computer is no longer able to process the available data in a reasonable time. "[133]

If huge amounts of data can no longer be processed or only insufficiently processed with classical databases or other data management tools, we are talking about mass data. This results in the great challenge of recording different data formats, update rhythms and data sources and converting them into a relevant data stream.[134] This challenge can be characterized by the following four dimensions: Mass, Diversity, Speed and Accuracy [135].

The dimension mass refers to very large amounts of data that are collected and analyzed in a company in order to improve decision-making.[136]

The dimension diversity refers to the different data formats and data sources. Especially with the explosive spread of social networks and sensors in the *Internet of Things*, data from a wide variety of

---

[133] Vgl. Holland 2014, S. 243.
[134] Vgl. Kreutzer und Land 2013, S. 81 f.
[135] Vgl. Schroeck, et al. 2012, S. 4.
[136] Ebd., S. 4.

sources is generated in countless formats.[137] A distinction must be made between structured, unstructured and semistructured data. [138] [139]

The velocity dimension describes the effect on the time period between the acquisition of the data and the point in time at which they can be accessed. Data must be processed in real time where possible (e.g. fraud detection).[140]

As mentioned at the beginning of this chapter, the quality of knowledge depends on the accuracy of the data collected. For this reason, that dimension refers to the reliability of information associated with a particular type of data.[141]

High data quality is the basis for handling mass data. Data of the highest quality is essential, especially for high-quality forecasts, since incorrect or even

[137] Vgl. Bartel, et al. 2014, S. 12.

[138] Unstructured data is data that cannot be stored in a database or data structure (e.g. photos), audio files, e-mails, Word documents, PowerPoint files, etc.). Up to 90% of the data in the coming years are unstructured (cf. Intel 2012). Structured data can easily be integrated into databases or tables can be structured and sorted (e.g. connection data).

[139] Vgl. Geisler 2014, S. 495.

[140] Vgl. Schroeck, et al. 2012, S. 4.

[141] Ebd., S. 5.

inaccurate data can create uncertainty and thus have a negative influence on decisions.[142]

Above all, technological and economic changes, which develop in a short period of time, accelerate the growth of these data volumes enormously. Not only the *Internet of Things*, which with its billions of sensors enables a continuous stream of data in real time, generates enormous amounts of data, but also the very widespread use of mobile phones and the massive use of social networks[143]. But also the possible reintroduction of the controversial data retention of the German Federal Government, which provides for the storage of extensive data from communication services of all citizens of Germany without any reason, will lead to massive data growth[144]. The same applies to the mass surveillance programs in other countries. During the existence of data retention in Germany in 2010, telecommunications providers had to store many terabytes of metadata within six months, such as location data or call logs.[145] It could be shown that only three months of location data from mobile phones are sufficient to predict,

---

[142] Vgl. Bachmann, Kemper und Gerzer 2014, S. 161.

[143] Vgl. King 2014, S. 36.

[144] Vgl. Knierim-Moser 2014, S. 167.

[145] Vgl. Boie 2010.

among other things, the location of a mobile phone user at any given time with a probability of 93 percent.[146]

The main generator of data is particularly the private use of Internet services.[147] The data generated as part of the *computerisation of production technology and logistics* will also be another important area of application for the processing of mass data.[148] And last but not least, the storage of mass data was favored by the sharp drop in the price of storage space. Today, storing information on paper is 10,000 times more expensive than storing it on hard drives.[149] In 2003, storing one gigabyte of data[150] on hard disks cost 1.25 Euros (1,50 USD). Only ten years later, the same amount cost less than five cents.[151] New technologies for storing mass data are already being developed. In February 2016, researchers at the University of Southampton announced that they could store over 360 terabytes of data on a coin-sized glass disk. The data was written layer by layer into the

---

[146] Vgl. Knierim-Moser 2014, S. 35.

[147] Vgl. Cisco Systems 2015, S. 5.

[148] Vgl. Härting 2014, S. 23.

[149] Vgl. Geisler 2014, S. 393.

[150] One Gigabyte corresponds to approx. 30,000 e-mails in text format or 100 pieces of music in MP3 format.

[151] Vgl. Brandt 2014.

glass using a femtolaser. The durability of the data carrier is several billion years.[152] This storage technology is particularly suitable for the digitization and conservation of libraries, national archives or museums.

3.3 Cognitive Computing Systems and Machine Learning

Data that is in a context of meaning is information that serves to prepare decisions.

According to analyst firm *Gartner*, in the near future machines will be intuitive enough to process human intentions and respond to instructions.[153] *Microsoft* founder Bill Gates also predicted in 2005 that in the future there will be sophisticated algorithms capable of automatically sorting huge amounts of data in order to identify meaningful connections and trends. In addition, software will be able to draw conclusions about human behavior through intensive interaction with people. These algorithms are able to learn which information is used by people and which is not used

---

[152] Vgl. University of Southampton 2016.
[153] Cole, Digitale Transformation: Warum die deutsche Wirtschaft gerade die digitale Zukunft verschläft und was jetzt getan werden muss! 2015, S. 37.

to make decisions.[154] The term *cognitive computing* is used here.

Today, almost 15 years later, it is possible to simulate some cognitive performances of humans in computers to support human thinking. Through intensive and complex interaction between humans and computers, so-called human-computer systems are created in which a computer system assumes the role of a virtual assistant. The machine learns from experience through continuous interaction with people. This process is called *machine learning*. In their paper "Data Mining" the authors JÜRGEN CLEVE and UWE LÄMMEL state that machine learning aims at an understanding of contexts and backgrounds. New knowledge is generated.[155] [156] [157] This represents a further step towards machine evolution.

Current cognitive systems learn primarily in two ways. In so-called supervised learning, thousands or millions of images of an object or living creature are given to the machine in turn for storage. The machine is now able to recognize the object or living being on the basis of its structure and special features and to

---

[154] Vgl. Gates 2005.
[155] Vgl. Cleve und Lämmel, Data Mining 2014, S. 13.
[156] Z. B. das das Erkennen von Mustern und Abhängigkeiten.
[157] Vgl. Cleve 2014, S. 15.

name it correctly.[158] *Google* used this method with its neural network called *DeepDream*. *DeepDream* is permanently fed with large amounts of images and thus trains to find objects, animals or people on photos with many motifs. The name derives from the ability of *DeepDream* to recognize patterns in previously unknown images. Like a person who finds familiar patterns in clouds in the sky, *DeepDream* sees what it already knows. The result often looks surreal to humans because the machine uses only those features that are essential to them and neglects other features that would be essential to human understanding.[159] Figure 3 illustrates this. On the left side there are two dogs of the breed Yorkshire Terrier.[160]. On the right side you can see the view of *DeepDream*. If you take a closer look you can see that DeepDream recognizes a fish, a chicken head and other animals in the photo, because it has already learned these animal forms.

---

[158] Vgl. Gershgorn 2016.

[159] Vgl. Hildebrand 2015.

[160] The dogs are called Susi and Juli and belong to the family of the author.

Figure 3 Googles *DeepDream* Generator.
Quelle: http://deepdreamgenerator.com

In 2014, Facebook announced that its *DeepFace* software would recognize 97.25 percent of human faces on images. For comparison: human test subjects had a recognition rate of 97.53 percent in the test.[161]

The second currently preferred applied methodology of machine learning is the use of decision tables with the characteristic values "Yes / No".[162] The answers are stored and evaluated in decision tables.[163] [164] What is essential, however, is not the decision table itself, but the auto-adaptation process that allows it to develop. In addition, the quality of such a yes/no test is the most important concept. Quality is based on the understanding of *information*. The American mathematician, after whose name the unit for the information content of a message was named, defines it in this way[165]:

---

[161] Vgl. Simonite 2014.
[162] Vgl. Schoenebeck 2015.
[163] Vgl. Schulte-Zurhausen 2014, S. 602.
[164] Vgl. Harrach 2014, S. 52.

„Information is the resolution of uncertainty."

- CLAUDE SHANNON

The information content of a message depends on the probability of occurrence of the message itself. The less likely the message is to occur, the higher its information content will be.[166] This means that the information content of a message corresponds to the number of yes/no questions asked that are required for reconstruction.[167] This is illustrated by a very simple traffic light example. Two questions are needed for the traffic light: Is it red? Answer: no. Is it green? Answer: no. The machine enters the question and answer in a decision table and comes to the conclusion: the traffic light must be yellow. As you can see, the information content at a traffic light is very small, since only a few colours are possible. Also because traffic lights often adhere to programmed rules ("green wave"), the colors are relatively predictable and not surprising.[168] The big advantage of learning with decision tables is that they are robust against noise.[169] Incorrect training data

[165] Vgl. Devasahayam 2013, S. 297.

[166] Vgl. Hundt 2015, S. 12.

[167] Vgl. Harrach 2014, S. 56.

[168] Vgl. Todesco o. J..

[169] Vgl. Als Rauschen wird nutzlose Information oder geringer Informationsgehalt bezeichnet (Vgl. Bisanz, 2011, S. 196).

only slightly interferes with the auto-adaptation process. The machine is also able to process incomplete decision tables, which make only approximately correct statements. This is the case when the procurement of information is too expensive or not possible.[170]

When both types of learning are combined, the result is that machines are perfectly capable of learning according to human patterns. Because we also observe, we draw conclusions and we store everything in our knowledge storage.[171]

3.4 Deep Learning

In 2015, *Google* proved the technology of deep learning by combining both types of learning with its neural network *DeepMind*. Here, the network was equipped with a video camera which *observed* old game classics such as Breakout or Pinball. *DeepMind* recognized the success strategy applied by people while playing and learned it. After a short time of watching *DeepMind* was able to break the highscore in all games and was far superior to its human competitors. On January 28, 2016, *Google* again

---

[170] Vgl. Harrach 2014, S. 58.
[171] Vgl. Gershgorn 2016.

demonstrated the capabilities of neural networks.[172] At five to zero, the self-learning network called *AlphaGo* beat the multiple European winner in the board game *Go*. Previously, *AlphaGo* was trained with 30 million *Go* moves until it could predict human moves with 57 percent probability. The special thing about *Go* is that it is many times more complex than chess and requires *intuition*. In games like chess, previous machines could only win by very quickly calculating the probability of all possible and logical moves. In the game *Go*, however, more moves are possible than there are atoms in the universe. This number is currently not calculable even for modern computing systems. Instead, *AlphaGo* is based on two synchronous neural networks, uses advanced algorithms from deep learning technology and uses the computing power of 1,920 parallel main processors and 280 graphics card processors[173]. These are managed via *Google's* data cloud platform.[174] *AlphaGo* was trained in advance, in which it had to play *Go* against itself for several months.

In mid-March 2016, the machine competed against 33-year-old *Go* World Champion LEE SEDOL. It

---

172 Vgl. Google AlphaGo 2016.
173 Vgl. Handelszeitung CH 2016.
174 Vgl. Google Official Blog 2016.

won in four out of five games.[175] This victory is regarded as a further milestone on the way to artificial intelligence.[176] It was the first time that a machine has completely defeated a human player in a *Go* game. According to the experts, this should not be the case for ten years at the earliest. [177]

Deep learning is a special form of machine learning. Here the relatively old technique of artificial neural networks (ANN) is used. This is a research object of neuroinformatics, the beginnings of which go back to WARREN MCCULLOCH and WALTER PITTS. In 1943, almost at the same time as the beginning of programmable computers, the two described a kind of neurological network. With its help it was possible to calculate practically every logical and arithmetic function. Only four years later they described the possibility of spacial pattern recognition. Artificial neural networks are based on biological models: the human brain.[178] Similar to the brain, these networks learn from experience by changing the simulated neuron connections to fit exactly. As early as the 1950s, the first artificial intelligence researchers used

---

[175] Vgl. Spiegel Online / cis 2016.
[176] Vgl. Wunderlich 2016.
[177] Vgl. Jimenez 2016.
[178] Vgl. Rauschner 2004

the ANN algorithm to develop the vision of a self-thinking computer.[179] However, there was a lack of computing power and digitalised mass data in particular in order to carry out actual deep learning, as is possible today. Today, sufficient computer resources and enormous amounts of data are available to successfully use deep learning in speech and image recognition.[180]

The opportunities and risks of this technology cannot yet be fully assessed, as its development is still in its infancy.

A great chance of cognitive computing systems is the high degree of automation of routine tasks that can be performed by machines. The high reliability and speed also open up high potential for time-critical applications, for example in the field of passenger transport or medicine.[181]

On the other hand, neural networks also have a weakness. It is the lack of transparency and the possibly limited acceptance of the results.[182] Neural networks are highly complex. It is often difficult or

---

[179] Vgl. Jones 2014
[180] Vgl. Petschar 2014
[181] Vgl. Süße und Rodner 2014
[182] Vgl. Kunze 2007, S. 313; Kammerer 1999, S. 47.

impossible to understand which data has been processed by the machine, how, in order to make a decision.[183] This poses major challenges for banks, among others. While *LGT Bank* has been using neural networks for price forecasts since 1986, *Deutsche Bank* rejected the use of neural networks due to the lack of transparency.[184] Further disadvantages are the necessity of lengthy learning patterns from mass data and the high demands on computing power and energy consumption.[185]

Another serious danger could be so-called *Deepfakes*. *Deepfake* is a blend where *Deep* is associated with Deep Learning technology. The term has been in use since 2017. This technology is based on artificial neural networks and can produce deceptively real-looking images or videos that are not real. The software analyses the transcripts of a video and can use them to change what a person says. It is capable of changing a person's mouth movements, exchanging or removing words in a sentence, or creating entirely new sentences in the same pitch of the person's voice in the video. This can lead to a massive distortion of

[183] Vgl. Tripathi 2015, S. 23.
[184] Vgl. Laucker 1996.
[185] Vgl. Zakharian, Ladewig-Riebler und Thoer 1998, S. 43.

our physiological perception or to misinformation of whole societies ("fake news").[186]

"Everything I have accepted up to now as being absolutely true and assured, I have learned from or through the senses. But I have sometimes found that these senses played me false, and it is prudent never to trust entirely those who have once deceived us."

RENE DESCARTES
(1596-1650)

3.5 Criteria for Machine Learning

The basis for machine learning and cognitive computing systems are the mass data described above. And just like these, cognitive systems are also characterized by four criteria: Adaptivity, interactivity, iterativity and contextuality.[187]

The *Adaptivity* criterion describes learning when information, goals or requirements change. The aim is to process data in almost real time and to resolve ambiguities.

---

[186] Vgl. Kaeser, 2019
[187] Vgl. Holtel 2015, S. 15.

Interactivity is about simple interaction with users so that they can comfortably formulate their needs. This also includes the ability to interact with other processors, devices and people.

Iterativity helps to define and specify a problem by asking questions or finding other sources if a problem description is ambiguous or incomplete. This also includes remembering information from previous interactions that is suitable for finding solutions.

The criterion *contextuality* includes drawing conclusions from various sources of information. This includes structured or unstructured data as well as data from sensors in the *Internet of Things* (e.g. visual gestures, voice commands).[188]

3.6 The need for Data Centers

Currently, only ten percent of the mass data collected is actually converted into knowledge and used.[189] The reason for this is that the evaluation of unstructured data requires enormous computing capacities. In order to process such data efficiently, cognitive computing systems require not only very powerful processors, but also fast and reliable data transmission

---

[188] Ebd.
[189] Vgl. IBM 2015.

networks and high-performance storage systems. These properties can be found in data centers.[190] If a customer only wants to use the services of such systems, it is not necessary to operate an own computer center. Services from remote data centers can be obtained via the Internet. This is called *cloud computing*.

3.7 Services Forms in Data Clouds

The experts agreed on three types of data cloud organisation: public, private and hybrid.

Public: If all IT resources and their operation are owned by an external service provider, this is referred to as a public data cloud. In principle, any number of companies or users can obtain services in this form. Highly standardized business processes, applications or IT infrastructures are made available here on a usage-dependent fee system. In this way, the costs for operation by the service provider can be divided among a large number of users. The user is thus in a position to obtain these services extremely cost-efficiently. The fact that the user of a public data cloud can never ensure at which physical location his data is currently stored is also associated with a high

---

[190] Vgl. Hintringer 2014, S. 31 ff.

risk with regard to data protection, data security and reliability.[191]

Private: In order to minimize the above-mentioned risks of the public data cloud, more and more companies are installing their own solutions. In doing so, the company's own IT environments are enriched with the features of cloud computing. The aim should be to make full use of features such as flexibility, resource allocation and cost savings through virtualisation and to operate all data and IT infrastructures in-house at the same time. Providers and users are located within their own organization. Access to the private data cloud is only possible via the intranet for employees, authorized business partners, customers and suppliers.[192] The risk of operating a private cloud is the higher costs associated with the plus in security and exclusivity. This form of service is particularly suitable for companies whose interest is to place particularly high value on the protection of personal data.

Hybrid: The hybrid cloud is a combination of the advantages of private and public data clouds. Although the company operates its own private data

---

[191] Vgl. Plass, et al. 2013), S. 39 f.
[192] Vgl. Plass, et al. 2013, S. 40.

cloud here, it also obtains services from the public data cloud. The particularly sensitive and business-critical data remain stored in the private part of the data cloud. If required and for non-personal data, the advantages of the dynamic and above all rapid expansion of IT resources from public data clouds can also be used. According to a study by the industry association *Bitkom*, hybrid clouds will increasingly be used in business practice in the future. The challenge in operating such hybrid technologies is to integrate one's own IT environment, the private cloud and the public cloud in terms of security and service.[193] By combining security from the private cloud and flexibility from the public cloud, the hybrid cloud is particularly suitable for medium-sized companies, as the cost effects of both technologies are exploited here. In a study published by *IBM* in February 2016, it was proven that the use of hybrid data clouds leads to a higher return on investment in nine out of ten companies.[194]

A study by the auditing firm *PricewaterhouseCoopers* has shown that experience with the various forms of service in companies has

---

[193] Ebd., S. 41 f.
[194] Vgl. Karpovich, et al. 2016, S. 4.

been very positive. These are in particular the high cost savings, the low upfront investments and the shorter time to market.[195]

According to a forecast by *Cisco*, the global data volume for data cloud technologies will more than quadruple by 2019. It is particularly noteworthy that devices from the *Internet of Things* will produce almost 50 times more data than data centers will process in 2019.[196]

The possibility of dynamic adaptation of IT infrastructures leads to a paradigm shift in the IT and software industry due to the tertiarisation of IT services.[197] The provision of computing capacity, storage space and software as a service via the Internet as a usage-based fee model opens up many opportunities, but also risks, for small and large companies. They can very quickly and dynamically expand or even completely outsource their own IT and thus react to changing market situations or customer wishes in the shortest possible time.[198] [199]

---

[195] Vgl. Vehlow, Resetko, et al. 2015, S. 28 ff.

[196] Ebd.

[197] Vgl. Kemper, Pedell und Schäfer 2012, S. 168; Bedner 2013, S. 27.

[198] Vgl. Keuper, et al. 2013), S. 103.

[199] Ebd., S. 37 und S. 50; Vehlow und Golkowsky 2013.

This helps entrepreneurs to introduce new business models or to optimize business processes. [200] [201]

Data clouds are a good basis for digitization. Due to their performance, they are able to collect, store and process the constantly growing mass data from sensors.[202] Only the reservations of some companies about the high complexity and the potential data protection risks are currently hampering growth.

3.8 The Need for Information Quality

In 2013, a street light in New Zealand received a reminder from the local electricity supplier to pay the outstanding bill. It turned out that the cause was a number shifter in the address.[203] The public television contribution service (formerly GEZ) sends requests for payment to pets[204]. The assassin from the Boston Marathon in April 2013 was able to flee to Russia unnoticed because of a spelling mistake of his name..[205] The Rhine is suddenly 90 kilometers shorter than assumed for 50 years. The customer of a French telecommunications company receives a telephone

---

[200] Ebd., S. 423 ff.
[201] Ebd., S. 247.
[202] Vgl. Buxmann 2016.
[203] Vgl. panorama 2013.
[204] Vgl. focusonline 2015.
[205] Vgl. TagesAnzeiger CH 2013.

bill for 63.3 million Euros [206] and in the Black Forest a low-income woman should pay back an incredible 4.6 trillion euros to the German pension insurance company [207].

These curious examples have one and the same cause: incorrect information quality. It is obvious that good information quality is an important factor and competitive advantage. In the US economy alone, the poor quality of information leads to annual losses of over 600 billion dollars. In Germany, this corresponds to almost 190 billion Euros in damage - per year. Incorrect address data, for example, leads to wasted postage costs or even to the loss of the customer. But also the subsequent cleaning up of defective data records costs a lot of time and money. The cause of faulty data often lies in the companies themselves. Usually there is a lack of persons responsible for data management or of guidelines for the administration of data. But also ignorance of human employees when dealing with data or inadequate databases and technical information processing tools contribute to this.[208]

---

[206] Vgl. dertagesspiegel 2008.
[207] Vgl. sz.de 2015.
[208] Vgl. Wendehorst 2013.

To ensure quality, it is now necessary to filter information by relevance. The more relevant the information is to the company's progress, the higher the demand for quality of information.[209] This means that information must be correct, complete and unambiguous. The *German Society for Information and Data Quality* defined a total of 15 dimensions, which are based on a study by the Massachusetts Institute of Technology (MIT).[210]

The quality management standard DIN EN ISO 9001:2015, revised in September 2015, takes particular account of the quality of data and information due to digitisation and the steady increase in mass data.[211]

It is not uncommon for information preparation and cleansing to take up to 80 percent of the project duration. But the effort is worth it, because a high quality of information leads to a high level of decision-making security and a decisive competitive advantage.[212]

---

[209] Vgl. Knauer 2015), S. 59.
[210] Vgl. Hildebrand, et al. 2015), S. 32 ff.; AZ Direct AG o. J.
[211] Vgl. DGQ 2016.
[212] Vgl. Walters 2015.

The study shows that useful, high-quality and secure information can only be obtained through the interaction of mass data, utility, semantics, quality, security and data protection.[213]

---

[213] Vgl. Jähnichen 2015.

4 Data protection and data security

The terms data protection and data security are often used synonymously. However, this is not correct. Data security is the technical protection of all data against unauthorized access. Data protection, on the other hand, is much more complex. It refers to the comprehensive protection of personal data and is anchored in Germany in the Federal Data Protection Act (BDSG). IT security is the technical implementation of security concepts taking into account economic aspects.[214] In the Anglo-American area, the term privacy is also used to be translated as privateness and to be assigned to data protection.[215] In general, the topics of data protection, data security and IT security are also summarised as *information security*.[216]

In 1983, the German Federal Constitutional Court passed the so-called census judgement. It is still regarded today as a milestone in data protection, as the basic right to informational self-determination was derived from it. Everyone should be able to

---

[214] Vgl. Neunteufel 2014, S. 14.

[215] Vgl. Dinger und Hartenstein 2008, S. 276.

[216] Vgl. Neunteufel 2014, S. 14.

decide for themselves when and within what limits information about themselves may be recorded and stored. People who feel or are constantly monitored show a clearly abnormal and disturbed pattern of behaviour. They do not know what information already exists or has been recorded about them. They adapt their behaviour so as not to attract attention. A study published in February 2016 by *Wayne State University* confirms that people who are under observation or who feel secretly monitored are much more reluctant to express their own opinions if they deviate from the majority opinion.[217] Even today, one third of all Germans feel restricted in their freedom of expression.[218] This has serious implications not only for the individual but also for the common good of a democratic society.

The BDSG also provides for a number of other paragraphs which are intended to serve data protection. These include the prohibition subject to permission, which requires the storage of personal data only with the consent of the data subject, or the transparency requirement, which gives the data subject the right to request, delete or correct the

---

[217] Vgl. Stoycheff 2016, S. 8 ff.
[218] Vgl. Grieß 2016.

disclosure of the information stored about him at any time. New technologies such as cyberphysical, globally linked and cognitive computing systems as well as mass data from sensors, video and audio systems were not foreseeable in the preparation of the BDSG. These technologies affect our informational self-determination in an unprecedented way.[219] The principles and legal regulations for automated data processing laid down in the BDSG can hardly or no longer be complied with due to inexpensive and ubiquitous Internet technologies. Examples include companies such as *Google* and *Facebook*. These make the collection and automated processing of all user data their business model. Global surveillance activities by government intelligence agencies also show that these principles can no longer be upheld. Such sometimes dubious business practices are clearly in conflict with the current German Law, but are nevertheless accepted by many users in favour of comfort and benefit.[220] A modernised basic data protection regulation may improve this situation. The Europe-wide data protection directive known as the *EU Data Protection Basic Regulation* (GDPR) has been in force since May 2018.[221] This creates a

---

[219] Vgl. Bullinger und Hompel 2007, S. 371 f.
[220] Vgl. Bittner, et al. 2014, S. 63.

common data protection framework in the European Union, taking into account modern data business practices.

With tiny miniature sensors, cheap microchips and wireless communication, connected computing systems can be extended into everyday life in ways previously unimagined. In the future, many billions of devices will be connected with each other. The physical world is merging with the virtual. The digitization of entire areas of business and life is making great strides forward.[222] And despite the biggest data protection scandal in the history of the world, uncovered by EDWARD SNOWDEN in 2013, we continue today to use supposedly free services, often unconsciously passing on personal and private data to governmental and private-sector organizations and giving little thought to complex encryption methods.[223]

A further security risk is caused by device manufacturers, who want to bring their connected products to market as quickly as possible. According to OREBAUGH, manufacturers are trying to save

---

[221] Vgl. Caspar 2016.
[222] Vgl. Fleisch und Mattern 2005, S. 335.
[223] Vgl. Seemann 2013.

time by using inadequate or even missing safety methods. Manufacturers of embedded computer systems have hardly had to worry about the security of their modules, since these systems were not part of the Internet.[224] With the *Internet of Things*, they now face new challenges. A North American research team had tested the security of embedded systems in March 2016 and found serious security deficiencies in over ten percent of all tested devices.[225]

Information security is an economic factor that companies and organisations must reckon with. If measurable damage is prevented by suitable protective mechanisms, this can be seen as virtual revenue. The costs for more information security can be offset by possible damages and thus economically justified.[226] The analysis company *Gartner* expects the average security budget to rise from one to 20 percent in the next five years due to the *Internet of Things*.[227]

[224] Vgl. Orebaugh 2015.
[225] Vgl. Schmidt 2016.
[226] Vgl. Neunteufel 2014, S. 14.
[227] Vgl. Drilling 2016.

4.1 The Privacy Paradox

Over 58 percent of Germans fear that their personal data could be misused on the Internet.[228] More than two thirds state that they deliberately do without online services as soon as personal information is requested. When using these services, almost 80 percent agree with the privacy statements, although they have not understood them.[229] Over 87 percent use providers that they do not trust to comply with legal data processing requirements. Three-quarters of them consider the usefulness of the service more important than their own data protection, one-third consider data protection to be less important, and the rest see themselves *forced* to use the service. In social networks, almost 80 percent of users voluntarily state their correct first and last names and age. Well over half even publish their portrait photo and current relationship status.[230]

Despite the revelations from SNOWDEN, the use of services such as *Facebook* or *Google* continues to grow strongly. Although the majority of all users in the surveys express great concerns about the privacy

---

[228] Vgl. Eurobarometer 2015, S. 25.
[229] Vgl. Rohleder 2015, S. 6.
[230] Vgl. statista 2011.

of such service providers, they continue to pay the *price of the free.*[231]

Few have switched to secure email or short messaging services with strong encryption capabilities after the data protection scandals in the past five years. The reasons for this behaviour are a lack of competence, a lack of motivation and a high degree of uncertainty with regard to constantly changing terms and conditions.[232]

The privacy paradox describes the observation that while privacy and data protection are regarded as extremely important issues in surveys and personal conversations, hardly anyone is prepared to do anything about them.[233]

4.2 Information security on the Internet of Things

The increasing miniaturization of computer technology means that in the future, more than ever, the smallest sensors and processors will be integrated into all kinds of everyday objects. Classic peripherals such as mice, keyboards and monitors will disappear

---

[231] Vgl. Becker und Knop 2015, S. 141.
[232] Vgl. Becker und Knop 2015, S. 143.
[233] Vgl. Seemann 2013.

and be integrated directly into our clothing, vehicles, furniture, wristwatches and pens in order to communicate with other people's devices at the same time. This is referred to as wearable computing, which is explained in more detail in Chapter 6.2.11. It is obvious that this development has a major impact on information security and especially data protection. In addition, comprehensive networking has an oppressive monitoring potential.

A further complicating factor is that most conntected everyday objects hardly have any acoustic or visual signaling devices with which they can draw attention to the user during active monitoring. Even the multitude of seemingly banal measured variables, such as the recorded cadence, room temperature or the number of eyelashes of a person, can be correlated by sophisticated cognitive computing systems in order to obtain more sensitive information.[234]

An example: In 2014, *Google* bought *Nest Labs*, a manufacturer of connected thermostats and smoke detectors, for $3 billion. In addition to a thermometer, the thermostat also has a humidity sensor. The recorded measured values are transferred wirelessly into *Google's* data cloud and evaluated using complex

---

[234] Vgl. Langheinrich und Mattern 2002.

algorithms. The system thus learns when someone is in the house and when not. Accordingly, it independently regulates the temperature and leads to considerable energy savings. In practice, this works so well that it is possible to measure and calculate exactly when and how many people are in the room or will be in the future.

If the topics of the *Internet of Things*, mass data and data cloud technology are brought together, the following fields arise from the point of view of information security: Regulations, secure communication channels and authentication of all parties involved.[235]

The variety of devices on the *Internet of Things* increases the attack surface for hackers and malware immensely. Every device on the *Internet of Things* has different ways of interacting. The more possibilities and interfaces are offered, the higher the attack surface. This also includes the built-in sensors, which can be manipulated depending on what they measure. The central system with which the device communicates or from which it is controlled and supplied with software updates also offers attack potential.[236]

---

[235] Vgl. Kranawetter 2015.

These findings have an impact on the entire production process of such a device. This is because manipulations, e.g. in the switching process, can already be carried out during manufacture. A few additional lines of code in the control chip enable later remote access to the hardware. Such so-called hardware Trojans are seldom or even impossible to track down later and can put users in mortal danger or cause high damage through industrial espionage. It was not until the last *Chaos Communication Congress* at the end of 2015 that the *Chaos Computer Club* pointed out the great dangers of such Trojans in an emphatic manner.[237] Experts assume that by 2020 a black market of counterfeit and corrupted sensors will develop that will allow data to be replaced or manipulated at will unnoticed.[238]

So before well over 50 billion devices can be connected on the Internet by 2020, the following risk factors must be considered:[239]

Uncertain design: As described above, manufacturers of embedded systems have not had to worry about security mechanisms because they have no access to

---

[236] Vgl. Kranawetter 2015.
[237] Vgl. Krempl 2015.
[238] Vgl. Drilling 2016.
[239] Vgl. Evans 2011, S. 3.

the Internet. This is changing with the *Internet of Things*. Many devices lack basic security features or are shipped with very insecure default settings. For this reason, it makes all the more sense to identify potential data protection problems at the device development stage and implement data protection mechanisms in advance at the device development stage, rather than painstakingly troubleshoot them afterwards. This is called "Privacy by design".[240] In January 2016 did many media again report on the search engine shodan.io, which has been established for many years and automatically searches for unsafe devices on the Internet and lists them. These include webcams in bedrooms, private network storage devices and electronic door locks that can be opened remotely.[241] During a demonstration at *T-Systems HackerDay* in Bonn, Germany, the author himself was able to see for himself how easy it is to access third-party devices. Standard passwords are a frequent weak point. Many devices are delivered with predefined standard passwords, which can be found in the corresponding manual. With the help of such a standard password it was possible to open the room door of a hotel equipped with an electronic lock. A

---

[240] Vgl. Schaar o. J.
[241] Vgl. Kühl 2016.

secure design must therefore also include an individual password, which must be changed by the user himself upon activation. As a result, the end user also has to ensure the security of the devices he uses.

Missing possibility for software updates: No software is without errors. For example, it is imperative to have a way to update devices when vulnerabilities become known. In February 2016, a serious security vulnerability was discovered in the *Simplisafe* connected alarm system. Insufficient encryption made it possible to read the deactivation code and deactivate the system completely. Since the hardware was equipped with memory modules that could only be written to once, this security gap could not be eliminated by a software update. Only the complete hardware exchange of the system could eliminate the problem.[242] Even with systems that can be updated remotely via a software update, care must be taken to ensure that the update interface is adequately protected against manipulation.

Insecure data: The protection of communication paths with modern encryption methods must be just as self-evident as the encryption of locally stored information.[243]

---

[242] Vgl. Zonenberg 2016.

Unsecure networks: Many devices will connect to each other even with partially unsecured networks. Here it is necessary for the devices to be able to communicate with each other via secure and trustworthy channels. Virtual private networks (VPN) play an important role here.[244] Via so-called VPN tunnels, devices in public networks can exchange encrypted information.

Insecure data storage: Since the devices in the *Internet of Things* send their data to remote data centers for processing, it is necessary that the central data storage is also sufficiently protected. More details in the following chapter.[245]

Due to the high importance of information security, it is necessary that security mechanisms are already taken into account during development and are not added later as an extra.

Challenges for the security of devices in the *Internet of Things* are among others:

- *The low power consumption*. The devices must often be able to be operated with a single

---

[243] Vgl. Kranawetter 2015.

[244] Ebd.

[245] Ebd.

battery for up to ten years. This is only possible with low-power processors. However, a more secure encryption requires high computing power.

- *The low costs*. The devices must be cheap to manufacture. A manufacturer who produces a sensor for one Dollar may seldom invest another Dollar in security features. This does not allow large memory or processor power. Also because of this hurdle, strong cryptography is difficult to implement.

- *The long lifetime*. In ten years of a sensor's lifetime, the computing power will have multiplied according to Moore's law. Decryption will probably be many times faster in the future. Weak points that have been discovered but cannot be closed could also pose a problem.

- *Physical access*. Sensors and other hardware are often easily visible and tangible for the attacker. Here, too, hardware interfaces must be reliably secured against unauthorized access from outside.

The author concludes that the *Internet of Things* provides real-time insights not only into people's private lives, but also into industrial and business processes.[246] In DAVE EGGERS novel "The Circle" the effects of the full storage and evaluation of everyday activities and confidential information are well described.

The authorized and unauthorized correlation of information with other data sources also poses great risks. An insurance company would certainly be very interested in the leisure activities, nutrition and health status of its members.

Data protection plays an even greater role in the design of connected devices. With televisions or most electronic devices commonly used today, people are sensitized and immediately recognize the technology. In the case of connected everyday objects, such as clothing or product packaging, this is not easily recognizable.[247] Personal data must be subject to appropriate data protection controls. The

---

[246] Vgl. Kranawetter 2015.
[247] Vgl. Dittert 2016, S. 38.

legislator is required to do this when it comes to outdated security and data protection regulations. An obligation to label mechatronic systems that are suitable for monitoring is conceivable. When the EU Data Protection Directive comes into force, at least RFID chips will be labelled accordingly.[248] A government and private-sector total monitoring through the storage of all data without cause should not be the goal.[249] Data processing organizations must make the commercial use of their customers' data as transparent as possible and adhere to the highest possible data protection standards, such as are common in Germany. Rules on anonymisation and pseudonymisation are also important. This means that business models based on mass data can be implemented in a data protection-friendly way. But the consumer himself can also help to ensure that his data is processed as securely as possible. Data security must establish itself as a decisive purchasing criterion and the consumer must develop an awareness of who he wants to disclose which data to.[250] In most cases, a smartphone application for a torch does not require geo-information.[251] Smartphone

---

[248] Ebd., S. 38.
[249] Vgl. Langheinrich und Mattern 2002.
[250] Vgl. Kranawetter 2015.
[251] Vgl. Özbicerler 2016.

applications often form the springboard for hackers to enter all systems.[252]

4.3 Information security in the data cloud

The company *Mattel* developed with "Hello Barbie" an interactive doll. Wirelessly connected to the Internet, children can talk to this doll in natural language and promptly receive a suitable answer. The language input of the children is transported by the doll into the data cloud, evaluated and stored for two years. The doll listens continuously and scans its surroundings for input signals. Even the most intimate secrets or personal conversations can be recorded and saved from the children's room. At the end of 2015 it became known that it was possible for an American hacker to gain access to this sensitive data in the data cloud with relatively little effort. Among other things, it is possible to manipulate the voice output of the doll and, for example, to ask for the presence of the parents or to make requests. Access to the conversations stored in the data cloud was also possible.[253] In a similar example, hackers from a Chinese toy manufacturer were able to access over

---

[252] Vgl. Handesblatt 2015.
[253] Vgl. nbc chicago 2015.

190 gigabytes of private photos of parents and children as well as personal conversations.[254] From this it can be deduced that in the production of such conntected toys, care must be taken to ensure the data protection of minors.

Section 9 of the Federal Data Protection Act stipulates that the protection of personal data requires appropriate technical and organisational measures.[255] This also applies to providers of data cloud technologies. ISO/IEC 27018 also regulates the protection of personal data in public data clouds.[256] However, the question of location remains open here. Different countries have different regulations on how access by government agencies is regulated. Companies domiciled in Germany are obliged by law to guarantee government agencies access to accounting data stored in the data cloud at all times.[257] However, personal data may only be accessed with the reservation of a judge. Outside Germany, it may be the case that government agencies make the encryption of sensitive data a punishable offence.[258]

---

[254] Vgl. Beuth 2015.

[255] Vgl. Bundesdatenschutzgesetz o. J.

[256] Vgl. Dinnes 2014.

[257] Vgl. M. Weber 2010, S. 51.

[258] Vgl. Gillberg 2015.

In France and Great Britain, legal policy reactions in the context of the fight against terrorism have considerably facilitated the access of state authorities to private and sensitive data in the data cloud.[259] American providers must pass on the data to government agencies if either a judge has issued an order or the FBI forces the provider to do so by means of a National Security Letter. At the same time, the providers are prohibited by a prohibition order from informing those affected or speaking about it in public.[260] In Australia it does not need a judge, because only a minister is allowed to order the release of data. In Spain, the police are already allowed to access data without judicial authority, and in Ireland, too, data can be accessed for serious offences without a judge's reservation.[261] There is a tightrope walk between the protection of the general public and the freedoms of the individual.

Worldwide, only in Japan and Germany is the investigative competence of state authorities limited to the data centers located in their own countries. In all other countries, authorities can also access servers

---

[259] Vgl. Carl 2012.
[260] Ebd.
[261] Ebd.

outside their own country, provided the service provider has a branch in their own country.[262]

The location of the data cloud provider is thus a decisive criterion for the data protection of personal or company-relevant data. The local providers of data clouds can gain market advantages from the location in countries with a high level of data protection. According to a representative survey by the Institut für Demokopie Allensbach, Deutsche Telekom is by far the most trustworthy company when it comes to handling personal data.[263] More and more foreign companies are therefore relying on data centers located in Germany.[264]

The General Data Protection Regulation, which is established by the EU Parliament in 2018, could be a great opportunity for Europe and give European companies a considerable competitive advantage in the international environment.[265] One of the consequences of this would be that non-European service providers who violate European data protection law would have to pay fines of up to EUR

---

[262] Ebd.

[263] Vgl. Lindlar und Schweinsberg 2015.

[264] Vgl. Kroker, Darum drängen alle IT-Giganten in die deutsche Wolke 2015.

[265] Vgl. Rebiger 2015.

20 million or up to 4 % of the total annual worldwide turnover in the previous financial year, whichever is the higher.[266] The new Regulation can enable privacy-friendly and new digital business models.

With regard to the *Internet of Things* and the expected explosion of connected devices, data cloud providers are forced to handle a significantly higher number of concurrent connections and larger amounts of traffic. If the providers are unable to provide the necessary resources, the entire security system could fail.[267]

Not only should data centers be protected against unauthorized virtual access, but also against physical access. Modern high-security data centers are protected from floods, fires, lightning strikes and unauthorized access. Trained security personnel, high-security fences, alarm systems or fire alarm and extinguishing systems should be a matter of course.[268]

4.4 Protection of cyberphysical systems

A cyberphysical system (CPS) is the fusion of the physical world with the information technology world. It is an embedded software system that is part

---

[266] Vgl. Bub und Wolfenstetter 2014, S. 11 f.

[267] Vgl. Kranawetter 2015.

[268] Vgl. Telekom.com 2016.

of equipment, buildings, transportation, manufacturing facilities, medical processes, or logistics and management processes. By means of sensors and actuators they collect physical data and can influence physical processes. The collected data enables them to interact actively or reactively with the digital and physical world and to exchange information with each other worldwide via digital communication devices. They are equipped with human-machine interfaces.[269]

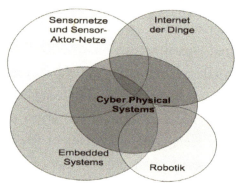

Figure 4 Composition of cyberphysical systems
Source: Hof o. J.

As can be seen in Figure 4, cyberphysical systems use existing technologies. With the help of sensors, actuators and robotics, they record their environment and act on it. With the help of technologies from the

---

[269] Vgl. acatech - Deutsche Akademie der Technikwissenschaften 2011, S. 13.

Internet of Things they depict objects in the information technology world and with the help of embedded systems they perform tasks such as monitoring, control, regulation or signal processing.

The integration of these technologies into production plants poses corresponding security challenges. Previously, these systems were isolated for a long time. For many current and future scenarios, such as telemetry-controlled quality assurance of industrial plants or their maintenance and optimization options, these systems must be fundamentally connected. Missing security measures of such systems can have a direct effect on us humans through manipulation. Life-threatening are the consequences of external intervention on e.g. controllable medical devices or human prostheses.[270]

In 2010, the computer worm STUXNET achieved media fame. The malware was specially developed for monitoring and controlling technical processes in production plants. This made it possible, among other things, to manipulate the motors in nuclear power plants, air conditioning technology or pipelines remotely. STUXNET thus transformed entire

---

[270] Vgl. Kranawetter 2015.

industrial plants into a cyberphysical system. The potential dangers are obvious.[271]

The dominant topic when dealing with CPS is the safety for life and limb of people.

CPS collect a variety of data via sensors. Whereas human beings have so far been unable to act in order to protect their privacy, the inaction of individual users is irrelevant for these systems. Nevertheless, they collect. This could become a problem as CPS is increasingly used in public areas. Although paragraph 3a of the Federal Data Protection Act (BDSG) provides for data economy, the collection of all data is the goal of every CPS.

In order to prevent or restrict this, the functioning of CPS must be completely transparent for the user and operator of such systems. This is prescribed by the BDSG. Legal responsibilities must be clearly defined. Those affected must have the opportunity not to feel at the mercy of such systems, but to intervene. And when personal data is stored in data clouds, the data subjects must also be granted the right to delete, correct and block the data. In order to achieve this, a CPS must be completely or at least partially

---

[271] Vgl. Frank 2011, S. 108.

switchable. Manual operation and direct contact with the operator are also required.[272]

In order to avoid a possible profiling of individual individuals, the collected data and processes from different contexts must not only be anonymized or pseudonymized, but also physically separated from each other. Local encryption must be as self-evident as encrypted data exchange.[273]

The German Federal Office for Information Security (BSI) sees a growing threat especially in industry and manufacturing. The following five key threats have been identified for cyberphysical systems: [274]

- Infection of control components with malware via office networks
- Introduction of malware via removable media and external hardware
- social engineering
- Human misconduct and sabotage
- Burglary via remote maintenance accesses

Particularly outdated software versions play a role here. But also insecure passwords or standard

---

[272] Vgl. Hof o. J.
[273] Ebd.
[274] Vgl. Bund 2014.

passwords, missing monitoring of your own network, missing interface controls when using mobile data carriers, unencrypted mobile end devices and missing change documentation are dangerous weak points.[275]

The following events illustrate the effects of inadequate security management.

In 2014, an insecure password gave hackers administrator access to the company's *Code Spaces* data cloud. The attackers then demanded a lot of money from the operator, which the operator did not respond to. The attackers then deleted all data, including backups and machine settings. After seven years, the company was forced to completely shut down. The recovery costs and compensation claims of the customers could not be met.[276]

The HAVEX malware program, which became known in the same year, introduced itself specifically into industrial plants, similar to the STUXNET worm described above. The program already attached itself to legitimate software on the download server and installed itself unnoticed. In Germany, several dozen industrial companies were infected as a result.[277] [278]

---

[275] Vgl. Eckert 2015.
[276] Vgl. Bund 2014.
[277] Vgl. Neunteufel 2014, S. 64.

Such scenarios can be avoided by reducing the number of attack surfaces, identifying weak points and designing technology. In access systems, for example, the attack surface can be reduced by more secure storage systems and unique identification (e.g. by fingerprint). Automated testing of smartphone applications before they are installed in the corporate network also contributes to greater security. Access control and authentication of network components should also be a matter of course.[279]

In addition, awareness of data security must be created, especially in the management. According to a study by the eco association, only 29 percent of managing directors see data protection in cyberphysical systems as a relevant driver in IT security.[280]

Security challenges also include a number of legal issues. Contract law, liability law, data protection law, IT security law and labour law play an important role in the implementation of appropriate security measures for cyberphysical systems.[281]

---

[278] Vgl. Bund 2014.
[279] Vgl. Eckert 2015.
[280] Vgl. Müller 2016.
[281] Vgl. Eckert 2015.

4.5 Information Law in the Internet of Things

Storage media, processors and communication devices are already built into many everyday objects. By 2018, every second person on Earth will own a modern smartphone.[282] This innovation means that different areas of law meet or become blurred. New legal constellations are emerging. The reason for this is that in the *Internet of Things* physical objects are not only objects, but also carriers of intellectual property and personal data.[283]

The basic question with regard to the *Internet of Things* is therefore: who owns the data?

The fact that the data on the computer's hard disk belongs to the owner of the hard disk is undisputed. It is irrelevant whether this data is personal or machine data. But in the course of digitalisation, more and more machine data can be linked to people. The refrigerator provides information about the owner's eating habits, the vehicle data reveals the driver's driving habits and the industrial machine stores

---

[282] Vgl. Liu 2015.
[283] Vgl. Heun und Assion 2015.

information about the machine operator. At the latest since *Google* photographed and mapped all buildings with "StreetView", we know that building data can also be easily linked with information about owners and residents, thus creating a personal reference.[284]

But it's not just about the data, but primarily about the rights to use this data and the associated added value. When the vehicle, refrigerator or industrial machine sends the collected information to the manufacturer via the Internet, the manufacturer is able to evaluate this data and develop new business models from it. He could resell the information to garages and other third parties and derive further economic benefits from it. If the collection and transfer of personal information takes place without the consent of the user and without the possibility of stopping it, manufacturers run the risk of quickly getting into legal difficulties. Such action can, for example, violate the right to informational self-determination as well as a number of other laws from the BDSG.[285] There is a risk that unauthorized data retention constitutes a material defect, which has a negative effect on the sales law.[286]

---

284 Vgl. N. Härting 2016.
285 Vgl. Oberlandesgericht Hamm 2015.
286 Vgl. N. Härting 2016.

It is clear from the previous studies that Internet law still leaves many questions unanswered. Communication law provisions meet property law and information law provisions. The manufacturers of devices for the *Internet of Things* are well advised to include these aspects of information law in the risk assessment and drafting of their chewing contracts.[287]

---

[287] Vgl. Assion 2016.

5 Informatization of Production Engineering (Industry 4.0)

As a student, the author worked during the holidays on the production lines of an Bavarian factory for cardboard boxes. The machines were inspected by a machine operator. Three other employees loaded the machine with cardboard blanks and stacked the finished printed cartons on pallets at the end of the machine, where they were packed in foil and pulled to a warehouse by pallet truck. For each new customer order, the shift supervisor handed the machine operator a piece of paper with the folding and printing pattern requested by the customer as well as the quantity to be produced. The operator then manually reloaded the printing plates and reprogrammed the machine for the job. This process was repeated for each job and was unique for each print and folding pattern. If there was a technical problem with the changeover due to a defective component, there were further delays, which were to the detriment of the piecework wage of the machine operator. The employees searched in panic for the type of component in documents and later reported this to the shift supervisor, who had to take care of the replacement. This process was very time-consuming.

Every downtime of a machine caused high machine downtime costs for the company.

Two different problems are described in this scenario, which are to be solved, among other things, by computerizing production technology and logistics. The following technologies have already been partially implemented in the above-mentioned cardboard box operation today[288]. In the age of so-called Industry 4.0, the customer is independently able to send the order directly to the machine via the Internet. Thanks to modern colour laser technology, the cartons are printed with individual patterns during production without the machine having to be stopped and the printing plate having to be replaced. The cardboard blanks are equipped with tiny RFID chips, which can communicate independently and wirelessly with the machines. They therefore automatically know which machine needs replenishment and which patterns they need to be printed with. They are driven directly to the appropriate production line by voice-controlled and autonomous forklift trucks, while the machine simultaneously reports the demand for further blanks via the Internet to a machine in Poland and orders them.[289] Due to this highly flexible

---

[288] The author received this information from conversations with employees of the factory.

production, even small quantities are possible at the cost of mass production, without significant additional costs for operation.[290] Even batch size 1 should be possible, i.e. an economic production of only one piece by itself.[291] The machine standstill caused by the defective component described above can also be reduced. Using a mobile scanner, the machine operator is able to read the RFID information from the connected component. With this information, he can search for suitable spare parts on the company intranet at the same time and order them, if the machine itself cannot do this.

5.1 Definition of Term Industry 4.0

According to a representative survey conducted by the *Allensbach Institute for Public Opinion Research*, over 80 percent of Germans cannot assign the term "Industry 4.0" or heard it for the first time.[292] And even only 18 percent of German entrepreneurs have heard this term before.[293]

[289] Vgl. Stoller 2016.
[290] Vgl. Denner 2014.
[291] Vgl. Ulfers 2004, S. 43.
[292] Vgl. Lindlar und Schweinsberg 2015, S. 12.
[293] Vgl. Bertschek 2015.

For the first time the term Industry 4.0 was mentioned during the *Hannover Messe* in 2013. It describes the informatization of manufacturing technology and logistics. The numerical sequence 4.0 is supposed to indicate the fourth industrial revolution. In the fourth industrial revolution, earlier isolated solutions in factories are to be combined with each other. The goal is worldwide networking, communication and independent monitoring of all components involved in the production process. This is why these cyberphysical systems will be massively equipped with control chips, sensors, actuators and radio modules, so that an intelligent manufacturing swarm will be created.[294]

The German government supported the "Platform Industry 4.0" project with 200 million Euros. It is a central alliance of companies, associations and trade unions from the fields of science and politics. The focus is on bundling forces for the coordinated shaping of digital structural change.[295]

Industry 4.0 is a subset of the *Internet of Things*, since devices outside the manufacturing industry and logistics are or will be connected with each other.

---

[294] Vgl. Weckbrodt 2015.
[295] Vgl. Finger 2016.

These include smartphones, connected household appliances, vehicles, clothing, watches and glasses.

5.2 Opportunities for Europe and economic potential

„ Those who do not learn history are doomed to repeat it. "

- GEORG SATAYANA

In 1982, the *Frauenhofer Institute for Integrated Circuits (IIS)* in Erlangen, Germany, developed a compression format for audio files. Only a few years later the format became the industry standard in the music industry and the first portable players for MP3 files were available.[296] However, American companies such as *Apple*, in particular, have benefited from this German invention.

In its algorithm, the American search engine giant *Google* was largely inspired by the inventions of MASSIMO MARCHIORI, an Italian mathematician.[297]

---

[296] Vgl. Bach, et al. 2012, S. 113.
[297] Vgl. McCarthy 1999.

And even the World Wide Web and its HTML markup language were developed predominantly in French-speaking Switzerland.[298]

Many years before *Facebook*, the German Bielefeld-based student PHILIP OETKER developed a social network for students with the support of *Deutsche Telekom*, with the aim of unifying the communication of the digital world with the real world.[299]

With *Industry 4.0*, Europe, once again has the opportunity to actively accompany one of the most important revolutions in the digital age, and this time even to play a leading role in shaping it. It is in the hands of the European players to make good use of this opportunity and to develop appropriate solutions before non-European competitors take over. The largest competitor in the development of connected production machines is the *Industrial Internet Consortium* in the USA, already mentioned in Chapter 2.4, with members from an international environment. The project "Platform Industry 4.0" aims at a German solution, which is written by predominantly German companies and exclusively in German language. However, this limits the visibility

---

[298] Vgl. Taglinger 2003, S. 25 f.
[299] Vgl. Unispiegel 2000; (Schoentahler 2000).

and influence of the platform on the international market.[300]

By the year 2025, a digital failure of Europe could result in a loss potential of over 605 billion euros. This would hit the European automotive industry particularly hard with a third of its value added and the logistics industry with around half of its value added. The internationally highly regarded European mechanical engineering, electrical engineering and medical technology industries also face a loss of over 215 billion euros in gross value added over the next ten years. Only the chemical industry, some of which is already very process-oriented and computer-supported, faces a comparatively low threat potential of 40 billion euros.[301] A successful digital transformation could lead to productivity leaps of up to 30 percent in the German mechanical and plant engineering industry alone.[302] In the logistics and chemical industry, there is potential of up to 20 percent.[303]

These figures illustrate the urgency of action by German and European companies to introduce

---

[300] Vgl. Pasqua 2015.
[301] Vgl. Bloching, et al. 2015, S. 12.
[302] Vgl. Shafranyuk, et al. 2015, S. 30.
[303] Vgl. Shafranyuk, et al. 2015, S. 40.

connected factory buildings and production systems. At present, entrepreneurs see the lack of resources, high initial costs, security risks and lack of specialist knowledge as the greatest obstacles.[304]

In order to fully exploit the above-mentioned potential, Europe needs its own strong digital industry. The European starting position is still good. According to ALEXANDER DOBRINDT, the Federal Minister for Digital Infrastructure, Industry 4.0 with its connected production processes and machines is a German invention that knows how to integrate data sensibly into industrial processes. The same applies to the automotive industry. German carmakers are international pioneers in automated and connected driving.[305] Currently, Germany has a strategic advantage of over two years over its international competitors overseas. In order to avoid the high loss potential, too long experiments or waiting should be avoided. Europe currently has the opportunity to continue to exist as one of the world's leading technology suppliers and to further expand this role. According to DORST, politics, society, science and industry must recognise this and pull

---

[304] Vgl. IBM Whitepaper 2015.
[305] Vgl. Dobrindt 2015.

together.[306] Reliable European framework conditions for investment, research and development and the correct orientation of a European industrial policy are essential prerequisites for the prosperity and economic success of *Industry 4.0* in Europe.[307]

Savings in production costs, better production planning, higher machine utilization and availability, faster response to market changes and real-time evaluation of machine data are just some of the benefits that Industry 4.0 promises.[308] However, the driving forces behind the networking of the company's own production facilities are not only cost savings, but in particular higher productivity, sales increases, flexibility in production and the development of new business models.[309]

One of the most important prerequisites for the industrial consolidation of Europe's position is the rapid alignment of the digital infrastructure. Mobile Internet access for high-performance and interference-free connectivity of sensors and actuators must be promoted, as must the further development of existing communication infrastructures.[310] Here the

---

[306] Vgl. Dorst 2015.

[307] Vgl. Gabriel 2016.

[308] Vgl. IBM Whitepaper 2015.

[309] Vgl. Weiß und Zilch 2014.

efforts of the Federal Government with its "Digital Agenda" are mentioned, among others. This primarily includes providing rural regions with broadband Internet access.[311] Highly available and quality-assured broadband access is an essential location factor for manufacturing companies and a basic requirement for connected production.[312]

According to measurements by *Cisco Systems*, Germany already meets the minimum requirements for a broadband society, but some of its European neighbors have significantly faster data networks.[313] According to *Cisco*, this backlog must be made up quickly.

German start-up companies, such as *EightyLeo* from Munich, also demonstrate the high innovation potential in the Industry 4.0 sector. In order to globally network exclusively German factories and their machines, the start-up wants to set up a global communications network in space based on hundreds of small satellites in the coming years. The project is supported by the Federal Network Agency. The fact that the servers are located in Germany gives

---

[310] Vgl. Geisberger, et al. 2011.
[311] Vgl. BMWi, BMI, BMVI 2014.
[312] Vgl. Grosser 2016.
[313] Vgl. Gurlow und Jordans 2015.

EightyLeo a decisive data protection advantage over its competitors in the USA.[314] There, *Tesla* founder ELON MUSK also plans to launch 4,000 satellites into space in order to equip even the most remote areas of the world with Internet access.[315]

The opportunities offered by Industry 4.0 bring enormous opportunities for the German and global economy. This applies in particular to maintaining international competitiveness. Individual employees also benefit, among other things, from greater room for manoeuvre, age-appropriate work arrangements, improved ergonomics, a better work-life balance and not negligible job security.[316] Faster product lifecycles, shorter lead times and greater transparency in production ultimately force all major market players to use connected cyber-physical production systems.[317] The fact that Industry 4.0 is currently also subject to limits was most recently demonstrated by *Mercedes Benz*. In the production of the new S-Class, the automobile manufacturer is increasingly replacing robots with human employees, as robots are currently

---

[314] Vgl. Henry 2015.
[315] Vgl. Vallancey 2015.
[316] Vgl. Kurz 2014), S. 7.
[317] Vgl. Hiller 2016.

still too inflexible and cannot cope with the high degree of individualization.[318]

Last but not least, it should be mentioned that according to a current study more than one million new jobs can be created by Industry 4.0 in Germany alone. Especially in the IT management of production plants, extensive IT competence is necessary due to the higher process complexity.[319] The loss of jobs caused by demographic change can be partially offset by increased productivity. Colleges, universities and employers are already called upon to counteract a worsening shortage of skilled workers with timely qualification measures. The acceptance of the new technologies and permanent networking must be increased, especially among young people.[320] But new skills for planning and control are also required in management positions.[321] Repetitive and physically demanding work will decrease in favour of creative workplaces.[322]

---

[318] Vgl. Schroeder 2016.

[319] Vgl. Dobrindt 2015.

[320] Vgl. Bielmeier 2016.

[321] Vgl. Schütte 2014.

[322] Vgl. Weber o. J.

5.3 The role of the medium-sized companiesin Germany

The author VOLKER BRÜHL states in his book *"Economy of the 21st Century"* that small and medium-sized enterprises (SMEs) in particular must take advantage of the opportunities offered by Industry 4.0. Germany still has a great advantage in global competition with its strong SMEs. Thanks to this, Germany is the world leader, especially in mechanical engineering and electrical engineering. By the use of Industry 4.0 as well as by suitable qualification measures and a challanged top management this position can be hold.[323]

According to a recent study by the market research institute *International Data Corporation* (IDC), small and medium-sized businesses are growing faster than their competitors through the extensive use of digital hyper-connected technologies.[324] They rely on conservative technologies. Almost 40 percent of these companies confirm that participation in the digital economy over the next three to five years is crucial for the survival of the company. The study clearly shows that the use of digital technologies has a major

---

[323] Vgl. Brühl 2015, S. 220.
[324] Vgl. IDC/SAP 2016; In der Studie wurden 3.210 kleine und mittelständische Unternehmen aus elf Ländern befragt.

impact on the business success of small and medium-sized enterprises.[325] And yet, almost a quarter of Anglo-American entrepreneurs have not yet invested in digital transformation. Companies in Asia-Pacific and Europe also have great reservations about the use of digital technologies.[326] Almost every second company expressed concern that decisions were being made too much on the basis of data.[327]

In a report published in 2016 by the *Expert Commission on Research and Innovation* (EFI), it was confirmed that the manufacturing industry in particular was still too hesitant in the use of automation technologies.[328] Small and medium-sized enterprises in particular are not innovative enough and invest too little in research projects. While companies in Sweden invest almost 2.5 percent and Finland almost 2.0 percent of their turnover in innovation activities, the figure in Germany is less than 1.2 percent. Only the UK invests even less, at 0.8 percent. The trend shows that German SMEs in particular are spending less and less on innovation. Some reasons for this are high costs, high economic

---

[325] Vgl. n-tv.de 2016.

[326] Vgl. Merz 2016

[327] Vgl. IDC/SAP 2016, S. 8.

[328] Vgl. Expertenkommission Forschung und Innovation (EFI) 2016.

risk, lack of suitable specialists and legal regulations. In particular, the threat of a shortage of skilled workers due to demographic change is a major obstacle to innovation for SMEs. Here, state support for small and medium-sized enterprises can counteract this by means of tax incentives. Germany does not yet have any tax incentives for research and development. For this reason, the Federal Ministry of Education and Research has announced a ten-point programme which, among other things, aims to increase the funding volume for small and medium-sized enterprises to 320 million euros by 2017. In addition, the expert commission also recommends recruiting specialists from abroad in order to counteract demographic change. According to the EFI, the professional qualification of refugees is also decisive.

The German Federal Ministry of Economics and Energy has also recognised that there is still a lot of catching up to do, especially for small and medium-sized enterprises. For this reason, it opened "*Mittelstand 4.0 Competence Centres*" throughout Germany at the beginning of 2016. These centres are designed to provide local support to small and medium-sized enterprises in the digitisation, networking and application of Industry 4.0 solutions.[329]

German SMEs are coming under pressure due to the increasing saturation of the domestic market, which makes the internationalisation of the business model and the use of new, digital technologies indispensable. More than 3.3 million medium-sized companies are counted in Germany.[330] Many of them miss out on decisive growth opportunities due to their strong home orientation. On the one hand, licensing agreements with a partner company in the export country are suitable. The foreign partner supplies only a few relevant parts and takes over finishing and sales. Later, these products can be expanded to include services and thus developed into hybrid products. Physical goods with the addition of services are particularly suitable for customers of system solutions. Savings can be achieved here through lower factor costs in the export country.[331] On the other hand, hybrid data cloud technologies are suitable for realizing high cost savings in the IT environment, especially in small and medium-sized enterprises. Further information on hybrid data clouds was described in Chapter 3.7. The use of modern decision support systems through cognitive neuronal

[329] Vgl. Nußbaum 2016.
[330] Vgl. Merkle und Kreutzer 2008, S. 356.
[331] Vgl. Bieger, zu Knyphausen-Aufseß und Krys 2011, S. 138 ff.

computing systems can lead to a further release of capital in medium-sized companies.[332]

---

[332] Vgl. Mack und Vilberger 2016, S. 2.

6 Business Models

„Who controls the data controls the innovation. "[333]

- TIMOTHEUS HÖTTGES

As early as 1957, the US economist PETER F. DRUCKER stated in his book *"Landmarks of Tomorrow"* that future organizations are above all one thing: complex information and decision-making systems. In his opinion, decisions are based on information from the corporate environment and from the company itself. A permanent problem is that the time span until an effective decision is made can take many cost-intensive years. And further years until the decision pays off at best.[334] Companies therefore need competence above all to recognize correlations and patterns where people only see data chaos.[335]

The *Internet of Things* and digitalization offer many new options for businesses to make money. More than 80 percent of German entrepreneurs have recognized that information technology is having an

---

[333] Quote spoken during a presentation at the conference "Digital Transformation" in Cologne on 19.2.2016.

[334] Vgl. Drucker 1957, S. 92.

[335] Vgl. Cole, Digitale Transformation: Warum die deutsche Wirtschaft gerade die digitale Zukunft verschläft und was jetzt getan werden muss! (1. Auflage) 2015), S. 34 f.

ever greater impact on their business model and that one in two believes they need to change it in order to remain successful.[336] Especially the convergent use of social media, cloud computing, analysis of mass data, security and optimization for mobile devices are important tools for the transformation of more conservative into digital business models.

In particular, the well-trained digital natives, i.e. the generation that grew up with the Internet, show a particularly high affinity to innovation.[337] A further role is played by the full flexibility of the own IT infrastructure, which can be scaled arbitrarily and according to the market situation by using technologies from the data cloud.[338] The Internet is already a basic prerequisite for the success of every second business model of German companies.[339] This chapter deals with the term business model. Proven innovative and disruptive models are presented and the possibilities of a so-called Sharing Economy are discussed. In addition, the effects of these technologies on the world of work are explained.

---

[336] Vgl. Breitenreuter 2015.
[337] Vgl. Schulenberg 2016, S. 205
[338] Vgl. Felser 2016.
[339] Vgl. Dänzel und Heun 2014, S. 69.

6.1 Definition

There are still enormous differences in the understanding of the term business model in the literature. PETER F. DRUCKER also stated most vividly here which questions must be asked when defining a business model.[340]:

- What benefits does the company provide to its customers and key partners involved in value creation?
- How does the company deliver this benefit?
- How does the company make money?

DRUCKER understands a business model as the design of connected activities to achieve entrepreneurial value creation and customer benefit.[341]

The authors OSTERWALDER and PIGNEUR are of the opinion that a business model is best described on the basis of nine basic building blocks [342]:

Customer segments: Mass market, niche market, segmented or diversified markets.

---

[340] Vgl. Schermann, Siller und Volcic 2013, S. 84.
[341] Ebd., S. 84.
[342] Vgl. Osterwalder und Pigneur 2011, S. 25.

Value offers: This includes tailor-made products and services that are tailored to special customer requirements.[343] This has become particularly important with the introduction of cyberphysical systems in production (keyword: lot size one[344]).

Channels: Offers are made to the customer through communication, distribution and sales channels.[345]

Customer relationship: Customer relationships are established and maintained with each customer segment.[346]

Revenue streams: Possibilities for this are the classic sale of assets, the demand of a user fee or membership fee, rental, hiring, leasing or licence fees.[347]

Key resources: For example, physical assets, patents and copyrights, partnerships, human resources or guarantees and credit lines.[348]

---

[343] Ebd., S. 27.

[344] Lot size 1 means using intelligent information technology to create flexible manufacturing systems that can enable customized, tailor-made production from one piece to the cost of mass production (Vgl. Brühl 2015, S. 62).

[345] Vgl. Osterwalder und Pigneur 2011, S. 31.

[346] Ebd, S. 33.

[347] Ebd, S. 35.

[348] Ebd, S. 39.

Key activities: These are any activities required to deploy the elements described above.[349]

Key partnerships: optimization and volume advantage, risk mitigation and acquisition of specific resources and activities.[350]

Cost structure: Cost-oriented models focus on maximum cost reduction in order to create the leanest possible cost structure. Value-oriented models attach great importance to value creation. This includes first-class value offers and a high degree of personal service.[351]

Simplified a business model can be defined in which it is described as a basic principle according to which an organization creates, conveys and captures values.[352]

6.2 Innovative models

Many of the existing business models have grown historically. They are based on proven and traditional principles. By creatively designing previously unused or unknown contexts, new ways can be found to open up previously unattained sources of revenue.[353] Mass

---

[349] Ebd, S. 41.
[350] Ebd, S. 43.
[351] Ebd, S. 45.
[352] Ebd, S. 18.

data, dematerialization and hyper-connected machines are ideal prerequisites for innovative business models.

6.2.1 Use of Mass Data from Social Media for Marketing and Customer Care

As entrepreneurs have more and more difficulties to design their products unique by differentiation, the competition among each other intensified. Companies try to gather as much information as possible about their customers in order to offer tailor-made services. With this information the needs of the own customers are to be seized and differentiated by a high quality at customer-referred processes from the competitors. If the needs of the customers are known, it is easier and cheaper to acquire new customers and to develop and/or hold existing customer relations. For this reason, the idea of Customer Relationship Management (CRM) was already established in the 1990s. Customer data is collected and managed in a CRM system in order to improve the quality of contact with the customer. The aim is to increase customer satisfaction and loyalty and thus increase the company's profit. The concept of a classical

---

[353] Vgl. Weis 2014, S. 69.

customer relationship management is therefore based on a purely economic understanding.[354]

Social networks are a new source of valuable customer information and image building. As digitalization progresses and Internet access via smartphones is available virtually everywhere, consumers today have the opportunity to compare prices in real time and choose the cheapest provider at the same time. This makes it all the more important for a company to be able to bind customers emotionally to its own brand and to inspire them. This is especially true for the service sector. Unlike physical goods such as smartphones or cars, it is much more difficult to arouse emotions in the service sector (tertiary and quaternary). A car brand or smartphone manufacturer can trigger positive emotions through the unique design of its products alone. *Deutsche Telekom* has proven that this is also possible in the service sector. In February 2016, the brand was named the most popular telecommunications provider brand in an independent *Forsa* survey. According to NEUHETZKI, it is not only the price that is decisive for the customer, but also the creation of a unique digital experience in

---

[354] Vgl. Wilde und Hippner, Grundlagen des CRM: Konzepte und Gestaltung (2. Auflage) 2006, S. 21.

which a consistency of brand promise and brand behavior is important.[355] The customer in the digital age expects full service and personalized services across all communication channels.[356] According to MERKLE and KREUTZER, emotions, passion and enthusiasm may play a decisive role in differentiating brands and companies in order to reach and retain customer potential.[357]

With the help of a functioning customer relationship management the needs and wishes of the customer can be recognized and thus positive emotions can be aroused with the contact with the brand. By documenting and managing orders, inquiries or quotations placed, the customer approach can be optimized and customer satisfaction and loyalty can be increased.[358] Chapter 6.3.6 addresses the fact that an optimal customer approach can lead to significantly increased sales figures. Here, too, customer data from the CRM system formed the basis.

---

[355]   Vgl.   Neuhetzki,   Deutsche   Telekom   beliebteste Telekommunikationsanbieter-Marke 2016.
[356] Vgl. Deutsche Messe AG 2016.
[357] Vgl. Merkle und Kreutzer 2008, S. 21.
[358] Vgl. Naumann 2015, S. 53.

However, knowledge is not only stored in forms, but also in free text documents or social media. If this data from the classic customer relationship management of companies is enriched with mass data from social networks such as *Facebook*, *Twitter* or *Instragram*, there are further possibilities for collaborative exchange between companies and customers.[359] For the first time, an immediate dialogue with the customer at eye level is possible. Companies can also use these networks to analyse their customers' behaviour, cultivate their image or advertise new products. In addition, it is possible to receive direct customer feedback on development information and to analyse the opinion of one's own brand in detail.[360] With the help of this additional information, new target markets can be opened up, target group-specific or new service offerings can be developed or previously unfulfilled or cross-product group customer wishes can be fulfilled. The possibility of benchmarking, i.e. comparison with competing companies, is also particularly valuable.[361]

Other opportunities for so-called social customer relationship management are the large database of

[359] Vgl. Mack und Vilberger 2016, S. 23.
[360] Vgl. Fachschule Osnabrück 2011, S. 19.
[361] Vgl. Naumann 2015, S. 58.

personal data, the high level of detail of the data and the fact that users update this data themselves. This helps customer segmentation and supports target group analysis, up-/cross-selling analysis, loyalty analysis and churn analysis.[362]

Social customer relationship management is establishing itself as another important instrument for preparing for a changed competitive environment, changed market structures, price wars and political framework conditions.

Modern CRM systems, in which data is processed in a central data cloud, also offer the opportunity of mobile access for sales representatives. An employee can use a smartphone or tablet to update or add relevant information from the call to the customer data master during a customer appointment and make it available centrally at the same time.

Mass data can not only be used for the analysis of customer relationships. The data generated by machines also provides valuable information, such as the condition or possible impending maintenance.

---

[362] Vgl. Mack und Vilberger 2016, S. 48.

6.2.2 Predictive Maintenance

The intrinsic value of mass data is particularly evident in the use of predictive maintenance. Here, data measured by sensors is collected in real time from the various components of a complex machine and then stored centrally. This data is correlated and analyzed based on rules. Complex algorithms are thus able to predict the failure probability of a component or the entire machine in good time.[363]

The proactive maintenance allows the machine running times to be extended and unplanned machine downtimes to be avoided. This results in constant adherence to product quality and a reduction in maintenance costs.[364]

The market success of this foresighted technology depends on how intelligently the process and machine data are recorded and linked with each other.[365] This is because knowledge about how long individual machine components last is partly stored in individual knowledge silos and is therefore difficult to access. In many cases, it is necessary to cross company boundaries. However, data correlation problems can

---

[363] Vgl. Hackmann 2013.
[364] Vgl. Schlatt 2014, S. 2.
[365] Vgl. Schlatt 2014, S. 2.

also arise within a company if warranty terms, spare parts lists or contact persons are stored in different systems or are not available in digital form. The biggest challenge is to decide when to stop a machine and which customer order to postpone.[366]

A further development of this computerized system maintenance is the so-called *Condition Based Maintenance*. Sensors measure the vibrations of components subject to wear, as is the case, for example, in wind turbines subject to heavy loads. These data are analysed in real time by mathematical methods in high-performance computers in order to predict a possible failure. Automobile manufacturers such as *BMW* also rely on this method. Text and data mining solutions are used, which perform extensive pattern recognition by analyzing all available data. This involves linking technical data from the vehicle's own database with data stored by the vehicle itself and feedback from dealers. The current i3 electric vehicle from *BMW* also stores and transmits data such as engine speed, triggering of the belt tensioner by sharp braking manoeuvres, operating hours of the vehicle lighting, seat positions, start times and the last 100 parking positions.[367] Expensive repairs or serious

---

[366] Vgl. Hackmann 2013.

vehicle failures can be predicted with very high probability with the help of such and similar data and larger damages can be avoided. The vehicle itself can inform the driver when which component needs to be replaced before any actual damage occurs.[368] This data also serves to optimize the design of new vehicle models.

The difference between forecasting and traditional business intelligence tools is that modern predictive maintenance technologies not only access structured data, but also unstructured data from sensors, documents or natural language.[369] For airlines, for example, current weather data as well as the temperature of the starting point and destination are included in real time for predictive maintenance.[370]

Based in Coburg, Germany, *KAESER* offers a particularly innovative business model based on Industry 4.0 technologies. The compressor manufacturer offers its customers the availability of compressed air on the basis of Service Level Agreements. Invoicing is based on a fixed price for one cubic metre of compressed air including all costs.

---

[367] Vgl. Wimmer 2016.
[368] Vgl. Weiss 2012.
[369] Vgl. Haufe Online / Mindbreeze 2015.
[370] Vgl. Mauerer 2015.

The systems are connected via the Internet, permanently monitored and failures detected in advance. The collected data flows into the machine operation center in Coburg and is analyzed with the help of mathematical models and the machine running times are optimized on the basis of this.[371]

6.2.3 Remote maintenance of globally distributed machines

The example of the German company *Dürkopp-Adler* shows that the global networking of one's own production plants can pay off. The company produces industrial sewing machines at worldwide locations, which are used, among other things, in the automotive industry for the production of airbags. In cooperation with *Deutsche Telekom*, all of the manufacturer's production plants abroad were equipped with sensors, configuration software and IoT modems. If sensors and software measure an imminent machine failure or irregularities in production, this information is uploaded to the data cloud in Germany in real time via the local mobile network. There *Dürkopp-Adler* has the possibility to manage and control the machines centrally and to evaluate the information. In

---

[371] Vgl. Kaufmann 2015, S. 29.

the past, specialized employees had to be flown to the respective country in order to repair or check the machine, but today's modems offer the possibility of reconfiguring the machine from Germany or importing software updates. This makes expensive on-site technician visits obsolete. Among other things, this leads to a significant reduction in travel costs and production downtimes.[372]

6.2.4   Tracking in Logistics

Swiss logistics company *Die Post* has also recognised the trend towards the *Internet of Things* and is planning to optimise and support its national logistics on the basis of energy-efficient radio standards. With the help of the Long Range Wide Area Network (LoRaWAN) radio standard recently developed by *IBM* and *Cisco*, it is possible to connect vehicles, parcels or letterboxes to the Internet very cost-effectively and with minimal energy consumption. The LoRaWAN antennas specially designed for this network have a range of up to 15 kilometers. *Die Post* wants to offer innovative, intelligent and customer-friendly services based on this network. Scenarios such as alarm messages are conceivable as soon as

---

[372] Vgl. Digital Manufacturing Magazin 2015.

sensitive items are opened without permission or the maximum permissible temperature for a medicine is exceeded. GPS sensors can be used to determine the exact location of the shipments at any time to the nearest metre and track the progress of the shipment. The advantage of this technology is that it requires neither the SIM card of a mobile phone provider nor a connection to the power grid. The sensors operate on batteries for up to five years. In March 2016, the company began conducting the first field trials in a pilot network between Berne and Biel.[373]

6.2.5   Predictive Policing

Similar to predictive maintenance, it is possible to foresee and prevent some crimes by using computer algorithms. In the USA such methods are already common practice under the term "predictive policing". But also in Germany and Europe extensive and automated surveillance measures by computer systems are increasingly being applied. The basis are statistical calculations of offences already committed as well as freely accessible data sources such as structural conditions in urban districts, infrastructure and weather data.[374] In an area marked out by the

---

[373] Vgl. Die Schweizerische Post 2016.
[374] Vgl. Brühl und Fuchs 2014; Thomas 2014.

police, computer systems collect data from video cameras and mobile phone cells. If the surveillance system detects the simultaneous presence of transport vehicles with foreign license plates and the use of foreign mobile phone cards, a cognitive computing system calculates the probability of an imminent break-in in this area and, if necessary, alerts the local police forces. In the future, automated facial recognition will also make it possible to compare persons with databases in real time, or cognitive computing systems will be able to calculate the person's mood image in order to determine a potential criminal offence. These methods have already been successfully tested by American police authorities. Such systems are also in pilot operation in German cities such as Munich, Duisburg, Berlin and Cologne.[375] In order to clarify the statistical calculations, it is conceivable to extend the data sources to include the real-time data collected by vehicles, as described in the following chapter.

In March 2016, the news magazine *Bloomberg* reported that the Chinese government wanted to establish a comprehensive monitoring program for all population groups. It commissioned *China*

---

[375] Vgl. Seitz 2014.

Electronics Technology to develop software that could collect, store and process data on each citizen's professions, hobbies, buying patterns and habits. This also includes checking bank accounts, health reports from health insurance companies, employer assessments and telephone behaviour. The system is supported by a profound sensor network based on the technology of the *Internet of Things*. With the help of a data analysis platform, these mass data are to be monitored for behavioural irregularities of citizens and impending criminal offences are to be prevented before the crime is committed.[376]

The military also uses data for behavioral pattern analysis and probability calculation.[377] Under the term "Patterns of Life", US military personnel collect metadata from mobile phones and enrich them with further surveillance measures. It collects information about recipients and senders of short messages, location data and calls made. If this information indicates a calculated probability that the wearer of the mobile phone is a terrorist, he will be killed by remote drone attacks.[378] Since this type of counter-terrorism is not completely error-free and morally

---

[376] Vgl. Oster 2016.
[377] Vgl. Lobo 2015.
[378] Ebd.

questionable, the proceedings came under criticism at the latest since the announcement that these drones were controlled from Germany.[379]

6.2.6 Insurances

Another example of innovative business models is the collection of sensor data in a vehicle. If the vehicle sensors report frequent and strong braking and high acceleration, the correlation of these three data can be used to generate the knowledge that the driver must be at increased risk. This knowledge is particularly interesting for insurance companies, for example, in order to make a decision about the amount of the premium. Already today, many automobile insurers, especially in the western industrial nations, offer so-called telematics tariffs. The amount of the premium thus depends on the actual driving behaviour determined by the sensors.[380] In the automotive industry, sensors are already recording data from the vehicles sold. These include speed, engine temperature and driving behavior. These data can be analyzed by car manufacturers in near real time and thus be useful in vehicle development, among other things. The vehicle owner's data can also be used to

---

[379] Ebd.
[380] Vgl. Sonderegger und Hartmann 2015, S. 8 f.

adapt marketing campaigns to the social milieu or to optimize one's own logistics.[381]

6.2.7 Medical technology

Cognitive computing systems are a further development on the way to artificial intelligence and represent a promising foundation for the meaningful processing of large mass data in medicine. These possibilities were first made known to the general public in 2011. The *Watson* computer system developed by *IBM* was able to hold its own against two top human players in the quiz show "*Jeopardy!*". This quiz is about solving a complex and ambiguous task within a few seconds by linking different information. *Watson* understood human language, responded within just three seconds and even understood complex word games. The algorithm simulated higher thinking skills. *IBM Watson* is currently one of the most powerful cognitive computing systems in the world[382]. It was not until mid-December 2015 that *IBM* opened its global headquarters for the *Watson* supercomputer in Munich, thus making one of the largest investments

---

[381] Vgl. Knauer 2015, S. 25.
[382] Vgl. Lomas 2014.

in the last 20 years. The goal at the new location is to advance the development of the *Internet of Things*.[383]

By analyzing huge amounts of data from all over the world, *Watson* is already able to provide a physician specializing in cancer treatment with therapy recommendations that are precisely tailored to the patient's personal situation and clinical picture.[384] To do this, *Watson* accumulates the patient's data with existing data from around the world, such as other patients' medical records, multilingual research reports, and other medical data.[385] As a result, the system delivers a 90 percent correct therapy recommendation within a few seconds. For comparison: In a study by the insurance company *WellPoint*, human experts chose the right therapy in only 50 percent of cases.[386] This shows that the goal of a common health telematics infrastructure must be the exchange of information across locations and thus represents a strategic factor for treatment and operational control in medical technology.

---

[383] Vgl. IBM 2015; Riedel 2015.
[384] Vgl. Cole, Digitale Transformation: Warum die deutsche Wirtschaft gerade die digitale Zukunft verschläft und was jetzt getan werden muss! (1. Auflage) 2015, S. 36.
[385] Vgl. Osman, Anouze und Emrouzejad 2013, S. 125.
[386] Vgl. Upbin 2013.

The *Internet of Things* with its many sensors also simplifies the lives of severely disabled people. One example is the Lorm-Hand developed at the *Berlin University* of the Arts. Deaf-blind people communicate exclusively with the Lorm alphabet. Letters with typing and stroking movements are written on the palms of the other person's hands. If a person does not master this Lorm-Alphabet, there are no further communication possibilities. The Lorm-Hand is a glove which is equipped with sensors and can translate the German Lorm alphabet into digital text and vice versa. Deafblind people are thus able to send messages electronically to mobile phones, computers or other Lorm gloves via pressure sensors in their hands. With this *Internet of Things* technology, deafblind people are even able to consume digital audio books and communicate with the outside world and physically absent people.[387]

6.2.8 Risks for business models

Information is a resource that allows a company's management to make decisions with a higher probability of occurrence and less variance. They

---

[387] Vgl. ZDF 2015.

have strategic significance and are decisive for the ability to act and agility of a company. [388]

However, many global corporations have a wide variety of methodological approaches to handling information, which results in a high degree of fragmentation as the volume of data increases. Some companies speak of an information infarction due to the unmanageable amount of information.[389] According to KNAUER, the reason for this is that some information is still managed using the same methods from the 1990s. The increasing digitalization, the flood of data from the sensors of the *Internet of Things* and the mass data from the social media present companies without modern information management with an existential risk.[390]

Technological progress makes it possible to access huge amounts of data and process them sensibly thanks to cognitive computing systems. For this reason, the question in modern information management should not be about technology, but about the formulation of meaningful questions. A competitive edge can only be achieved today and in

---

[388] Vgl. Knauer 2015, S. 3.
[389] Vgl. Knauer 2015, S. 24.
[390] Ebd., S. 24

the future by asking the right questions. The gut feeling, which many managers still use as the basis for their decisions, becomes obsolete.[391]

Enterprise Search

Since knowledge does not only occur in structured form such as in forms or tables, but also in free text documents, e-mails, notes, calendar entries or social networks, there is a possibility of processing information with the computer-supported content-oriented and company-wide search, the so-called Enterprise Search. Here, similar to an Internet search engine, a small computer program indexes the digital areas of the company.[392] This also includes Word documents, calendar entries, forums, photos, PDFs or e-mails. Regular indexing ensures that the data is up-to-date and enables employees to quickly search for relevant information from structured and unstructured data.[393] Modern enterprise search products are able to display the information found in a 360-degree view. The most important core information is displayed and additionally enriched with knowledge from internal and external databases. This gives the searcher an all-

---

[391] Ebd., S. 26
[392] Dieses wird auch Crawler genannt.
[393] Vgl. Becker, Schwaderlapp und Seidel 2012, S. 100.

round view and does not have to click through long result lists. The results are put into context with the user. If an employee in the personnel department searches for the keyword "invoice", he or she receives, for example, pay slips or travel expense slips. The system automatically recognizes what the user is primarily interested in. The Enterprise Search option gives companies the opportunity to deal efficiently with large mass data and to use the knowledge available in the company correctly. [394]

The risk of modern information management lies in the initial phase. The basic prerequisite for the establishment of such a system is complete transparency. In many companies, individual departments have no interest in transparency, as their tried and tested local methods are sufficient and information is not shared with other departments. In such cases, extensive convincing of the added value of the new approach helps.[395]

6.2.9 Mobile working via WiFi

Chapter 2.2.1 described that the number of WiFi - enabled devices will increase to over 20 billion by

---

[394] Vgl. Kogler 2016.
[395] Vgl. Knauer 2015, S. 166 f.

2017. The reason is simple. Consumers are always looking for stable and broadband connections to the Internet to access the information they need around the clock. While the younger generation in particular is using the Internet to exchange media in social networks or for data-hungry streaming services, the increasing digitalisation of the world of work demands an increasing mobilisation of employees.[396] [397] They need stable broadband connections also via WiFi on business trips or in telecommuting. In cooperation with *Deutsche Telekom, Deutsche Bahn* already offers so-called WiFi hotspots on many high speed trains with which travellers can go mobile online.[398] Since 2011 *Lufthansa* has also been offering a WiFi service on board the aircraft in cooperation with *Panasonic Avionics*.[399]

6.2.10 Precise Control of Time Critical Applications in the 5G Network

With the requirements for the 5G network described in Chapter 2.2.5, many scenarios are conceivable, such as cross-border surgical operations performed by

---

[396] Vgl. Trick und Weber 2015, S. 7.

[397] Vgl. Papmehl und Tümmers 2013, S. 191.

[398] Vgl. Deutsche Bahn 2016.

[399] Vgl. Deutsche Lufthansa 2016.

a robot connected to a specialist or remote-controlled drones in crisis areas. Autonomous vehicles are also dependent on low latency times in order to be able to calculate and prevent dangerous situations in real time. These and many other applications require extremely low latency times of less than one millisecond.[400]

Projects such as *Google SkyBender* show just how important 5G technology is for the network supply of large and inaccessible areas. In January 2016, it became known that *Google* was already successfully testing unmanned aerial drones that could supply remote areas with data rates of several gigabits per second using 5G technology. Since 2014, the US military has been working on a similar method to provide broadband to ground troops in remote areas.[401]

6.2.11 Wearable Computing

One of the most important innovations from the *Internet of Things* is wearable computing. These are miniaturised and connected computer systems that are used in the immediate vicinity of people, e.g. sewn into clothing or in the form of wristwatches, glasses

---

[400] Vgl. Erfanian und Hattachi 2015, S. 16 f.
[401] Vgl. Harris 2016.

or jewellery.[402] With the help of sensors, memories and processors, body and environmental data can be recorded, collected and processed. If previously defined threshold values are exceeded, alarms can also be triggered and the rescue service or relatives can be informed. It is also conceivable to alert the wearer if he or she is in a dangerous situation or in a dangerous area.[403]

First and foremost, wearable computing is used to increase or expand people's sensory perception. For example, glasses with a built-in microphone, data modem, GPS system, camera and infrared mode are conceivable. The infrared mode could also enable the wearer to see in the dark. A zoom and macro function also allows the wearer to see things far away or close up.[404]

Google is already conducting research on an electronic contact lens that determines the wearer's current glucose level every second and informs the wearer of any abnormalities. Diabetics are spared the need to determine their blood sugar level by taking blood samples.[405] In addition, blind people should

---

[402] Vgl. Roßnagel, et al. 2012, S. 1.
[403] Ebd., S. 2.
[404] Ebd., S. 2.
[405] Vgl. Otis und Parviz 2014.

also benefit from these lenses. In a US patent, *Google* describes how these lenses can be equipped with tiny sensors and microcameras.[406] By recognising colours and movements, modern image processing software in cognitive computing systems enables them to recognise certain situations and inform the wearer via an external device such as a smartphone. For example, they could warn of a busy road or use face recognition algorithms to identify the human counterpart.

In 2014, *Samsung* applied for a patent for a contact lens that enables the wearer to take photos by the blink of an eye and then transmit them to the smartphone[407]. You can also project information from your smartphone, such as photos, videos, or text messages, directly into your eyes retina.[408] The wearer benefits from a computer-aided expansion of the perception of reality. Applications such as navigation services or video conferencing are conceivable.

---

[406] Vgl. Williams 2014.
[407] Vgl. Williams 2016.
[408] Ebd.

6.3 Disruptive Business Models

"As turbulence and instability become the norm in business, the most effective survival stance is a constant but highly selective disruption that we call innovation. "

– Kevin Kelly[409]

In 1998, the 18-year-old student SHAWN FANNING wrote a small software program called *Napster*, which enabled a worldwide exchange of music files via the Internet.[410] Within just a few months, over 70 million users exchanged music free of charge via the Internet and within a very short period of time, the established music industry suffered sales losses of more than 40 percent.[411]

Innovations that make established technologies and business models obsolete are referred to as disruptive.[412] Traditional structures are rigorously broken down and inefficient process steps are radically eliminated. There is a massive change and influence on the value promise of existing goods and services.[413] Disruptive

---

[409] New Rules for the New Economy: https://kk.org/newrules/
[410] Vgl. Kurp, Hauschild und Wiese 2002, S. 99.
[411] Vgl. Roebers und Leisenberg 2010, S. 102.
[412] Vgl. Bloching, et al. 2015, S. 15.

innovations have particularly high potential where special customer requirements are discovered, solutions are found and made accessible to the general public.[414] As a rule, such innovations begin in small and often non-industry niche companies. Through capital investments, they can completely displace established companies and their products from the market after only a short time. According to a study published by *IBM* in November 2015, one in two CEOs now sees their business model threatened by non-industry companies.[415] Often, established companies leave the lucrative business to the so-called start-ups because they lack an eye for revolutionary innovations and the possibilities of cognitive computing systems and powerful data clouds are not fully exploited.[416] [417]

With its disruptive business models, digitization has a massive influence on all industries. The driver exchange platform *Uber* is regarded as the world's largest taxi company, but does not own its own vehicles. The accommodation broker, *Airbnb*,

---

[413] Vgl. Schönefeld 2015.

[414] Vgl. Knöchelmann 2014, S. 11.

[415] Vgl. IBM Institute for Business Value 2015.

[416] Vgl. Brock und Bieberstein 2015, S. 97 f.

[417] Vgl. IBM Institute for Business Value 2015.

generates more than half the turnover of the entire *Hilton* hotel chain, but does not own a single room.[418].

Skype is one of the largest telecommunications companies in the world and does not have its own network.[419] *Facebook* is considered the most popular media company, but does not produce its own content.[420] *Wikipedia* is considered today as the world-wide largest encyclopedia and is free of charge.[421] And the world's largest software vendors, *Apple* and *Google*, rarely write their applications themselves.[422] Such business models are called disruptive.

A small selection of particularly successful and disruptive innovations is presented below.

6.3.1 Uber

Uber is a company founded in 2009, which provides a worldwide driver exchange platform for driving services with its smartphone application.[423] Private persons who own their own vehicle can register as a driver with *Uber*. The application then provides real-

---

[418] Vgl. travelnews 2016.

[419] Vgl. Zühlke 2016.

[420] Vgl. Hohensee 2016.

[421] Vgl. Bauer 2010, S. 29.

[422] Vgl. Kennedy 2015.

[423] Vgl. F. Hackmann 2014.

time driving information to people who are currently looking for a driving opportunity. The drivers act on their own account and pay a 20 percent brokerage fee to *Uber*.[424]. For customers, these rides often cost only half the local taxi fare. Payment is convenient and cashless via smartphone.[425]

With a market value of over 90 billion US dollars, *Uber* is considered the most valuable start-up company in the world.[426] The prerequisites for success were already in place: Smartphones with GPS sensors, drivers with cars, mobile phones and data clouds. The intuitive smartphone application and the lower price resulted in a strongly accelerated market penetration.

Uber led to massive sales losses for local taxi entrepreneurs.[427] This disruptive effect led to some violent riots by taxi drivers in France and further protests in other countries.[428] In addition, legal reasons ensured that the service had been banned in Germany since the beginning of 2015 by the Higher Regional Court of Frankfurt/Main.[429] It was not until

---

[424] Vgl. Rungg 2014.

[425] Vgl. dpa - Spiegel Online Wirtschaft 2015.

[426] Vgl. MacMillan 2015.

[427] Vgl. Soper 2015.

[428] Vgl. Mosler 2016.

the beginning of 2019 that this service became available again in some German cities. The protests of the taxi drivers in London made the application public in the mass media. The number of new customers rose by 850 per cent as a result.[430]

Almost 80 percent of Germans consider their own vehicle a luxury good.[431] It steadily loses its value as a status symbol for under 34-year-olds.[432] European carmakers are therefore under massive pressure to continue building desirable cars and digitalizing processes at the same time. This is precisely where disruptive companies like *Uber* come in.

In March 2016, it became known that *Uber* had apparently ordered a fleet of over 100,000 S-class vehicles from the Stuttgart-based automobile manufacturer *Daimler* for over ten billion US dollars.[433] The condition for this contract was that the vehicles be fully autonomous, i.e. without a human chauffeur. The vehicles should be able to drive independently in the areas with the highest demand in order to reduce waiting times. *Uber* already uses the software for this

---

[429] Vgl. Willmroth 2015.
[430] Vgl. Withnall 2014.
[431] Vgl. Knab, Pezzei und Dancu 2014.
[432] Vgl. Oakes 2015.
[433] Vgl. Feitag 2016.

purpose for its human drivers. *Daimler* thus received the largest order in the company's history. However, the software is not expected to be ready for the market before 2020.

Although *Uber* has a highly disruptive character for the taxi industry, such business practices can form the basis for innovative business models. Luxury goods, such as *Daimler's* S-Class, will continue to be in greater demand in the future. The short-term rental of such goods also gives less affluent customers the opportunity to use them.[434]

6.3.2   *Transport of passengers*

Self-driving cars, trucks or public transport are no longer a vision of the future. The Nuremberg subway in Germany has been running completely autonomously since 2008. Since 2012, fully autonomous cars produced by *Google* have also been allowed to drive on public roads in the US state of Nevada. In *Tesla's* current vehicle model, owners can already download a software update for 2,500 US dollars, which enables the vehicle to drive semi-autonomously.[435] [436] In the future, vehicles will

---

[434] Vgl. D'Arpizio 2015, S. 11.
[435] Vgl. Hemmerich 2012.

increasingly be equipped with cognitive properties from the deep learning process.[437] They independently learn the meaning of traffic signs and rules, recognise people, wild animals and other obstacles and react automatically in hazardous situations within a few milliseconds - if they have not already calculated and avoided them. The only hurdle here is the lack of a legal framework.

In addition, alternative mobility concepts from the Sharing Economy, such as those offered by *Uber*, *BMW* or *Daimler*, will continue to gain in importance. Particularly in urban areas, people will increasingly use transport options with low-cost, minute-based or distance-based utility billing and less own or use their own vehicle.[438]

6.3.3 Amazon

Amazon is regarded as a strong disruptor in various industries. One example is the Kindle - a portable reader for electronically stored books. *Amazon* recognized people's need for more mobility, price reductions and faster book shopping in good time.[439]

---

[436] Vgl. Tesla Motors 2016.

[437] Vgl. Kirk 2015, S. 207 f.

[438] Vgl. Bundesverband Carsharing 2016.

[439] Vgl. Blümlein 2013, S. 69 ff.

Initially, the market remained a niche market that generated hardly any sales after so-called e-readers. The reasons for this were a too small number of electronic books and a lack of acceptance among potential buyers. In 2007, *Amazon* offered its e-reader along with an online library from which the owners of such a device could download numerous electronic books at a uniform price model. With this overall concept as a provider of technologically mature hardware and a multitude of content, *Amazon* established itself as the leading supplier of digital books and at the same time strengthened its perception as the place where books are purchased.[440] Today *Amazon* is regarded as the world's largest bookseller.[441] While the sale of printed books in the stationary trade is constantly decreasing, the sale of digital books is continuously increasing. [442] [443]

Kindle users will not be able to read purchased books on third-party devices. This type of customer loyalty is also known as the "lock-in effect", which is also used in *Apple's* and *Google's* ecosystems.[444]

---

[440] Vgl. A. Aaker 2013, S. 82.
[441] Vgl. Probst, et al., 2012.
[442] Vgl. Börsenverein des deutschen Buchhandels 2013, S. 19.
[443] Vgl. Börsenverein 2016.
[444] Vgl. Galitz, et al. 2012, S. 228 f.

6.3.4 Social Networks

So far, companies such as *Facebook, Google, Amazon, XING* or *Linkedin* have understood the principle of Business Intelligence (BI) and have turned the analysis of data into their business model. The evaluation of motion profiles and data from installed applications on smartphones has long since become an economic phenomenon.[445]

After *Google, Facebook* is the most visited website in Germany and has more active members worldwide than the Catholic Church.[446] [447] It should be noted that the individual benefit increases proportionally to the size of the social network and provides for a constantly increasing attraction for non-members. With a market share of over 85 percent, *Facebook* clearly dominates among social networks.[448] This also applies in particular to *Facebook's* purchased startups *Instagram* and *Whatsapp*.

The market capitalization of social networks *Facebook* and *Google* amounted to 568 billion US-

---

[445] Vgl. Knauer, 2015, S. 24.

[446] Vgl. comScore 2014.

[447] Vgl. facebook Investor Relations 2016; Deutsche Bischoskonferenz 2015.

[448] Vgl. StatCounter 2016.

dollars in 2014. These companies were worth more than *Bayer, Volkswagen, SAP, Siemens, Daimler, BASF* and *Deutsche Telekom* combined.[449]

Contrary to what is often assumed, the business model of social networks does not consist of the sale of personal information, but of the analysis of user behaviour, expressions of interest and the resulting possibilities of individual and targeted advertising.[450] The better the network knows the interests and behaviour of its users, the more valuable the user profile becomes. This allows advertisers to target highly personalized ads by bidding for the coveted ad space in real time.[451] The advertiser can determine exactly which target group his ad should be aimed at. For example, *Facebook* uses user activity to calculate the potential income of its users, knows the exact location, detailed interests, contacts and purchases made in online shops.[452] A user profile, on which just a health problem was announced, is interesting thereby particularly for the pharma industry and accordingly more expensively in the advertising auction. If the user announces the relationship status,

---

[449] Vgl. Dimitz 2014.
[450] Vgl. Funk, et al. 2012.
[451] Vgl. Jiw 2015.
[452] Vgl. Twenga Solutions 2015.

then the value of the profile rises, the nearer a relationship-relevant event moves, e.g. Valentine's Day or wedding day. This is, for example, of interest to florists. It is particularly remarkable that these networks are able to recognize situations from uploaded pictures and videos by the use of modern picture recognition algorithms and to fade in advertisement according to contents. If the uploaded medium shows, for example, a person with a beer mug in his hand, it is possible that the profile visitor sees advertisements of a brewery.[453] The author has recreated this function in a self-experiment on *Facebook*. How this procedure works was explained in Chapter 3.

While the net advertising volume for offline advertising is steadily decreasing, the advertising expenditure for advertising on social networks will rise from 17 billion euros in 2016 to almost 27 billion euros by 2020.[454] [455] There is a creeping dematerialization of advertising media.

---

[453] Vgl. Pfeifer 2015.
[454] Vgl. Schickler Media Index 2015.
[455] Vgl. statista DMO 2015.

6.3.5   WhatsApp

WhatsApp is a smartphone application released in 2009 that enables free messaging and media exchange with other users worldwide.[456] In 2014 they used 450 million people. In the same year, the company with only 57 employees was sold to *Facebook* for 19 billion US dollars.[457] Since the beginning of 2016, more than one billion people have already used the service and exchanged almost 21 billion short messages every minute.[458]

The application had a massive disruptive effect on the classic SMS short message service of mobile phone providers. In 2013, for the first time, more short messages were sent via *WhatsApp* than via classic SMS.[459] This led to a massive drop in revenue for the established mobile communications providers. More than $54 billion in revenue lost due to the spread of alternative short messaging services.[460] Money that the mobile communication industry urgently needs to expand its networks.

---

[456] Vgl. Kneussel 2016.
[457] Vgl. Paukner 2014.
[458] Vgl. Nier 2016.
[459] Vgl. Dialog Consult / VATM 2015, S. 30.
[460] Vgl. Kölnische Rundschau 2012.

WhatsApp wants to generate revenue through communication applications between consumers and businesses. It is charging a fee to companies that want to reach their customers through their application. Services such as customer support are one way to reach customers faster and more effectively. In particular, the company is working on business models for the *Internet of Things*. For example, a connected washing machine could send a message to the owner of the washing machine when the washing process is complete or when detergents need to be replenished. The South Korean company *LG* is already working on such a solution.[461]

6.3.6   *Marketing*

The use of cognitive computing systems also makes sense in marketing. Since 2010, for example, *Persado* has been working on software that uses semantic and statistical algorithms and language analyses to formulate highly effective marketing messages. Various variables, such as style or structure, are analyzed in order to later generate a customer-specific advertising message. This is intended to evoke personal emotions in the recipient. When the software

---

[461] Vgl. Klug 2016.

was used in a mobile communications company, the individual texts written independently by the machine led to 200 percent higher click rates in electronic advertising messages. Sales of terminal devices also more than doubled as a result of the direct address.[462]

6.3.7 Services from the data cloud

Capital-weak, small or medium-sized companies no longer have to invest in expensive telephone systems and the associated maintenance and installation work. The extensive achievements of a modern telephone system can be obtained over Internet from the data cloud. Payment is only made per workstation and according to the service actually used.[463] The telephone system has been dematerialised and is no longer available on site. This not only saves space in the company, but also frees up investment capital previously tied up in operation and acquisition. Over the next four years, every second telephone system in the world could be obtained from the data cloud. Classic providers of permanently installed telephone systems are therefore irrelevant.[464]

---

[462] Vgl. Gador 2015, S. 86; Levine 2015.

[463] Vgl. Rittinghouse und Ransome 2010, S. 30; Telekom Deutschland 2015.

[464] Vgl. Donner 2016.

This paradigm is called *cloud computing*. This is a concept in which computer resources from external providers can be used without extensive installation or configuration work. The hardware and software as well as the entire infrastructure are not visible to the customer. The customer accesses the resources in a data cloud that is opaque for him, so to speak.[465] This enables a concrete economic benefit: the capital costs can be converted into operating costs and are immediately tax-effective.[466]

Google Docs is a well-known example of calculating in the data cloud in broad society.[467] Since 2006, *Google* has provided free text- and spreadsheet processing software that can be used by one or more users at the same time.[468] An installation on the local computer is not necessary for this. The prerequisites are simply any web browser and Internet access.[469] When using such services, a user should be aware of the risk that all data can always be stored, read and evaluated by the provider.

---

[465] Vgl. Beckers 2012, S. 7.

[466] Vgl. Cole, Digitale Transformation: Warum die deutsche Wirtschaft gerade die digitale Zukunft verschläft und was jetzt getan werden muss! (1. Auflage) 2015, S. 37.

[467] Vgl. Manhart 2011.

[468] Vgl. Press 2006.

[469] Vgl. Buyya, Vecchiola und Selvi 2013, S. 363.

Service Models for Calculating in the Data Cloud

In order for IT paradigms such as cloud computing to bring potential benefits and suitability to the enterprise, it is essential to address service models. Due to a lack of a clear definition, it was agreed in expert discussions to divide the data cloud into three models that can be used by the user: Software-as-a-Service (SaaS), Platform-as-a-Service (PaaS) and Infrastructure-as-a-Service (IaaS).

SaaS is the delivery of out-of-the-box software to the customer. However, the infrastructure required to run the software is the responsibility of the vendor. In contrast to the classic software distribution model, the customer pays only for the actual use of the software and no fixed license fees for the local installation on his own computer.[470] The outsourcing of internal company applications to external infrastructures results in potential cost savings and a high degree of flexibility, as the application is not linked to a specific location and can be used from any location with access to the Internet. Known business models for this are *Apple iCloud, Google Docs* or *Microsoft Office 365.*[471]

---

[470] Vgl. Borges und Schwenk 2012, S. 47.
[471] Vgl. Katzer und Crawford 2014, S. 319.

With PaaS, the vendor virtually provides a complete infrastructure to which application developers have access via standardized interfaces. The developer transfers his application to the data cloud, which then handles the processing itself (e.g. database access, synchronization with distributed systems). New applications can often be introduced to the market much faster. Administrative tasks and costs for operating your own platform on site are eliminated. If more powerful platforms are required due to strong customer growth, these can be easily upscaled. Here, too, the customer only pays for the services actually used. Examples of PaaS are *Windows Azure* from *Microsoft* or *AppAgile* from *T-Systems*.[472]

IaaS is the provision of computing, storage and network capacity. The user of such services does not have to worry about sufficient hardware or network capacities, as these are the sole responsibility of the service provider. The necessary IT resources can be negotiated in contractually agreed service level agreements with the provider and are freely scalable at any time. When completely outsourcing the IT infrastructure to external providers, the security aspect cannot be neglected. The largest provider of

---

[472] Vgl. Borges und Schwenk 2012, S. 46 f.; Murtz 2015.

such services at present is *Amazon* with "EC2" for computing power or "S3" for data storage.[473] Since March 2016, *Deutsche Telekom* has also been offering such infrastructure services from the data cloud as a European alternative that is less questionable under data privacy law. In the business model known as the "*Open Telekom Cloud*", the telephone system described above is also operated.[474]

In March 2016, the *European Organization for Nuclear Research* (CERN) announced its intention to obtain massive computing power, high data transfer bandwidths and storage space for processing scientific data from *Deutsche Telekom's* data clouds. With this contract, the nuclear research institute wants to test the performance and flexibility of commercial data cloud providers for scientific calculations. The aim is to establish an interdisciplinary scientific data cloud and to accelerate the research of such sourcing models.[475]

In addition, there are a number of other service models. These are called XaaS. The X represents a placeholder for any service. One example is Human-

---

[473] Vgl. Münzl, Pauly und Reti 2015, S. 10; Chatfield 2014, S. 165.
[474] Vgl. Marwan 2014; Rottinger 2016.
[475] Vgl. Schindler 2016.

as-a-Service (HuaaS), also known as crowdsourcing. Tasks that cannot be performed by machines are broken down into smaller task packages and offered for solution by human intelligence on the Internet.[476]

6.3.8 Information security in the data cloud as a business model

As already indicated, the use of public clouds of data still entails a risk of data protection and data security. If all data about product technologies and production processes, i.e. those data that make up the competitive advantage, are stored online in public data clouds, then all the industrial secrets that make up the prosperity of a leading industrial nation like Germany are also located there.

At the latest since the revelations of SNOWDEN, which describe a large-scale industrial espionage by Anglo-American secret services, companies should be aware that the careless use of online data storage can cause high economic damage.[477] This is another reason why 83 percent of European companies rely on service providers whose data centers are

---

[476] Menschliche Intelligenz besitzt gegenüber Maschinen (noch) die Fähigkeit der Kreativität.

[477] Vgl. Wolfenstetter, Bub und Deleski 2015, S. 2.

physically located in Germany.[478] Germany provides a very high level of data protection internationally due to its strict data protection laws.[479] *Deutsche Telekom* has also recognized this. It uses the location advantage as a business model by making data cloud technologies from its own data centers available to partner companies.[480] In November 2015, for example, the *Handelsblatt* newspaper announced the joint cooperation between *Microsoft* and *Deutsche Telekom*. In the future, the Anglo-American company *Microsoft* will store all customer data of European users exclusively in highly available high-security data centers of *Deutsche Telekom* located in Germany.[481]. Among other things, the aim is to prevent the spying out of state secret services and to increase the attractiveness and growth potential of services from the data cloud.[482]

The business model stipulates that *Deutsche Telekom* acts as a data trustee and has sole physical and technical access to the personal customer data of its business partners. *Microsoft* therefore only has

---

[478] Vgl. Pols und Heidkamp 2015, S. 32.

[479] Vgl. Haag 2014.

[480] Vgl. DTAG Medien 2016.

[481] Vgl. Abolhassan, Big Data und Cloud Computing gehören zusammen 2013.

[482] Vgl. Kerkmann und Karabasz 2015; Clauß 2016.

temporary access to customer data in accordance with the contractual agreement or permission of the customer.[483]

In addition, large information and communications service providers operate business models that provide that security functions such as firewalls, attack detection systems, network communication interfaces or virus protection programs can also be rented from the data cloud. This means that inquiring companies have the option of renting these as required and without having to purchase their own hardware or maintenance. This flexible sourcing model for information security is increasingly being used in a meaningful and useful way in business life, as consumption-based performance billing and end-to-end service level agreements in the security sector offer added value especially for small and medium-sized enterprises.[484]

The fact that the protection of industrial plants in particular must be given top priority was demonstrated not least by *Siemens* with the construction of its Cyber Security Operation Centers

---

[483] Vgl. Rath 2016.

[484] Vgl. Abolhassan, Kundenzufriedenheit im IT-Outsourcing: Das Optimum realisieren 2014, S. 92 f.

in Lisbon, Munich and Milford. From there, so-called industrial security specialists monitor all industrial plants of *Siemens* customers worldwide for possible security threats to the machines or the industrial infrastructure. If necessary, proactive countermeasures are coordinated, with priorities based on the criticality of the expected impact on the customer's business.[485] Since 2017, *Deutsche Telekom*'s Security Operation Center (SOC) has also been offering a professional threat analysis and defense service, which can also be used by small and medium-sized enterprises.

6.3.9 Personal Assistants

Even large IT companies are aware of the potential of cognitive computing systems. *Apple* developed the virtual language assistant Siri, *Google* developed Google Now, *Amazon* relies on Echo, *Microsoft* on Cortana and *Facebook* is currently investing in the development of an artificial intelligence called "Memory Network".[486]. All systems are based on human voice input. Through frequent use, these virtual assistants learn a human understanding of their environment by correlating, for example, location

---

[485] Vgl. Petry 2016.
[486] Vgl. facebook Inc. 2015.

data from the GPS sensor of the mobile phone, movement intensity from the activity sensor, phoning behaviour from the call list, written texts and typing speed. With "MoodScope", *Microsoft* has already developed a prototype that uses the above information to calculate, predict and simultaneously announce the current mood of a person on social networks with an accuracy of 93 percent.[487] According to a study by the American market research institute *IDC*, half of all consumers are expected to interact with self-learning cognitive computing systems by 2018.[488] For the year 2021, the number of worldwide users of virtual digital assistants is forecast at around 1.8 billion. Films such as "Her", "Odyssey in Space", "Terminator" or "Ex Machina" show that the opportunities and risks of advanced, cognitive computing systems in particular inspire people's imagination.[489] In "Ex Machina", an artificial neural network is created from the correlation of mass data of social networks and search engine queries, which develops the ability to interpret and manipulate human emotions through distinctive deep learning methods. Current technologies are able to take over simple organizational tasks. They

---

[487] Vgl. Likamwa, et al. 2013.
[488] Vgl. High 2015.
[489] Vgl. Kleingers 2014.

respond to natural language or foresighted, based on probabilities.[490]

6.3.10 Financial technology

"Banking is necessary, Banks are not." This Bill GATES said in 1994 and already predicted the upcoming disruption in the classic banking business.

According to SCHRÖDER and BUKOWSKI, traditional banks have not produced any further innovations in recent years, with the exception of online banking.[491] In addition, private investors have lost confidence in the traditional banking system due to the recent economic crises. Only a quarter of private customers still consider their bank advisor to be highly trustworthy.[492] Only the possession of a banking licence gives those banks an advantage over alternative credit institutions from the digital world.[493]

According to a study published by *Pricewaterhouse Coopers* in March 2016, 83 per cent of traditional financial services providers currently see parts of their business as severely threatened by financial

---

[490] Vgl. Engelien 2014.
[491] Vgl. Schröder und Bukowski 2015, S. 77.
[492] Vgl. Handelsblatt / dpa 2014.
[493] Vgl. Schröder und Bukowski 2015, S. 77 ff.

technology companies.[494] These so called *FinTechs* is the umbrella term for technologies that revolve around web-based or data-based financial products. These include mobile banking transactions via smartphone, innovative loans, insurance, portfolio management concepts or digital currencies.[495] As with most disruptions, the technology-driven and often non-industry players are starting where the customers of traditional banks feel the greatest potential for frustration. They focus on simple and customer-friendly innovations in the service sector. One example, well known to the general public, is *Paypal*, a company founded by ELON MUSK in 1998, which now processes more than 200 billion US dollars annually.[496] The company demonstrated how simple and customer-oriented payment transactions can be designed in the digital, globally connected and mobile age and thus hit the nerve of customers.

Digital currencies such as Bitcoins or IOTA, which rely on complete decentralization, also pose a threat to the classic banking system in the medium and long term. This currency, which is based on strong cryptography, enables largely anonymous electronic

---

[494] Vgl. Kashyap, et al. 2016, S. 19.
[495] Vgl. Kornstädt 2015.
[496] Vgl. paypal 2016.

payment transactions between two parties. This makes it possible, for example, for consumers of music to pay the creative artist directly via crypto currencies without incurring a transaction fee or other costs. A central credit institution is not necessary. [497]

The World Economic Forum predicts a strong disruptive effect on the banking sector over the next five to ten years, especially for African countries.[498] Digital currencies have the potential to significantly reduce corruption and provide more transparency in payment transactions.[499] This gives back valuable confidence in payment transactions, especially to the African economy. The *Melinda & Bill Gates Foundation* invests in African start-up companies for digital currencies.[500] According to *Microsoft* founder Bill Gates, digital crypto currencies also offer the poorest people in the world the chance to participate in electronic payments. More than 2.5 billion people currently have no bank account due to poverty.[501]

It shows that value creation processes and business models of time-honoured banks are not only affected

---

[497] Vgl. Kuo 2016.
[498] Vgl. Gould 2016.
[499] Ebd.
[500] Vgl. Bergmann 2015.
[501] Vgl. M. a. Gates 2015.

in part by digitisation, but in their entirety. These banks are well advised to use modern data analysis methods driven by algorithms as well as seamlessly integrated sales models and to align themselves with an all-encompassing digitization strategy.[502] Digitisation has become visible. This is also reflected in the massive downsizing of local bank branches. While there are more bank branches than petrol stations in Germany, FinTechs rarely have their own branches.[503] Fewer and fewer customers see the need for personal on-site advice through online offers and mobile payment methods. By 2030, German banks will close more than 40 percent of their branches.[504]

But there is also a risk. If you feed machines with large amounts of data, they learn additional standard processes. They become more intelligent. Digital financial technologies will determine the future of the financial industry. But what happens when these algorithms produce errors and who is responsible? This question has not yet been clearly clarified and will not only continue to occupy the financial world.

---

[502] Vgl. Dapp 2014.
[503] Vgl. Krause 2015.
[504] Vgl. Luttmer 2014.

174

6.4 Sharing Economy

At present, the term *Sharing Economy* is only known to every second German citizen.[505] Millions of people are already using offers from this hybrid market model. The best known representatives of the Sharing Economy are the companies *Airbnb* and *Uber* mentioned in Chapter 6.3. Almost 90 percent of users believe that such offers will become more popular in the future and will make a significant contribution to environmental protection.[506] Manufacturers of vehicles or other consumer goods may be forced to design their goods to be more durable and of higher quality as the Sharing Economy becomes more widely used. This means that fewer products are needed that work longer and therefore cause less waste and resource consumption.[507]

Instead of owning things, more and more people see advantages in saying goodbye to the burdens of ownership and using things only when they are really needed.[508] Almost every second German can imagine

---

[505] Vgl. Gfk Verein Compact 2015, S. 1.
[506] Ebd., S. 7.
[507] Vgl. Strobel, 2015.
[508] Vgl. Granig, Hartlieb und Lingelhel 2016, S. 8.

borrowing tools, sports equipment or entertainment electronics over the Internet instead of buying them.[509]

This disruptive type of consumption harbours risks, but also opportunities for new business models. Instead of being repressed, established companies are encouraged to develop models that allow them to profit from this trend. Already in 2010, the economic potential of the Sharing Economy was estimated at over 100 billion US dollars per year.[510] With the right investment strategy, even large companies have the opportunity to benefit from it.[511] *Google, General Electric, Citigroup* and *Avis* are already investing heavily in start-up companies in this industry. While 300 million US dollars were invested in such companies in 2010, by 2014 the figure had risen to over six billion US dollars.[512]

The advantages are obvious: falling search and transaction costs as well as greater flexibility and convenience for the consumer. With the help of a smartphone application, the user checks the local availability of the goods or services he is looking for and often benefits from significantly lower prices

---

[509] Vgl. Pentsi und Miosga 2015.
[510] Vgl. Granig, Hartlieb und Lingelhel 2016, S. 120.
[511] Vgl. Deloitte Studie 2015.
[512] Ebd.

compared to conventional rental offers. Unlike in the past, this modern form of market and exchange economy among private individuals is based on current Internet technologies such as data clouds, smartphones, sensors and digital payment options.[513]

However, not only cars, tools, housing, land or work are offered in the Sharing Economy, but credit transactions are also possible. *Lending Club*, for example, has brokered over seven billion US dollars in loans since 2007. Credit seekers can use a smartphone application to search for private savers and borrow money. A bank is no longer necessary. Here, too, a disruptive character is discernible.[514]

The legal framework represents a risk. Since within the Sharing Economy everyone becomes relatively simply a provider in the legal sense, there are still open questions regarding taxes and security standards. As mentioned in Section 6.3.1, *Uber's* business practice has been partly prohibited in Germany. The basis for this is that private drivers cannot prove that they have a valid taxi license and thus violate the German Passenger Transport Act. However, business models such as *Airbnb's* housing

---

[513] Vgl. Deloitte Studie 2015.
[514] Vgl. Deloitte Studie 2015.

agency also quickly reach their legal limits. In Germany it is forbidden to rent out one's own private apartment if the landlord does not allow it.[515]

Even sharing your own WiFi network is not always possible without further ado. A worldwide unique phenomenon in the operation of wireless Internet access is the German "Störerhaftung". This is a regulation laid down in the German Telemedia Act which makes the operator of a wireless network personally liable for all activities of the connected devices. If, for example, the guest of a holiday home commits a copyright infringement on the Internet via the WiFi network shared by the owner, the guest is not prosecuted for this offence under German law, but the connection holder of the network is prosecuted.[516] Although this law has been partially repealed in 2019, many connection holders will continue to be liable for illegal activities of their users in 2019. This can lead to a forced shutdown of your own connection. For this reason, the spread of free Wi-Fi networks in Germany is severely affected. The unrestricted sharing of the own Wi-Fi network is therefore not legally secure. The Association of the German

---

[515] Vgl. Aulich 2015.
[516] Vgl. Digitale Gesellschaft e.V. o. J.

Internet Industry fears that this regulation will hinder the expansion of open wireless networks in Germany.[517]

Commercial providers of rentals or services have further disadvantages due to the often strict legal requirements. Hoteliers must comply with hygiene and safety regulations, while this is left to the private housing agents of the Sharing Economy. In Germany, professional passenger transporters have to undergo regular health checks and have their vehicles inspected annually by the Technical surveillance association (TÜV). Private drivers, such as those mediated by *Uber*, do not have to do this.[518] There are two solutions for this. The existing regulations of the respective countries could be critically questioned and laws that are no longer up to date or superfluous could be deleted. Alternatively, the companies concerned can seek dialogue with the providers of Sharing Economy platforms and work together on innovative concepts.[519] One example of this is *Daimler's* cooperation with the German start-up company "*My-Taxi*", which provides taxi drivers via a smartphone application. Daimler has owned 100 percent of this company since 2014.[520] In 2019, "*My-*

---

[517] Vgl. Landefeld 2014, S. 9.
[518] Vgl. TÜV Hessen o. J.
[519] Vgl. Deloitte Studie 2015.

Taxi" was renamed "*Free Now Ride*" and offers chauffeur services and other mobility services in addition to driving services. This puts the company in direct competition with *Uber*.

But the Sharing Economy also offers the opportunity to increase the prosperity of a society. One of the many examples of this is Car-Sharing. People who could not afford their own car have the opportunity to use it for small amounts. With its fleet of vehicles called *DriveNow*, BMW, for example, offers such an opportunity. Here, private individuals can reserve and use a nearby BMW vehicle at any time using a smartphone application. Payment is made by smartphone and only for the actual period of use per minute. The vehicles are monitored via machine-to-machine communication and the information collected during the journey is stored in data clouds and then analysed to improve the service quality.[521]

---

[520] Vgl. Hecking 2016.
[521] Vgl. Karlstetter 2012.

7 Changes in the world of work

„No one can escape the transforming fire of machines." [522] - KEVIN KELLY

When THOMAS NEWCOMEN invented the steam engine about 300 years ago, which was considerably improved a few years later by JAMES WATT, it was probably not yet clear that this would lead to the construction of the Berlin Wall. Further effects were shift work, increasing divorce rates and single mothers. [523]

During the first industrial revolution, human labor lost enormous value through the use of the steam engine. It became much more important to supply the machines with coal to keep them running. People were centralized around the engine, leading to rural exodus, working-class neighborhoods and cramped housing. The families became smaller and smaller. [524] The electric light bulb patented by THOMAS ALVA EDISON led to the electrification of the industry and made night work possible for the first time. [525] The

---

[522] Vgl. Hänisch, et al. 2016, S. 68.
[523] Vgl. Dumm und Schild 2009, S. 183.
[524] Vgl. Fuchs 2011, S. 82.
[525] Vgl. Myers 2014, S. 102.

consequence: the constantly changing working hours and 24-hour shift work led to the destabilization of the bourgeois family order. Divorces and more and more single mothers were the result.[526] The high capital expenditure for the machines and the high productivity fuelled capitalism. The simple workers could only oppose exploitation with solidarity, class struggle and trade unions. This resulted in socialist or communist social orders.[527]

Since then, three more industrial revolutions have taken place. This chapter explains the potential impact of the Fourth Industrial Revolution on the world of work. Whether it will have a similarly serious impact on the social and political order as the steam engine once did, and whether an unconditional basic income is an alternative to mass poverty, cannot be predicted with certainty.

The *Digital Transformation* and the *Internet of Things* have long since found their way into professional life. Topics such as mass data, cognitive computing systems, cloud computing, cyberphysical systems or crowdsourcing are becoming increasingly important for professional life. Without the

---

[526] Vgl. Heiden 2014, S. 323.
[527] Vgl. Uhlig 2008, S. 359.

possibilities of computer support and global networking, many companies would already be at a standstill today. Employees make agreements about social networks and digitally mapped processes simplify work processes. At the same time, administrative tasks are being increasingly automated, creating more time for essential tasks. Connected and automated processes enable more flexible working hours and more location independence for professional activities. Numerous risks are also emerging. More and more people are ordering their clothes, books and electronic items on the Internet. Service providers such as language teachers, financial advisors, sales staff, legal assistants, security personnel or bank employees are increasingly losing their social significance.[528] The platforms of the Sharing Economy place craftsmen at low prices. Working models such as crowdsourcing lead to considerable price pressure for simple services, as contractors have to compete with international prices. This leads to lower tax revenues. In addition, permanent availability and monitoring at the workplace can lead to stress-related illnesses and behavioural anomalies and thus cause high damage to society.[529] Since not only machines and things are

---

[528] Vgl. Peterson 2015.

connected in working life, but increasingly also people, this leads to questions of data protection and labour law, to which there is currently no answer. *Industrie 4.0* technologies are regarded as enormous productivity drivers, similar to the steam engine. Intelligent and connected machines are increasingly taking on monotonous and repetitive tasks and are not only displacing low-skilled people from production, but are also reliably performing routine tasks for academics, doctors, office and administrative staff.[530]

According to the *World Economic Forum*, more jobs will be lost than created in Germany as a result of digitisation and demography. The situation in the Asian economic area is quite different. In the next 15 years, significantly more jobs will be created there than will be lost.[531]

Since digitisation will have radical effects on a large part of the global world of work, only representative economic areas are described below for which a particularly high impact on the world of work can be expected.[532]

---

[529] Vgl. Siebert o. J.
[530] Vgl. Frey und Osborne 2013.
[531] Vgl. Prising 2016; Monck 2016.
[532] Vgl. Becker und Knop 2015, S. 34.

7.1.1 Manufacturing sector

Particularly in industries subject to global competitive pressure, it is important to ensure that wage costs are in line with productivity gains in order to secure the future of the location.[533] Here, technologies such as the cyberphysical systems of Industry 4.0 play a decisive role for the manufacturing industry in Germany. But even if Germany plays a leading role in Industry 4.0, it is to be expected that the demand for low-skilled and unskilled workers will continue to decline in the medium term.[534] The leaps in productivity brought about by technological innovations will be so great that fewer and fewer production personnel will be needed. There are, however, great development opportunities for highly qualified workers. Complex IT systems in production demand significantly higher demands on technical training as well as a high degree of personal responsibility and self-directed action. In the next five to ten years, routine tasks that can be easily automated will be subjected to further automation. In the future, production employees will increasingly take over controlling tasks and will be supported and

---

[533] Vgl. V. Brühl 2015, S. 3.
[534] Vgl. Statistisches Bundesamt o. J.

advised by digital assistance systems. These include e.g. data glasses, tablets or smartphones that display production-relevant information to employees in real time or display instructions for action with computer-aided reality enhancement.[535] Assistance robots will relieve employees of hazardous and monotonous tasks and create more time for creative thinking and action. Using deep learning algorithms, they automatically learn new assembly processes.[536] At CeBit in March 2016, the Chinese telecommunications supplier *Huawei* announced its cooperation with Kuka, a German manufacturer of industrial robots. In a joint research project, the aim is to expand robot technology to include deep learning techniques, cloud computing, the *Internet of Things* and the 5G wireless standard.[537]

The possibilities of 3D printers will also find their way into production. It is already apparent today that 3D printers can shorten computer-aided development and production processes from several years to just a few weeks. This significantly reduces complexity costs.[538] They enable the production of individual

---

[535] Vgl. IKT.NRW 2014.
[536] Vgl. V. Brühl 2015, S. 206 ff.
[537] Vgl. Sawall 2016.
[538] Vgl. V. Brühl 2015, S. 196.

pieces at the cost of mass production.[539] A well-known example of this is the manufacture of dental prostheses from the 3D printer. It is regarded as high-precision, fast and particularly cheap in production.[540] Dentures can be produced within minutes. This took days or weeks for human dental technicians. 3D printers are already being used not only in medicine, but also in vehicle and aircraft construction. The aircraft manufacturer *Airbus* had previously purchased all components from suppliers. In a current project, double-walled petrol pipes made of titanium are being printed. And only when they are needed. Storage is therefore no longer necessary. From mid-2016, components made of stainless steel and later aluminium will also be printed. At the same time, the aircraft manufacturer is training 55 engineers for this project, who will operate, assemble and monitor the printer.[541] In recent years it has already been successfully proven that it is also possible to produce fully functioning passenger cars and entire houses from the 3D printer at a reasonable price.[542] In the medium term, 3D printing technology will not completely replace the spare parts trade, but it will

---

[539] Ebd., S. 203.
[540] Vgl. Mörer-Funk 2014.
[541] Vgl. DPA/N24 2016.
[542] Vgl. Reek 2014.

complement it. Before production comes to a standstill, spare parts required very quickly will be printed on site.[543]

It should be noted that there are currently no confirmed empirical findings on the labour-relevant effects of such technologies. Nevertheless, it is to be expected that in the next five to ten years there will be highly automated, sensor-supported networking and increased information technology penetration of human-machine interaction. In the long term, product development and production will be virtual throughout.[544] Terminal devices such as tablets or smartphones, technologies such as data clouds, cognitive computing systems, virtual assistants, multimedia or social media are already widespread in the office world today and are also becoming increasingly important in the production environment.

---

[543] Vgl. Cole, Digitale Transformation: Warum die deutsche Wirtschaft gerade die digitale Zukunft verschläft und was jetzt getan werden muss! (1. Auflage) 2015), S. 113.

[544] Vgl. Kurz, Arbeit in der Industrie 4.0: „Besser statt billiger" als zukunftsfähige Gestaltungsperspektive 2014.

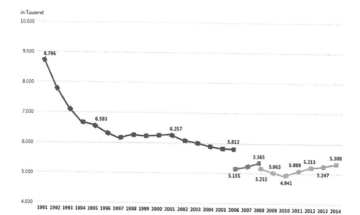

Figure 6 Development of employment in the manufacturing sector.
Source: Statistisches Bundesamt o. J.

7.1.2 Financial management

In November 2015, *Deutsche Bank* announced its intention to counter the attack by FinTechs. The bank is developing fully automated robots called "Robo-Advisor" to automate private and business customer advisory services in the future.[545] The client's investment strategy is adopted by software, taking into account the tax situation and risk tolerance. These robots are primarily used for customers who have not yet been able to afford a personal investment advisor.[546]

---

[545] Vgl. Kanning 2015.
[546] Ebd.

At the end of 2015, *Comdirect Bank* announced a cooperation with the *Connected Living Innovation Centre* to further expand its market-leading role as an innovative and digital bank. The aim is to expand the customer's living room into a digital bank branch with the help of connected building services. This means that all banking services can be provided from home without the need for personal advice.[547]

Future bank employees will therefore have to demonstrate highly specialised IT skills and fewer skills in business and finance. Trained experts for investment consulting are needed only to a limited extent and only for individual interests in the investment of funds as well as for the optimization and control of financial software.[548]

7.1.3 Stationary trading

According to a projection by the *Cologne Institute for Retail Research*, online sales will increase by twenty percent by 2020, while retail sales will decline by ten percent.[549] Nevertheless, stationary retail will remain the dominant sales channel in the coming 25 years,

---

[547] Vgl. Connected Living 2015.

[548] Vgl. Lorenz und Heumann 2015; Frey und Osborne 2013, S. 17.

[549] Vgl. Frankfurter Allgemeine Zeitung Nr. 82 2014, S. 26.

although it will have to implement new concepts. According to market researchers, in the future the smartphone will be developed into an all-encompassing shopping assistant that navigates customers to the nearest store, compares prices in real time and offers mobile payment options.[550] According to current findings, human customer advisors could continue to lose importance, as the smartphone uses machine learning algorithms to better understand the customer's individual purchasing behavior and can provide appropriate advice and recommendations.

Digital business models are often not feasible in stationary retail. In addition, sales are falling steadily. Customers often use retail stores only for fitting, trial and error or for advice. The goods are then ordered from the cheapest supplier on the Internet. For this reason, the retail trade must strive for new concepts in order to retain its employees. Any concept that is not geared to the exact needs of the customer will fail. One of these concepts could be to provide the offered goods only once in the shop in order to save rental costs. At the customer's request, the goods are delivered the same day directly from the central warehouse to the customer's desired location. For

---

[550] Vgl. V. Brühl 2015, S. 32.

comparison: The online retailer *Amazon* already plans a delivery within 90 minutes after ordering.[551] *Tesla* also pursues a similar model. The vehicle manufacturer only makes very few vehicles available in its shops. There they can be viewed and configured in virtual mirrors. Once the desired configuration has been completed, the car can be ordered online on site. The vehicle is then delivered to the desired delivery address.[552]

By offering wireless Internet access, customers were to be given the opportunity to order goods online in the shop and pay for them without cash. This also eliminates the need for point-of-sale. With the help of the beacons described in Chapter 2.2.3, the customer can navigate independently within the store and display recommendations, availability or additional product information via a computer-supported reality enhancement. According to a consumer survey conducted by the market research institute *Innofact*, one in two today can already imagine using virtual mirrors. The garments tried on by the customer on site are displayed in a mirror in different colours without the customer having to change them.[553] In the

---

[551] Vgl. T. /. Neuhetzki 2016.
[552] Vgl. Buvat und Subrahmanyam 2014.
[553] Vgl. eBay International AG 2015.

future, the retail trade will have to distinguish itself more than ever through high consulting competence in order to stand out from the online trade. These include, in particular, skills that are currently difficult or impossible for machines to adopt: a pronounced empathy for customers, active listening, negotiating skills and service orientation.[554] Shopping in stationary retail should be perceived as a positive experience for the customer.

7.1.4   Police, Justice and Military

Police

In parts of the USA, a fully autonomous robot called *Knightscope* has been successfully used for over two years to predict and prevent impending crimes in schools, business premises and neighborhoods. The robot, which weighs around 150 kilograms and measures 150 centimeters, is equipped with numerous sensors, microphones, an infrared and thermal imaging camera, and air quality meters. It regularly scans its environment, such as vehicle number plates and the faces of passers-by. This information is then compared with police databases using modern image recognition algorithms. It automatically detects noises

---

[554] Vgl. V. Brühl 2015, S. 32 ff.; J. Myers 2016.

such as broken glass or human cries as well as air pollution or life-threatening dangerous situations. If necessary, it alerts human emergency forces available at the same time. With the help of learning algorithms, it detects impending dangerous situations in advance and tries to prevent them by active intervention or acoustic alarms. *Knightscope* is rented by his development company for 6.25 US dollars per hour. This is far below the local minimum wage for human security personnel.[555] According to FREY and OSBORNE, up to 84 percent of human security personnel and one in ten police officers can be replaced by machines.[556]

Justice

In 2011, a research group investigated 1,112 verdicts of Israeli judges. The analysis showed that the number of sentences pronounced after the lunch break was significantly higher than before the break. It could be confirmed that the judges did not base their judgments exclusively on facts, but also on the time of day and their own well-being. It is obvious that machines are free of cognitive distortions, so-called bias, and can make decisions without reservation and

---

[555] Vgl. Buhr 2015.
[556] Vgl. Frey und Osborne 2013, S. 60 und S. 67.

more safely.[557] In his 2013 study "The Future of Employment", the economist CARL BENEDIKT FREY calculated a 40 percent substitution potential for judges. For judges and hearing officers specializing in administrative law, he even calculated a substitution potential of 64 percent. According to FREY, lawyers, on the other hand, are only 3.5 percent replaceable by machines, as this profession requires a high degree of creativity and social intelligence. According to the current state of science, these properties are not yet feasible by computers.[558]

Military

Technologies such as intelligent decision algorithms and machine learning are also used in the military. Computer algorithms have been supporting soldiers in surveillance aircrafts for many years. In the process, recommendations for action are calculated in order to avoid enemy attacks more quickly, for example.[559]

Flight drones are becoming increasingly popular not only in the private and commercial sectors. Also in the military, in secret services and in police

---

[557] Vgl. Spiegel Online: Wissenschaft 2011; Frey und Osborne 2013, S. 16.

[558] Vgl. Frey und Osborne 2013, S. 59 ff..

[559] Vgl. Klinger, et al. 1993, S. 60.

operations, they have been a proven means for many years to observe or eliminate suspected enemies without endangering their own human forces.[560] Due to the constant miniaturization of sensors, actuators, transponders and microchips, drones the size of insects are also possible today. For some years now, researchers have been working on equipping living insects with sensor packages, batteries and microphones for subsequent use in crisis areas for espionage or surveillance purposes in disaster situations.[561] Since living insects are difficult to control, the US military developed fully electronic flying drones that can be controlled from a distance or even fly autonomously.[562] In 2011, the US Department of Defense presented the *Nano Hummingbird* to the public. The *Nano Hummingbird* weighs 19 grams and is 16 centimeters wide. It not only looks like a hummingbird, but also imitates its special flight characteristics. Equipped with a camera, the *Nano Hummingbird* is able to transmit live images from the air for up to eight minutes.[563] In May 2013, a research group at Harvard University published the results of their *RoboBees*. These flying micro-robots

---

[560] Vgl. Grieß 2014.
[561] Vgl. Czycholl 2013.
[562] Vgl. Seidler 2008.
[563] Vgl. Gitlin 2011.

are flying drones the size of a paper clip and weigh only 0.1 grams. In the future, these drones will be equipped with an artificial swarm intelligence and will be used completely autonomously in flight for the pollination of crops.[564] In addition, there are applications in personal surveillance, search and rescue operations, weather and climate research as well as traffic and environmental monitoring.[565] The microdrones, which are equipped with microphones and cameras, have the potential to land independently on humans or animals, take DNA samples or inject nano-sized transponders with tiny needles. A similar procedure has been used for animal identification since the mid-1990s.[566] In the military field, autonomously executed espionage or killing missions are also conceivable.[567]

---

[564] Vgl. Spector 2014.

[565] Vgl. Harvard College o. J.

[566] Vgl. Bierwisch 2014, S. 34 ff.

[567] Vgl. Jain 2015, S. 73.

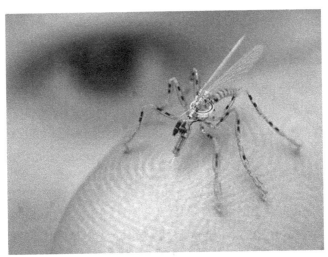

Figure 7 Model of a flying drone with needle.
Quelle: Johnson 2012.

In January 2016, the *University of Würzburg* announced, with the support of the *Volkswagen* Foundation, that it was conducting research on nano drones with light propulsion. The drones, made of monocrystalline gold, are precisely controlled by laser beams and simultaneously supplied with energy. These nano drones are so small that they can easily be introduced into the human organism. This opens up new fields of application, especially in medicine and the military.[568] [569]

---

[568] Vgl. Hecht 2016.
[569] Vgl. O'Mathúna 2009, S. 124.

7.1.5 Office and administration

According to the study by FREY and OSBORNE, machines can handle the tasks of administrative employees faster, more reliably and more efficiently.[570] Already today, many administrative tasks can be automated by automatic context recognition and sorting algorithms.[571]

In a study published in March 2016 by the IT industry association *Bitkom*, it was determined that half of the administrative tasks in German companies had already been digitized. Large companies even have a total digitization level of 70 percent. Process management and the scanning and archiving of paper documents are the most popular areas of application for digital technologies. The areas of accounting, finance, controlling and human resources are particularly permeated by the digital transformation. Medium-sized and smaller companies are currently still afraid of the high investment costs and fear unauthorized access to sensitive company data. In addition, they lack qualified personnel.[572]

---

[570] Vgl. Becker und Knop 2015), S. 43; Frey und Osborne 2013.
[571] Vgl. Zimmer 2007.
[572] Vgl. Biffar 2016.

According to FREY and OSBORNE's calculations, nine out of ten auxiliary personnel posts can be fully digitised and automated. In addition, the jobs of 30 percent of trained personnel developers are at risk.[573] A data-driven personnel strategy in human ressources is already an important competitive factor today.[574]

The fact that there is still great potential for digitisation in the administration of the German Federal Government has recently been demonstrated by the refugee crisis. Despite its extensive administrative staff, the Federal Government has great difficulties in completing the urgent tasks in the Federal Office for Migration and the Foreigners Authority in good time. For this reason, too, the Federal Government launched the so-called federal computer centre consolidation in January 2016 in order to merge the federal IT service providers. Through a stronger and nationwide networking and centralization of services as well as better IT solutions, the administration should bring greater efficiency and agility with it.[575] In September 2014, the Federal Government announced its "Digital Administration 2020" programme, which creates the

---

[573] Vgl. Frey und Osborne 2013.
[574] Vgl. Mamertino 2016.
[575] Vgl. Bock 2015.

framework conditions for ensuring the agility and financial viability of the administration.[576]

As a risk of a completely digital administration, it should be mentioned that with the background of the worldwide increasing attacks on IT systems, there is an increased risk potential for data security. A complete connected and digitalized administration increases the potential for attacks. This very sensitive data can be tapped, manipulated or destroyed by criminals or secret services.[577]

7.1.6   Programming and Software Developmen

Programmers, web designers or software developers will develop into the craft disciplines of the digital world, but their services will become standardized goods due to the high competitive- and price pressure. More and more large IT companies are already trying to limit their own staff of programmers to the necessary level and only use additional capacities from the Sharing Economy if necessary.[578]

Mastery of basic programming techniques could reach cultural engineering status by 2036 if even

---

[576] Vgl. Bundesministerium des Innern 2014.
[577] Vgl. Warislohner 2016.
[578] Vgl. V. Brühl 2015, S. 208 f.

children and pupils learn basic programming languages at school. Mastery of a programming language becomes just as natural as the knowledge of the four basic arithmetical operations. The proportion of software-intensive jobs could continue to rise significantly in the future. Despite their high qualifications, programmers have the potential to become the new assembly line workers of the 21st century.[579]

According to the calculations of FREY and OSBORNE, however, a differentiated picture emerges. According to this, every second workplace of a human programmer is at risk, since cognitive computing systems with their machine learning capabilities are very well capable of writing program code themselves in the future. Furthermore, machines can recognize and eliminate possible program errors much faster.[580] RAYMOND KURZWEIL, head of technical development at *Google*, already predicts the ability of self-programming machines in 2029.[581]

---

[579] Ebd., S. 206 f.
[580] Vgl. Frey und Osborne 2013, S. 19.
[581] Vgl. Kurzweil 2014.

7.1.7 Agriculture

Just as the tractor once replaced the horse and revolutionised agriculture, technologies from the *Internet of Things* will in future and already have a decisive influence on agriculture. Sensors measure soil moisture and light conditions and then deliver this data to the data cloud for calculation. The harvest is then carried out by autonomous or semi-autonomous machines. These are based on satellite-based location and weather data and calculate the optimum fuel consumption. Drones equipped with a thermal imaging camera detect possible animals or people in the fields and can pass this data on to the harvesters to prevent hazards. Not only the condition of the soil and plants is monitored by sensors, but also the machines themselves. In the event of overheating or maintenance intervals, they inform the human owner via the mobile phone network or independently request transfer wagons if the grain tanks are full. All in all, humans will play a more administrative role in future agriculture.[582] The demand for human farmers will fall by one fifth by 2022.[583]

---

[582] Vgl. Gropp 2016; Schindelar 2015; T-Systems 2013.
[583] Vgl. J. Myers, The Most Endangered Jobs in 2015 2015.

7.1.8   New job profiles

According to a *World Economic Forum* study, creativity, emotional intelligence, solving complex problems and critical questioning are among the four most important skills that employees must demonstrate in the next ten years. On the other hand, negotiating skills and flexibility will continue to lose importance in the future, as machines based on mass data will help us make decisions in the future. By 2026, cognitive computing systems should also be able to make decisions in the management levels of large corporations.[584] In addition, the *Institut der deutschen Wirtschaft Köln* (Cologne Institute for the German Economy) considers company- and professional experience, independence, communication skills and technical expertise as one of the most important qualifications for future employees.[585]

The digital transformation will lead to the emergence of more new job profiles and the disappearance of old ones. However, this does not necessarily mean that low-skilled people in particular will be unemployed in the future, but rather that they will work in the

---

[584] Vgl. Gray 2016.
[585] Vgl. Hammermann 2016

service sector.[586] Automation in the manufacturing industry frees up workers who find accommodation in new service areas. In an ageing society, health services will be as important as social services.[587] Since both parents will continue to work more frequently in the future, the need for family services is also increasing. The increasing networking with sensors is becoming very complex and involves a high susceptibility to interference. In the future, technical services for the installation and maintenance of billions of sensors will therefore increasingly be required.[588] The high degree of automation and networking could also make access to education more affordable for people in financial difficulties. But consulting services in application scenarios that are not yet known today will also experience an upswing. The connected world will bring new application possibilities and will result in new starting points for service offerings.[589]

According to a study published in January 2016 by the *Australian Advisory Council for Science and Industry*, pilots who perform their tasks from the

---

[586] Vgl. V. Brühl 2015, S. 210 f.
[587] Ebd., S. 211.
[588] Ebd., S. 211.
[589] Ebd., S. 212.

ground will be particularly sought after over the next 20 years.[590] In order to increase safety and efficiency, ships, boats, freighters, aircraft, drones and transport vehicles are increasingly controlled and monitored from a distance.[591] Although the majority of these vehicles will move autonomously, unforeseeable situations will occur again and again in the foreseeable future in which a person must intervene in a controlling manner. This requires very well trained personnel with aeronautical and meteorological abilities as well as a high sense of orientation.[592]

The digital transformation is not only driven by IT departments, but it is especially the task of upper management. This results in the completely new job description of the so-called Chief Digital Officer (CDO). This executive is responsible for the development and implementation of a digital strategy, develops new business models based on digital technologies and drives the transformation within the entire company. At present, one third of the companies either have the managing director himself or the IT manager take over this task. In another third of the companies surveyed, there is no coordination

---

[590] Vgl. Hajkowicz, et al. 2016, S. 78.
[591] Ebd.
[592] Ebd.

of digitization at all. Worldwide there are currently only 2,000 CDOs, which are primarily active in the Anglo-Saxon sector.[593] The vehicle manufacturer *BMW* has also admitted that it has a lot of catching up to do with its own digital transformation.[594] In March 2016, it became known that *BMW* had engaged the experienced *Google* manager JENS MONSEES to establish digital business models and a data-based ecosystem across the Group. He is responsible for topics such as mass data, vehicle IT, autonomous driving and data protection.[595] With the help of the CDO, the company wants to develop into a technology company in order to be able to face competitors from the technology industry such as *Uber* or *Tesla*.[596]

7.1.9 Summary

According to the US social theorist JEREMY RIFKIN, the first step was to replace muscle power with machines. In the next step, it will be the human mind that will be replaced by computer algorithms.[597]

---

[593] Vgl. Shad und Grimm 2016.

[594] Vgl. Greis 2016.

[595] Vgl. Nagel 2016.

[596] Vgl. Behrmann 2016.

[597] Vgl. Rifkin 2004, S. 57.

More than three-quarters of the workforce in Western industrial nations is engaged in routine work, which can be replaced by powerful computers, robots and automated machines.[598] Just as in agriculture the horse once disappeared with the introduction of the tractor, in the future man would disappear as the most important production factor.[599] Even JOHN MAYNARD KEYNES, one of the most important economists of the 20th century, predicted back in 1930 that progressive technology and its developments would lead to a working week of only 15 hours by 2030. The work steps carried out so far by humans would be carried out by machines.[600]

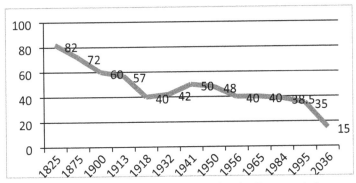

Figure 8 Development of weekly working time in Germany in hours with forecast up to 2036. The increase in working hours in the 30s and 40s is due to the Second World War.
Source: Strawe 1994. (own revision)

---

[598] Ebd., S. 57.
[599] Ebd., S. 57.
[600] Vgl. Kraemer und Nessel 2015, S. 158.

208

The Oxford scientists FREY and OSBORNE cited in the previous chapters come to the conclusion in their study "*The Future of Employment: How Susceptible are Jobs to Computerisation?*" published in 2013 that in the next ten to 20 years almost half of all current US jobs with a high degree of routine will be replaced by machines and software.[601] The employees of the future can be divided into two groups. Those who tell the machines what to do and those who do what they are told by the machines. The study also showed that there is a link between education, income and the risk of job loss. While academics and postgraduates are only 18 percent substitutable, people with low or no school qualifications are 80 percent substitutable. People with little or no school education will continue to be under greater pressure in the future.[602]

At the end of 2015, the management consultancy *A. T. Kearney* transferred the study published by FREY and OSBORNE to the German labour market.[603] It comes to the conclusion that a quarter of all occupational profiles in Germany also have a high automation risk. This means that in the next two decades up to 45 percent of all German employees

---

[601] Vgl. Frey und Osborne 2013, S .38.
[602] Ebd., S. 45.
[603] Vgl. Körner 2015, S. 1.

could lose their jobs to a machine.[604] There is particularly high substitution potential in secretarial, sales, catering and business management occupations, as well as in cooks and bank clerks. In contrast, it is difficult to automate occupations in childcare, health care and nursing and mechanical engineering.[605]

Most endangered professions (automation potential: > 70 percent)	Non-hazardous occupations (Automation potential: < 30 percent)
Office and secretarial staff	Childcare occupations
Sales professions	Health and nursing professions
Professions in the catering service	Supervisory and managerial staff
Professions in commercial and tech. Business administration	Occupations in mechanical engineering and industrial engineering
Professions in postal and delivery services	Professions in automotive engineering
Cooks	Professions in Sales
Bank clerks	Professions in social work
Occupations in inventory management	Occupations in nursing care for the elderly
Professions in metalworking	Professions in higher education / research
Accounting professions	Construction electrical professions

Table 1 Top 10 of the most endangered and safe professions. Source: Körner 2015, S. 2. (own representation)

---

[604] Ebd., S. 1.
[605] Ebd., S. 2

The above-mentioned studies clearly show how automation technologies are penetrating occupational groups that were previously reserved for human beings. Nevertheless, they should be viewed critically, as only existing occupations have been analysed, but not future occupations. The Centre for European Economic Research does not expect these occupational groups to die out to such an extent. This is due to the fact that the technical possibilities are often overestimated and that new technologies sometimes change existing jobs instead of destroying them. The working time freed up by automation can also be used for tasks that are difficult to automate. In addition, the macroeconomic adjustment processes, which can counteract the destruction of existing jobs, are left out of the studies.[606]

Technological leaps, such as those produced by the steam engine described above, force us to work differently. After the Second World War, about 50 percent of Germans worked in agriculture. Today it is less than two percent. Nevertheless, more is produced than is needed. Today it is the digital transformation that once again forces almost half of all employees to look for new jobs.[607] Fully autonomous vehicles, such

---

[606] Vgl. Bonin, Gregory und Zierahn 2015, S. 18.

as those currently being tested by *Google, Tesla, Daimler* or *BMW*, have the potential to revolutionize passenger transport and delivery traffic.[608] Human drivers are just as obsolete here as parking garages, traffic policemen or radar traps. Banks are increasingly focusing on mobile online business and computerized investment advisors based on artificial neural networks. Insurance policies are concluded exclusively online. Their trust is based less on people and more on mass data and algorithms collected by sensors. Parcel deliveries are handled by autonomous vehicles or drones, such as those introduced by *DHL* or *Amazon* in 2013. Letters are no longer sent to letterboxes, but electronically, encrypted and legally secure by electronic delivery.[609] [610] [611] The tasks of tax consultants, invoice verification or online bookings can already be automated to a large extent today. Electronic wristwatches or garments with built-in sensors assume vital monitoring functions and can detect whether a possible illness is present by means of measurement samples in real time and without having to visit a doctor.[612] Simple legal

---

[607] Vgl. Dueck 2016.

[608] Vgl. Doll 2015.

[609] Vgl. DHL Paketkopter o. J.

[610] Vgl. Kontio 2013.

[611] Vgl. BMI De-Mail o. J.

disputes, such as credit card cancellations, can be resolved using intelligent decision algorithms. Lawyers are only consulted in complex cases. Vehicles increasingly report their faults themselves, without a mechanic having to research or guess possible causes.

By automating routine tasks, complex professions such as doctors, lawyers, teachers, professors or educators will have more time in the future to communicate more intensively with their customers and patients. It is more important than ever to be particularly good at this. Professions with simple activities are now paid almost exclusively on the basis of minimum wages. The master painter becomes an interior designer who has the practical activities, which require less cognitive performance, carried out by simple workers. The well paid creative and the rather poorly paid executive side of the professions face each other.[613]

Another risk is that the smarter the machine becomes, the less the worker who operates it needs to know and earn. Highly paid are then only a decreasing number of specialized experts.

---

[612] Vgl. CeBit2016 2015.
[613] Vgl. Dueck 2016.

Not only the possibilities of Industry 4.0 technologies, but also the trend towards dematerialisation will lead to changes in the manufacturing sector. This trend describes the transformation of physical products into software. More and more people today use services for which they used to need hardware or even business. An example: many car manufacturers today offer a smartphone application with which the car owner can open his car with his smartphone. Physical car keys are no longer needed. Factories where plastic or metal parts for car keys are produced are becoming just as obsolete as the manufacturers of transponders, button batteries or printed circuit boards built into the keys.[614]

Germany has an international advantage as a location for highly qualified personnel thanks to its ideas of law and ethics.[615] The industrial and working culture established over decades in medium-sized businesses ensured that the last economic crises were largely overcome unscathed.[616] Although Germany is not at the top of the world in academic education, it is in classical education in medium-sized industry.[617]

---

[614] Vgl. Kreutzer und Land 2013, S. 16.

[615] Vgl. Deden 2004; Deutscher Ethikrat 2015, S. 12.

[616] Vgl. Rahmann 2011.

[617] Vgl. Bröker 2015.

German SMEs employ 84.2 per cent of trainees in Germany and make a significant contribution to the comparatively low international youth unemployment rate of 7.1 per cent (euro zone: 22 per cent).[618] German masters and well-trained apprentices are a valuable asset that must be combined with the technologies of Industry 4.0. Employees must remain in constant education and training and lifelong learning must be established within the companies. If, despite international pressure and accelerated innovation cycles, Germany and Europe can maintain or modernise its traditional industrial culture and its legal and ethical concepts, it has the potential for an attractive labour market in the future. Germany could become an attractive location for skilled workers from Silicon Valley, where working conditions are far removed from German and European ideas of law and ethics.[619] A recent study by *Glassdoor* shows that American employees in large technology companies increasingly want social benefits such as health insurance, pension contributions or sick pay. These benefits, which are legally anchored in Germany, are often only optional in American companies.[620]

---

[618] Vgl. BMWi German Mittelstand 2014, S. 2 f.; Jugendarbeitslosenquote 2015: eurostat 2016, S. 5.

[619] Vgl. Astheimer 2015.

[620] Vgl. Spiegel Karriere 2016.

This means that in the future, education and training in mathematics, computer science, natural sciences and technology will play a decisive role in international competitiveness. Already today, there is a shortage of more than 100,000 such specialists in Germany. This hampers the growth of digital innovation. Future jobs will be characterised by intelligent and comprehensively connected manufacturing and production technologies. The key role is played by the ability to interact between man and machine. Skilled workers must have a high degree of independence and abstraction as well as competences in solving complex problems.[621] Social skills such as communication, self-organisation and knowledge of information and communication technology are just as important as lifelong learning. These requirements apply not only to occupations in the IT and electronics sector, but to all occupations in all sectors of the economy.[622]

According to current knowledge, it cannot be clearly foreseen that the digital transformation will bring with it a fundamentally new social order, such as the invention of the steam engine described in the

---

[621] Vgl. J. Myers 2016.
[622] Vgl. Schlick 2015, S. 15.

introduction, but that changes will take place in the global labour market. The Indian consulting firm *Infosys* reported at the beginning of 2016 that countries with high demand for professions in the technology sector are particularly feeling the pressure of global competition.[623] According to the study, three quarters of young people in Germany and India see globalisation as the driving force for an increasingly competitive labour market. In addition, three quarters of French, British and Australian young people no longer believe that they will achieve a level of prosperity similar to that of their parents. In Germany, only one in two young people still sees themselves in a position to achieve a higher standard of living. In contrast, three-quarters of young people in Brazil, China, South Africa and the USA are much more optimistic about the future.[624]

At the end of 2015, *Deutsche Telekom* CEO TIMOTHEUS HÖTTGES opened the discussion on the unconditional basic income described by RIFKIN. The profits of the Internet companies are to be used to provide each citizen with a fixed amount of money - without consideration. This could be a long-term

---

[623] Vgl. Infosys 2016.
[624] Vgl. Armbrecht 2016.

option to maintain the social system in a changing society and world of work.[625] Whether or not the unconditional basic income is a definitive solution has not yet been clarified.

---

[625] Vgl. Hase 2015.

8 The future of European telecommunications operators

While classic telecommunications services such as voice telephony or SMS are becoming increasingly less important, so-called over-the-top services (OTT) such as *WhatsApp, Facebook, Instagram, Skype* or *iMessage* are becoming increasingly popular.[626] The distinguishing features between the telecommunications providers are reduced to the monthly basic price, included data volume, network quality and customer service.[627] In addition, large device manufacturers such as *Apple* or *Samsung* will in future rely more heavily on the so-called eSIM in order to simplify switching between network providers.[628] Even devices from the *Internet of Things* are partly equipped with eSIM cards to communicate over the Internet.[629] The eSIM is a chip card permanently installed in the device that can be programmed from the outside. With this disruptive technology, telecommunications providers are increasingly losing the close, central customer

---

[626] Vgl. VATM / Dialog Consult 2015, S. 23.
[627] Vgl. Loozen, Murdoch und Orr 2013, S. 10.
[628] Vgl. Wächter 2016, S. 24.
[629] Vgl. Venkataraman Krishnamurthy und Shetty 2014, S. 82.

relationship with device manufacturers.[630] The lack of innovative strength of telecommunications providers is therefore a core problem in a market with steadily shrinking profit margins.[631]

However, it is not only the lack of innovation, but also the strong regulation by the European Union and difficult legal conditions in the respective countries that make it difficult for network providers.[632] The excellent customer service provided by technology giants such as *Amazon* has enormously increased customer expectations and now also requires extraordinary efforts on the part of telecommunications providers to provide end customer services, which have often been neglected for years.[633]

In addition, there is strong competitive pressure from companies previously outside the industry. *Google, Facebook* and *Tesla* have long been working on their own data networks, some of which are to be made available worldwide and free of charge. In addition, the elimination of the controversial "Störerhaftung" (disturbance liability) in Germany could lead to more

---

[630] Vgl. Pallas und Spors 2016, S. 14.
[631] Vgl. R. Schindler 2015.
[632] Vgl. V. Brühl 2015, S. 133.
[633] Vgl. Franz-Rudolf 2016.

and more customers switching to open WiFi networks of private customers, retail stores or municipalities and being less dependent on commercial networks of large network providers.[634] [635] [636] [637]

Telecommunications providers overslept the first half of the digital transformation. The winners are *Facebook, Amazon, Google* and *Apple*, whose OTT services and devices are generating billions of dollars in revenue while leading to an exponentially growing volume of data in mobile and fixed networks.[638] The network providers, on the other hand, are forced to intercept these masses of data through capacity expansions and expensive network modernisations without significantly increasing prices.[639]

This chapter describes some hopeful business opportunities for European telecom operators as a result of digitisation and the *Internet of Things*, so as not to end up in the second half of digitisation as pure technology providers and data transport service providers for OTT services.

---

[634] Vgl. Google Loon 2013.
[635] Vgl. Eisner 2016.
[636] Vgl. Vallancey 2015.
[637] Vgl. Greif 2016.
[638] Vgl. Dialog Consult / VATM 2015, S. 20.
[639] Vgl. Kleinz 2016.

8.1.1 Cost reduction by virtualization

Major European network providers such as *Deutsche Telekom, Orange* and *Telekom Italia* have recognized the potential of dynamically adaptable IT infrastructures. By combining Network Functions Virtualization (NFV) with the Software-Defined-Network (SDN), network providers can outsource complete network nodes and large parts of their own network infrastructure to the data cloud.

NFV uses already established and extended IT virtualization technologies to virtualize network functions that were previously only feasible through the use of proprietary platforms and hardware manufacturers. This enables effortless scaling of capacities and load balancing across locations within the network. Energy consumption can be reduced by using standard hardware. SDN, on the other hand, separates data traffic from control. This simplifies network design and operation by allowing centralized control from a single point. Using a standardized interface, network operators are able to program and roll out new business models and innovative services directly and centrally in their network, thus responding flexibly and very quickly to customer requirements.[640]

According to a study by management consultants *Arthur D. Little*, European telecommunications providers can save up to 39 billion euros through the skilful use of this digitization strategy.[641] The savings potential results from greater process automation and a 26 percent reduction in operating costs.[642] IT fault management can also be greatly reduced or completely outsourced[643]. Network operators are thus able to react very quickly and flexibly to the introduction of new services and have an easier time to enter new market segments. This is mainly due to the fact that only one software module has to be implemented for new services.

In order to realise the vision of digitised networks, the network providers have formed a working group within the European Telecommunications Standards Institute (ETSI) to work together on digitisation concepts.[644] In March 2015, *Deutsche Telekom* was the first and only network provider in Europe to introduce a fully digitized and scalable network architecture in Croatia, Hungary and Slovakia. Its

---

[640] Vgl. Schnitter und Markova 2015, S. 69 f.; Portal, et al. 2015, S. 4.

[641] Vgl. Portal, et al. 2015, S. 2 ff.

[642] Ebd., S. 2.

[643] Vgl. Amdocs 2015, S. 4.

[644] Vgl. Boyer 2016; Nemat, et al. 2015; Lemke 2014.

network infrastructure in Germany is also to be digitized by 2018.[645]

The same company presented the *Next Generation Enterprise Network Alliance* (Ngena) industry model at the Mobile World Congress in 2016, which is based on the above technologies.[646] This is a technical platform that can provide telecommunications services in a highly automated and global manner. These services are resold to cooperating telecommunications companies, which can then develop their own services.[647] In the foreseeable future, other European network operators should also be able to resell their services via this platform.[648] *Ngena* thus becomes part of the Sharing Economy described in Chapter 6.4. In addition, the model has the advantage that the technical platform is operated in Germany and is therefore subject to German and European data protection law.[649] It has the potential to fundamentally change the corporate customer business, as telecommunications services can no longer only be offered nationally, but also

---

[645] Vgl. Nemat, et al. 2015.

[646] Vgl. Handelsblatt / dpa 2016.

[647] Ebd.

[648] Ebd.

[649] Ebd.

multinationally from a single source. This is particularly important in connection with the cross-border networking of devices on the *Internet of Things*.[650]

Already today, mobile network operators are able to create network slices through several virtually separate networks, with which they can develop industrial campus solutions within a licensed mobile spectrum. You could say that mobile operators can rent out their own network to large customers so that they can use their own dedicated network - including specially defined quality levels. At the same time, the public mobile radio network could be strengthened by network infrastructure elements specially installed on the customers site. Network infrastructure planning, setup and operation for the private and public networks are carried out from a single source.[651]

To sum up, telecommunications providers are revealing enormous cost savings potential through close cooperation with network infrastructure suppliers specializing in virtualization, terminal

---

[650] Vgl. Schamberg 2016.

[651] Vgl. https://www.t-systems.com/resource/blob/5360/ 8a6037cac33e721ed25913a34bfb32ef /DL-Factsheet-5G-Campus-Netze-t-systems-de-09-2019.pdf [5G Campus-Netze – LTE- und 5G-Technologie für lokale Firmennetze], called on 14.11.2019

equipment manufacturers and regulatory authorities. This results from the operation of networks based entirely on the Internet protocol. The capital freed up and the technical possibilities offered by the combination of NFV and SDN open up new ways for network operators to earn money with high-quality services and innovative business models. Particular attention should be paid to the IT security markets, cloud technologies and data transmission services for large and business customers.[652] *IDATE DigiWorld* predicts that Europe's largest market for NFV and SDN technologies will more than double in the next two years.[653]

Finally, it should not be concealed that the separation of hardware and software in such strongly virtualized networks also entails the danger of a complexity that is difficult to understand. Troubleshooting within the network can be an extreme task and orchestration errors of combined services can lead to catastrophic consequences.[654]

---

[652] Vgl. Portal, et al. 2015, S. 8.
[653] Vgl. IDATE DigiWorld 2015.
[654] Vgl. Ottenheimer und Wallace 2012, S. 239.

8.1.2 Mobile Payment

ABI Research predicts a market volume of almost 200 billion US dollars for electronic payment by smartphone for the coming year 2017 alone.[655] The IT giants *Apple, Facebook* and *Google* have already recognized this potential for years and are working on corresponding customer-friendly solutions.[656] These companies already have bank licenses are thus enter into direct competition with the established banks.

The development of mobile payment options has been relatively slow in recent years due to the large number of stakeholders involved.[657] In recent months, however, it has become apparent that the contactless payment method is becoming increasingly popular and is reaching its point of transfer. The largest German food discounters have already equipped their checkout terminals with NFC technology as a precautionary measure.[658]

---

[655] Vgl. ABI Research 2012.

[656] Vgl. Klotz, Mobile Payment in Deutschland: Warum Apple und Google den Markt unter sich aufteilen werden 2015.

[657] Vgl. Langer und Roland 2010, S. 206.

[658] Vgl. Klemm 2016.

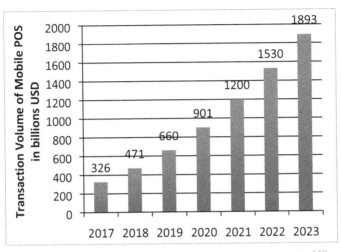

Figure 9 Transaction volume of mobile payment worldwide[659]

The challenge of mobile payment methods is to find a compromise between ease of use, cost and security. Previous mobile payment methods often fail in at least one of the three disciplines. A high level of security is often at the expense of convenience. In addition, the user should not incur any transaction costs. As in other payment models, the merchant making the offer pays any transaction costs incurred. Complete transparency of the fee models is essential here.[660]

---

[659] Vgl. https://de.statista.com/outlook/331/100/mobile-pos-payments /weltweit [14. Nov. 2019)

[660] Vgl. Brenner und Hess 2014, S. 195 ff.

Compared to device manufacturers, telecommunications providers have the major advantages of already having functioning billing channels, detailed payment information and experience with mobile payment methods.[661] These advantages must be exploited and converted into particularly user-friendly, terminal-independent and secure payment methods.[662] But for many years now, European telecommunications providers have been failing to provide customers with a decisive added value compared to paying by EC or giro card. The payment processes are not faster due to untrained cashiers or error-prone terminals. Many customers also feel that the barriers to entry are too high and impracticable. The payment model presented by *Deutsche Telekom, Telefonica* and *Vodafone* at CeBIT 2016 requires the use of an NFC-enabled smartphone with a specific version of the Android operating system. Use with an *Apple* iPhone is not possible. In addition, a SIM card and a proprietary smartphone application from the respective network provider are required, as is a further application from the *Volks- und Raiffeisenbanken*.[663] Therefore, the

---

[661] Vgl. Behrendt und Scholz 2013.
[662] Vgl. R. Schindler 2015.
[663] Vgl. Klotz 2016; IT-Finanzmagazin 2016.

solutions offered by network providers currently do not offer sufficient efficiency enhancements, added value or greater flexibility in mobile payment.[664] The existing solutions offered by the network providers are, without exception, systems based on the principles of traditional and fee-based card payment. This also means that there is no pressure on merchants to replace existing payment methods with cheaper ones.[665] This could easily create added value in which, for example, payment transactions could be separated between private and business and the electronic receipts for business trips could then be automatically booked in the accounting system and stored in digital form. Billing could be carried out via the mobile phone bill, as a direct debit authorization already exists.

Apple and *Google* are already offering mobile payment as a fixed feature in their operating systems. This can also be used without a SIM card and without additional installation of banking applications.[666] The payment functions of *Apple* and *Google* can already be used in many countries today. Since December

---

[664] Vgl. Strudthoff 2014.

[665] Vgl. Mosig und Sommer 2014, S. 32 f.

[666] Vgl. Klotz, Mobilfunkunternehmen stellen die Weichen für mobile Payment - schon wieder 2016.

2018, the *Apple* Pay service can also be used in Germany and most of Europe.[667] With its mobile payment method, *Apple* in particular is placing a major focus on Germany with its high purchasing power.[668] However, a study published by *Pricewaterhouse Coopers* in 2019 shows that Germans in particular have very strong reservations about mobile payment methods.[669] They are worried their mobile device might be misused, about identity theft and that mobile payment encourages them to buy more quickly. This is where the telecommunications companies, which are inherently experienced in payment procedures and often operate across countries, should come in and create a pan-european payment system. European telecommunications providers therefore urgently need to play to their advantages and establish their own secure, convenient and value-added payment methods - even before *Apple* and *Google* establish their own payment models in whole Europe.[670] According to a study by *Steinbeis University Berlin*, Europe's citizens

---

[667] Vgl. Fröhlich 2015.

[668] Vgl. Klotz, Warum du auch in Deutschland schon bald mit Apple Pay bezahlst 2015.

[669] Vgl. https://www.pwc.de/de/digitale-transformation/pwc-studie-mobile-payment-2019.pdf

[670] Vgl. Weberschläger 2013, S. 14 f.

will transfer eight times more money with mobile payment methods until the end of 2020.[671] This market must be conquered with sensible business models in cooperation with banks and manufacturers. There are currently no business cases with integrated process chains.[672]

8.1.3   Smart Home and Smart City

The so-called intelligent home control (Smart Home) is an essential component of the *Internet of Things*.[673] After the USA and Japan, Germany offers the largest market for Internet-connected devices for controlling, monitoring and regulating various functions in private households.[674] With expected sales growth of over 38 percent per year, almost eight billion euros in sales are forecast by 2020.[675]

Only one in four citizens would currently turn to their telecommunications provider to obtain smart home applications. Most of them are turning primarily to their electricity provider.[676] Telecommunications

---

[671] Vgl. Kleine, et al. 2012, S. 13.

[672] Ebd., S. 9.

[673] Vgl. Roth 2016, S. 26.

[674] Vgl. statista 2015.

[675] Ebd.

[676] Vgl. Statista-Research.com 2015.

providers have a decisive advantage when dealing with smart home applications. They have more experience in defining and billing more complex products.[677] Some telecommunications providers are already trying to prepare for this emerging market with their own offerings. For example, *Deutsche Telekom* was Europe's first telecommunications provider to develop the open, manufacturer-independent *Qivicon* smart home platform, which has been offered as a complete international solution since 2013.[678]

If European telecom operators are able to combine meaningful business models with their own portfolios, and if they additionally upgrade their own network infrastructure for technologies from the *Internet of Things*, they could take a leading position in the deployment and operation of smart home applications and generate additional high-margin revenues.[679]

The situation is similar with the networking of traffic-relevant urban applications and devices (Smart City). Here not only mobile radio capacities are needed, but

---

[677] Vgl. Schmidt-Wiedemann 2012.
[678] Vgl. Knöpke und Gerstner 2015.
[679] Vgl. Schmidt-Wiedemann 2012.

also fixed and cable networks. Telecommunications providers that can provide these three network technologies in parallel have another valuable revenue guarantee: data. By correlating anonymized location data from connected vehicles or smartphones, the paths and movements of people in groups can be traced and even predicted in real time through data analysis. These processed data can be developed into business models and resold to navigation software manufacturers or traffic authorities to improve traffic and transport flows, for traffic jam and traffic forecasting or for the coordination of mass events. Telecommunications providers have the advantageous role of being able to centrally oversee a large network of data points.[680]

8.1.4 Short Message Service (SMS)

The classic Short Message Service (SMS) distinguishes between two types. On the one hand there is the message exchange between two persons (P2P; Person to Person) and on the other hand between an application and a person (A2P).[681] For many years, telecommunications providers benefited

---

[680] Vgl. Bradley 2015.
[681] Vgl. Andersson, et al. 2006, S. 96.

from the seemingly unstoppable boom in SMS, which caused virtually no costs but generated high profits.[682]

A lack of further development of the service by the network providers and relatively high fees for the dispatch led to the fact that the free and Internet-based short message service *WhatsApp* completely replaced the SMS in the P2P business within only three years. Since 2013, more messages have been exchanged via *WhatsApp* than via SMS. Since then, telecommunications providers have failed to make up for the shortfall with their own modernized P2P short messaging service. New technical industry standards such as the *Rich Communications Suite enhanced* (RCSe) have not yet established themselves sufficiently despite their interoperability. RCSe is a new mobile communications standard for video telephony and the transmission of text messages, videos and photos. At Mobile World Congress 2016, *Google* announced that it would implement the RCSe standard natively in future versions of its Android operating system – for free.[683] In a joint initiative with the European telecommunications providers, the aim

---

[682] Vgl. Hagenhoff 2006, S. 5.
[683] Vgl. Spiegel Online: mbö/dpa 2016.

is to accelerate the spread of RCSe and make it the standard short message service of the future.[684]

However, the SMS service, which has now been sold off as an antique service, also holds a certain sales potential in the future, which should be exploited by the network providers. Because SMS plays a key role in many modern technologies and offers a number of advantages.[685] The market for A2P SMS services has been growing strongly for years. This is due to an increase in mobile services in retail, banking, gaming, travel and healthcare. These are primarily one-time passwords for money transactions (TAN) or two-factor authentication (2FA). However, SMS is also becoming increasingly important for parking ticket purchases, voting, online donations, order confirmations and information on parcel deliveries, credit card bills, flight and train connections and information services.[686]

SMS offers the following advantages over Internet-based OTT short message services:

---

[684] Vgl. GSMA Press Release 2016.
[685] Vgl. Absmeier 2014.
[686] Vgl. Tolentino 2015.

- High trustworthiness towards the sender[687]
- 90 percent of SMS are read within four minutes[688]
- Almost every SMS is also opened [689]
- Reception and dispatch is possible with the simplest cell phones [690]
- Four billion SMS users vs. one billion *WhatsApp* users worldwide [691]
- Requires no additional application [692]
- Delivery also possible without prior permission ("request for friendship") [693]
- Requires no data connection (text delivery via signalling channel) [694]
- Works even under difficult radio supply conditions
- Lower energy consumption as no active data connection is required [695]

---

[687] Vgl. Zheng 2015, S. 143.
[688] Vgl. Mana 2013, S. 25.
[689] Vgl. Tolentino 2015.
[690] Vgl. Tafazolli 2006, S. 35.
[691] Vgl. Beer 2016.
[692] Vgl. Amor 2002, S. 39 f.
[693] Ebd.
[694] Vgl. Boysen 2012, S. 19 f.
[695] Vgl. de Paly 2015; Schelewsky, et al. 2014, S. 76.

- Implementation and integration of SMS dispatch into existing IT landscapes is less time-consuming than connecting an application. [696]
- Encryption over the mobile network [697]

These advantages also qualify SMS for applications on the *Internet of Things*, such as time-critical and highly reliable alarm notifications, for energy-critical emergency power applications or as an emergency transmission channel in the absence of a data connection. Due to its high trustworthiness, read rate and interoperability, the A2P SMS service is particularly well suited for customer loyalty or marketing and advertising campaigns in the retail trade as well as in the wholesale business.[698]

[696] Vgl. Bullinger und Hompel 2007, S. 278; de Paly 2015.

[697] Vgl. Rajaraman 2010, S. 191.

[698] Vgl. Portio Research 2014, S. 53.

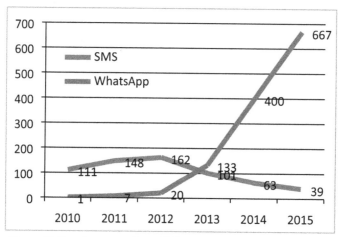

Figure 10 Development of sent P2P SMS and WhatsApp messages in millions per day

Source: VATM / Dialog Consult 2015, P. 30. (own representation)

8.1.5 Full service provider for information and communication services

A great opportunity for network providers is offered by a combination of high-quality and individual information and telecommunications services.[699] Especially in Europe's medium-sized companies, tailor-made complete offers for IT and communication services from a single source are important.[700] Those companies are often confronted with a lack of know-how, high maintenance costs and

---

[699] Vgl. Henkes und Praxmarer 2015, S. 6.
[700] Vgl. Erdkönig und Falkner 2014, S. 3.

incomplete functions in IT systems. In addition, there are high costs for the statutory data protection as well as for the administration and security of the data. Small and medium-sized companies therefore rarely have the capital to operate their own IT and outsource these services to external service providers.[701]

Full-service providers are those telecommunications providers who can offer IT services such as data cloud services (SaaS, IaaS, PaaS) in addition to fast, scalable and highly available fixed and mobile networks as well as high consulting competence.[702] Many European network operators have the conditions for such full services. They are already able to provide basic connectivity, sales, billing and consulting services, and have platforms to run software applications and Internet services.[703] If new technologies such as high-quality LPWA and 5G networks or scalable and powerful data clouds are added to these resources, the only thing missing is meaningful business models with excellent customer service, transparent tariff models and user-friendly data management and analysis platforms to ensure a valuable competitive advantage and stable long-term

---

[701] Ebd., S. 3

[702] Vgl. Hatton und Chua 2015, S. 30 f.

[703] Man spricht hierbei auch von sog. Hosting-Diensten.

revenue growth beyond the core business in the future.[704] In the future, business customers will place greater emphasis on comprehensive service ecosystems with very high-quality consulting and support services and less on purely physical network access.[705]

---

[704] Vgl. Rebbeck 2015), S. 7; Radke 2016; Dickgreber, et al. 2014, S. 4 f.

[705] Vgl. Dolata und Schrape 2013, S. 208.

9 Summary and outlook

„You can cut all the flowers, but you cannot keep spring from coming."[706]
- PABLO NERUDA

The *digital transformation* leads to serious changes in companies and society. The underlying elaborations show that many tasks in industry and administration can be automated or simplified. The data collected by sensor networks from the *Internet of Things* provides valuable information that was not previously used. This new information also creates new business models. As it turned out, these models not only focus on adapting to new situations, but above all on the economic benefits for companies. Conversely, this also means that these often disruptive innovations threaten or even replace traditional business models. A rethinking is therefore absolutely necessary for market stability, whether in the company itself or in politics.

Below is a brief summary of the results from the respective chapters.

---

[706] Vgl. Horden 2013.

Technical basics

The *Internet of Things* characterizes the combination of numerous technologies from different areas into a complete system.

The wireless networking of machines, houses or people results in a considerable savings potential. According to this, the elimination of cumbersome cabling leads to a reduction in installation and maintenance costs. This also makes it possible to network locations that could not previously be reached due to constructional inadequacies. RFID tags and NFC technology have proven to be future-proof networking technologies in this respect. It is foreseeable that the use of less expensive materials and mass production processes will lead to a sharp drop in prices in the manufacture of these technologies and thus to high market penetration.

Numerous technologies have already been established for data transmission between mechatronic systems in the close-up range. These are increasingly being tailored to the needs of sensor networks in the *Internet of Things*. WiFi is particularly suitable for applications that require relatively high bandwidths over long distances. The announced WiFi HaLow standard, which reduces the energy requirements of the often battery-operated and low-power mechatronic systems, is very promising.

Data transmission via light waves, the so-called Li-Fi, permits extremely high data transmission rates. However, this technology is only able to supply things that are in the same room or when there is visual contact. Therefore, there are currently no examples of applications worth mentioning in practice. It is not yet foreseeable in which areas Li-Fi will establish itself. Applications in closed rooms that require high bandwidths are conceivable.

The latest version of *Bluetooth* technology offers the best conditions for close-range supply. It has already been adapted by the industry giants *Apple* and *Google* and allows high data rates with very low energy consumption. The *ZigBee* standard, on the other hand, is unlikely to gain acceptance due to its limited distribution and known security risks.

In the medium term, GPRS will also provide the basic connectivity for data transmission from devices connected with each other on a supra-regional basis, as this is a standard available worldwide. Nevertheless, the forecast is negative. GPRS will probably be replaced by 5G technology, as its low-power wide-area properties guarantee extremely low latency times, while at the same time providing high data throughput and very low energy consumption. These requirements must be met with regard to the future use of autonomous vehicles, wearables, machines or drones.

A *world standard* for the interoperable exchange of information on the *Internet of Things* has not yet been established due to the large number of competing consortia and will probably be delayed even further. However, the first cooperations between American and German stakeholders are emerging. In the short and medium term, however, there will be mainly rival standards.

Information processing

Knowledge is the basis of all decisions. But especially in today's world, knowledge is also an essential success factor for companies, which must be treated just like raw materials, capital or labour from a business point of view. It is regarded as a motor in the value creation and innovation process. The underlying data is regarded as the fuel for the digital economy. It has turned out that technological and economic changes lead to a strongly accelerated growth of mass data in the private and industrial sector. At present, only ten percent of these mass data are used to generate knowledge.

The study shows that useful, high-quality and secure information can only be obtained through the interaction of mass data, quality and data protection. The more relevant information is to the progress of a company, the higher the demand for information quality. All industries need competence above all to recognize correlations and patterns where people only see data chaos.

Powerful computing systems and fast data transmission networks are required to evaluate mass data. Artificial neural networks help to process structured and unstructured data in order to recognize patterns or generate new knowledge. Through machine learning, these cognitive computing systems will in the near future be intuitive enough to process human intentions rather than just respond to instructions. However, this does not only bring advantages, because the decisions made by cognitive computing systems are often very difficult or even impossible to comprehend due to their high complexity. In addition, such systems require enormous computing capacities and a great deal of energy.

In order to relieve the computing capacities, computing systems of this kind are often outsourced to data clouds. A distinction must be made between public, private and hybrid data clouds. In public data clouds, there is a risk that the user will not be able to ensure at which physical location his data is stored. This is relevant, among other things, with regard to legal events concerning the storage of accounting and personal data abroad. Private data clouds are suitable for companies that place a particularly high value on the protection of personal data. The combination of the advantages of both types in the so-called hybrid data clouds would therefore exploit the full potential. The focus will also be on which geographic location for data centers is best suited for data processing. It turned out that only Japan and Germany have an excellent level of data protection. The General Data Protection Regulation (GDPR) which was introduced in mid-2018 by the European Union could lead to a considerable competitive advantage in the international environment with regard to data protection. The new regulation has the potential to enable data protection-friendly and new digital business models in Europe.

Information security

Information security is an economic factor. If measurable damage is prevented by suitable security mechanisms, this can be seen as virtual revenue. Until the end of 2021, the *Internet of Things* will increase the average security budget of companies from currently one up to 20 percent.

New technologies such as cyberphysical, globally connected and cognitive computing systems were not yet foreseeable when the Federal Data Protection Act (BDSG) in Germany was drafted. These technologies affect our informational self-determination in a way never before seen. The established principles and legal regulations for automated data processing are hardly or no longer observed by ubiquitous Internet technologies. It is also worth bearing in mind that this controversy is tolerated by many companies and private users because of its convenience and benefits. In addition, manufacturers of embedded systems will have to worry more than ever about the security of their modules. It has been shown that more than ten percent of such systems currently exhibit serious safety deficiencies.

The comprehensive networking offers an extraordinary monitoring potential. Particularly in view of data protection guidelines, certain measures must be taken here. This is because people who feel permanently monitored or are monitored show a clearly abnormal and disturbed pattern of behavior and are categorically more unwilling to express their own opinions if they deviate from the majority opinion. *This has serious consequences for the common good of a democratic society*. To counteract this, devices used for surveillance should emit acoustic or visual signals.

The variety of devices also increases the attack surface for hackers and malware. The study has shown that the *Internet of Things* provides real-time insights not only into people's private lives, but also into industrial and economic processes.

The previous paper shows that the law on the *Internet of Things* still leaves many questions unanswered. Communication law provisions meet property law and information law provisions. The manufacturers of connected objects such as vehicles or wearables are therefore well advised to include all legal aspects in the risk assessment and drafting of their sales contracts.

Industry 4.0

The presented results justify the statement that the use of hyper-conntected production machines can lead to highly flexible production, which enables even small quantities to be produced at the cost of mass production. Machine downtime can be reduced by analyzing the mass data collected, sales can be increased and new business models can be developed. The focus here is on bundling forces to coordinate the design of digital structural change. The use of technologies from the "Industry 4.0 Platform" offers Europe and Germanys SMEs in particular a great opportunity to continue to stand out from international competition in the future. Industry 4.0 will reduce repetitive and physically demanding work and create new jobs, especially in the IT management of production facilities. The prerequisites for this are suitable qualification measures, a challanged top management, highly available and fast data infrastructures and state subsidies for research and development. The years until the end of 2024 will be decisive for the survival of companies.

Business models

Mass data, networking, high-performance computing systems, data cloud technologies and comprehensive dematerialization form the basis for innovative business models. In addition, the use of social media enables detailed customer analyses. With the help of mass data and cognitive computing systems, events such as criminal offences or technical disruptions can be predicted. Manufacturing companies are increasingly developing into service providers, selling not only the product itself, but also the availability and quality of the service provided. This is recorded in service level agreements in order to give the customer the opportunity to decide transparently on the scope of the required quality and service. Insurance companies, for example, are particularly interested in supporting their decisions on the level of premiums on the basis of behavioural patterns. Vehicle manufacturers are also increasingly interested in the data collected in the vehicles in order to adapt marketing campaigns to the social environment or to optimise their own logistics and vehicle quality.

Cognitive computing systems are able to generate medical forecasts and therapy recommendations with very high hit probabilities. The study has shown that the goal of a health telematics infrastructure must be

251

the exchange of information across locations. The increasing volume of data poses great challenges, especially for medium-sized and smaller companies. The lack of competence in handling mass data in companies that do not pursue modern information management leads to existential risks. Therefore, the use of intelligent computing systems is just as essential as the correct question. The risk of a modern information management exists in the initial phase. It turned out that the specialist departments in many companies are not interested in complete transparency. However, this is a basic prerequisite for successful information management and can only be achieved through extensive persuasion of the added value of the new approach.

On the other hand, there are disruptive business models. They have the potential to displace established companies and their products from the market within a very short time. Every second managing director sees his business model threatened by companies from outside the industry. It has been proven that the digital transformation exerts massive disruptive influence on all industries and forces all companies to rethink. This includes large industry giants as well as small retail stores.

Changes in the world of work

Whether the digital transformation will have a similarly serious impact on the world of work and society as the steam engine did in the first industrial revolution was not confirmed in this paper. Here it is concluded that, in addition to routine tasks, tasks with high cognitive requirements can increasingly be performed by machines in the future. A study published by Oxford scientists FREY and OSBORN shows that until the end of 2030 half of all current US jobs will be replaced by machines. In Germany there is a substitution potential of 45 percent of all occupations. However, these studies must be viewed critically. Although they clearly show how automation technologies are penetrating occupational groups that were previously reserved for people, they neglect new occupational profiles. In the future, more workers than ever before will be needed to install and maintain billions of mechatronic systems. In an increasingly ageing society, more human resources will also have to be made available for non-automated health services and family services. In addition, the working time freed up by automation can be used to perform tasks that are very difficult to automate. Complex job profiles such as medical doctors, lawyers, educators, professors or teachers can communicate more intensively with those in their care when routine tasks are taken over by machines or algorithms. Good qualifications and advice are more important than ever. In particular, the need for aeronautical and meteorological capabilities to monitor autonomously moving vehicles such as drones, airplanes or sea ships and to control them remotely is growing. Germany has the opportunity to become an attractor for highly qualified employees due to its legal and ethical concept in the world of work. In summary, it can therefore be said that initial and further training in mathematics, computer science, natural sciences and technology will play a decisive role in international competitiveness. Future jobs will be characterised by intelligent and comprehensively connected manufacturing and production technologies. The key role is played by the ability to interact between man and machine. Independence and the ability to abstract and solve complex problems will be basic prerequisites for well-paid careers.

The future of European telecom operators

The initial hypothesis was that European telecommunications providers will only serve as data transport network service providers in the course of digitisation and the *Internet of Things* and will not be able to establish their own innovative business models. This thesis could be refuted in the context of this elaboration. With the help of comprehensive virtualisation strategies, European telecommunications providers can save up to 39 billion euros in costs. With these strategies they are able to react very flexibly to the introduction of new services and to open up new market segments more easily. The *Ngena* industry model offers the opportunity to offer telecommunications services not only nationally but also multinationally from a single source. The capital saved should be invested in the modernisation and expansion of network technologies in order to be able to offer a high-quality, high-performance network in the long term.

However, the separation of hardware and software means that there is a risk of complexity that is difficult to keep track of. Troubleshooting strongly virtualized networks can be an extreme task. Technical errors in the virtualization platform can trigger a chain reaction and thus lead to major disruptions of entire network areas.

Mobile payment also offers network providers great opportunities to generate new revenues. The challenge in mobile payment is to find a compromise between ease of use, costs and security. Based on the present studies, it becomes clear that there are currently no business models with end-to-end process chains. In order to keep up with international competition, European telecommunications providers should exploit their advantages even before *Apple* and *Google* establish their own payment models in whole Europe.

The Short Message Service, which is now regarded as antique, is also experiencing a renaissance. With A2P services, the Short Message Service can establish itself as a key technology in the *Internet of Things*. The market for A2P SMS services has been growing strongly for years. The reason for this is the increase in mobile services in the retail and healthcare sectors, among others.

The greatest opportunity for telecommunications providers lies in a combination of high-quality and individual information and communication services. For years, small and medium-sized enterprises have outsourced the operation of their own IT to external providers or have no resources for their own IT. Full-service providers are those providers who, in addition to fast, scalable and highly available fixed and mobile networks, can also offer IT services, e.g. from the data cloud. A pay-as-you-use fee model gives small and medium-sized enterprises access to affordable IT services. Most European telecommunications providers already have the necessary resources at their disposal. If modern technologies, such as LPWA and 5G networks, are added to these networks, it is only necessary to develop meaningful business models with excellent customer service, transparent tariff models and user-friendly data processing and analysis platforms. The aim is to create a mix of hybrid cloud models, fast connectivity and high security standards. This will ensure stable long-term sales growth beyond the existing core business. It should also be noted that high-quality service ecosystems with competent consulting and support services will play a greater role in the future than purely physical network access.

10 Reference

A. Aaker, D. (2013). *Markenrelevanz: Erfolgreich Wettbewerber ausschalten (1. Auflage 2013).* Weinheim: Wiley-VCH Verlag.

ABI Research. (18. Oktober 2012). *NFC Mobile Payment Transaction Spend to Hit the $100 billion Mark in 2016.* (A. Research, Produzent) Abgerufen am 21. Januar 2016 von http://de.statista.com/statistik/daten/studie/244 800/umfrage/prognose-zum-mobile-payment-umsatz-weltweit/

Abicht, L., & Spöttl, G. (. (2012). *Qualifikationsentwicklungen durch das Internet der Dinge: Trends in Logistik, Industrie und Smart House.* Bielefeld: W. Bertelsmann Verlag.

Abolhassan, F. (12. August 2013). *Big Data und Cloud Computing gehören zusammen* . (NetMediaEurope Deutschland) Abgerufen am 07. Januar 2016 von ZDNet / Cloud: http://www.zdnet.de/88165297/big-data-und-cloud-computing-gehoren-zusammen/

Abolhassan, F. (2014). *Kundenzufriedenheit im IT-Outsourcing: Das Optimum realisieren.* Wiesbaden: Springer Gabler.

Abolhassan, F. (2016). *Was treibt die Digitalisierung? - Warum an der Cloud kein Weg vorbeiführt.* Wiesbaden: Abolhassan, Ferri (Hrsg.); Springer Fachmedien.

Absmeier, A. (07. Oktober 2014). *SMS als Statusübermittler im Internet der Dinge relevant* . (ap Verlag) Abgerufen am 26. März 2016 von manage IT: http://ap-verlag.de/sms-als-statusuebermittler-im-internet-der-dinge-relevant/2703/

acatech - Deutsche AKademie der Technikwissenschaften. (2011). *Cyber-Physical Systems: Innovationsmotor für Mobilität, Gesundheit, Energie und Produktion.* Heidelberg: acatech (Hrsg.); Springer Verlag.

Adolphs, P., Conrady, H.-G., Dietrich, F., Frömel, G., Göddertz, J., Helm, W., . . . Thomer, H. (1993). *Sensoren in der Automatisierungstechnik (2. überarbeitete und erweitere Auflage).* Wiesbaden: Schnell, Gerhard.

Amdocs. (2015). *Bringing NFV to Life: Technological and Operational Challenges in Implementing NFV.* Abgerufen am 30. Januar 2016 von Amdocs White Paper: http://www.amdocs.com/solutions/network/documents/bringing-nfv-to-life-amdocs-wp.pdf

Amor, D. (2002). *Internet Future Strategies: How Pervasive Computing Will Change the World.* New Jersey, USA: Prentice Hall PTR.

Andelfinger, V., & Hänisch, T. (2015). *Internet der Dinge: Technik, Trends und Geschäftsmodelle.* Wiesbaden: Springer Fachmedien; Andelfinger, Volker (Hrsg.).

Andersson, C., Freeman, D., James, I., Johnston, A., & Ljung, S. (2006). *Mobile Media and Applications, From Concept to Cash: Successful Service.* Chichester, England: John Wiley & Sons.

Armbrecht, D. (29. Februar 2016). *Which country is most prepared for tech disruption?*. (WEF) Abgerufen am 21. März 2016 von World Economic Forum: Technology: http://www.weforum.org/agenda/2016/01/which-country-is-most-prepared-for-the-fourth-industrial-revolution?utm_content=buffer95435&utm_medium=social&utm_source=facebook.com&utm_campaign=buffer

Assion, S. (18. Februar 2016). *Internet(recht) der Dinge: 8 Thesen, Datenschutzverstoß als Sachmangel und OLG Naumburg zum "Dateneigentum".* (Telemedicus) Abgerufen am 1. April 2016 von Telemedicus: http://www.telemedicus.info/article/3052-

Internetrecht-der-Dinge-8-Thesen,-
Datenschutzverstoss-als-Sachmangel-und-
OLG-Naumburg-zum-Dateneigentum.html

Astheimer, S. (22. Dezember 2015). *Im Silicon Valley
ist niemand ausgeschlafen.* Abgerufen am 16.
März 2016 von Frankfurter Allgemeine:
http://www.faz.net/aktuell/beruf-
chance/arbeitswelt/interview-im-silicon-
valley-ist-niemand-ausgeschlafen-
13972099.html

Aulich, U. (30. Juni 2015). *Hoffnung für private
Airbnb-Vermieter Berlin könnte Verbot von
Ferienwohnungen lockern* . Abgerufen am 07.
März 2016 von Berliner Zeitung:
http://www.berliner-
zeitung.de/berlin/hoffnung-fuer-private-
airbnb-vermieter-berlin-koennte-verbot-von-
ferienwohnungen-lockern-1608940

AZ Direct AG. (o. J.). *Die 15 Dimensionen der
Datenqualität.* (arvato AZ direct) Abgerufen
am 13. Februar 2016 von AZ Direct CH:
http://www.az-
direct.ch/fileadmin/pdf/15_Dimensionen_Date
nqualitaet_DGIQ.pdf

Bach, N., Brehm, C., Buchholz, W., & Petry, T.
(2012). *Wertschöpfungsorientierte
Organisation: Architekturen – Prozesse –
Strukturen* . Wiesbaden: Springer Gabler.

Bachmann, R., Kemper, G., & Gerzer, T. (2014). *Big Data - Fluch oder Segen? - Unternehmen im Spiegel gesellschaftlichen Wandels.* Heidelberg: mitp Verlag.

Bartel, J., Böken, A., Buschbacher, F., Falkenberg, G., Feulner, J., Fuchs, G., . . . Wiesner, H. (2014). *Big-Data-Technologien: Wissen für Entscheider.* (T. u. Bundesverband Informationswirtschaft, Produzent) Abgerufen am 23. Januar 2016 von bitkom.org - Bundesverband Informationswirtschaft, Telekommunikation und neue Medien e. V.: https://www.bitkom.org/Publikationen/2014/L eitfaden/Big-Data-Technologien-Wissen-fuer-Entscheider/140228-Big-Data-Technologien-Wissen-fuer-Entscheider.pdf

Barth, A. P. (2013). *Algorithmik für Einsteiger: Für Studierende, Lehrer und Schüler in den Fächern Mathematik und Informatik (2. Auflage).* Wiesbaden: Springer Spektrum.

Bauer, D. (2010). *Kurzbefehl: der Kompass für das digitale Leben.* Basel: Echtzeit Verlag.

Bauernhansl, T., Hompel, M. t., & Vogel-Heuser, B. (2014). *Industrie 4.0 in Produktion, Automatisierung und Logistik.* Wiesbaden: Springer Fachmedien.

Becker, J., Schwaderlapp, W., & Seidel, S. (. (2012). *Management kreativitätsintensiver Prozesse:*

262

Theorien, Methoden, Software und deren Anwendung in der Fernsehindustrie. Berlin Heidelberg: Springer Heidelberg; Seidel, Stefan (Hrsg.).

Becker, T., & Knop, C. (2015). *Digitales Neuland: Warum Deutschlands Manager jetzt Revolutionäre werden.* Wiesbaden: Becker, Thomas (Hrsg.); Springer Fachmedien.

Beckers, A. (2012). *Szenariobasierte Evaluation von Open Source ESBs zum Einsatz in einer Cloud-basierten Softwareinfrastruktur.* Hamburg: Diplomica Verlag.

Bedner, M. (2013). *Cloud Computing: Technik, Sicherheit und rechtliche Gestaltung.* Kassel: kassel university press.

Beer, K. (02. Februar 2016). *WhatsApp hat eine Milliarde aktive Nutzer .* (heise) Abgerufen am 26. März 2016 von heise online: http://www.heise.de/newsticker/meldung/Wha tsApp-hat-eine-Milliarde-aktive-Nutzer-3089551.html

Behrendt, S., & Scholz, H. (November 2013). *Kampf der Giganten Deutsche Telekommunikationsanbieter im Fusionsfieber: Eine Analyse von DSP-Partners in Zusammenarbeit mit mobile zeitgeist.* (DSP-Partners, mobile Zeitgeist) Abgerufen am 28. März 2016 von Mobile

263

Zeitgeist: http://www.mobile-zeitgeist.com/wp-content/downloads/2013-11_Kampf_der_Giganten_-_Telekommunikationsmarkt_DSP_und_mobile_zeitgeist.pdf

Behrmann, E. (16. März 2016). *BMW Counters Apple Threat With Self-Driving, Electric Car Push* . (Bloomberg) Abgerufen am 16. März 2016 von Bloomberg: http://www.bloomberg.com/news/articles/2016-03-16/bmw-ceo-s-strategy-puts-focus-on-electric-luxury-vehicles

Belding-Royer, E. M., Agha, K. A., & Pujolle, G. (2005). *Mobile and Wireless Communication Networks - IFIP TC6/WG6.8 Conference on Mobile and Wireless Communication Networks (MWCN 2004) October 25-27, 2004, Paris, France.* Paris, Frankreich: Springer Science+Business Media. Von gta.ufrj.br: http://www.gta.ufrj.br/ftp/gta/TechReports/CCD04a.pdf abgerufen

Bergmann, C. (16. Juli 2015). *Bill Gates Stiftung investiert in kenianisches Bitcoin-Startup Bitsoko* . Abgerufen am 06. März 2016 von http://bitcoinblog.de/2015/07/16/bill-gates-stiftung-investiert-in-kenianisches-bitcoin-startup-bitsoko/

Bertschek, I. (23. Oktober 2015). *Industrie 4.0 ist in deutschen Unternehmen weiter kaum bekannt* . Abgerufen am 16. Februar 2016 von Netzoekonom: https://netzoekonom.de/2015/10/23/industrie-4-0-ist-in-deutschen-unternehmen-weiter-kaum-bekannt/

Beuth, P. (01. Dezember 2015). *Zu jung, um gehackt zu werden* . Abgerufen am 13. Februar 2016 von Zeit Online: http://www.zeit.de/digital/datenschutz/2015-12/hacker-vteck-spielzeug-datensicherheit

Bieger, T., zu Knyphausen-Aufseß, D., & Krys, C. (. (2011). *Innovative Geschäftsmodelle: Konzeptionelle Grundlagen, Gestaltungsfelder und unternehmerische Praxis* . Heidelberg: Springer-Verlag; Krys, Christian (Hrsg.).

Bielmeier, S. (17. Februar 2016). *Projekt „Industrie 4.0" stärkt die Arbeitsproduktivität bis 2025 um zwölf Prozent* . Abgerufen am 23. Februar 2016 von DZ Bank: Zusammen geht mehr.: https://bielmeiersblog.dzbank.de/2016/02/17/projekt-industrie-4-0-staerkt-die-arbeitsproduktivitaet-bis-2025-um-zwoelf-prozent/

Bierwisch, S. (2014). *RFID Radio Frequency Identification: Grundlagen und*

Einsatzmöglichkeiten. Hamburg: Diplomica Verlag.

Biffar, J. (15. März 2016). *Bitkom Digital Office Index 2016.* (Bitkom) Abgerufen am 16. März 2016 von Bitkom: https://www.bitkom.org/Presse/Anhaenge-an-PIs/2016/Maerz/Bitkom-Digital-Office-Index-PK-Charts.pdf

Bisanz, E. (2011). *Das Bild zwischen Kognition und Kreativität: Interdisziplinäre Zugänge zum bildhaften Denken.* Bielefeld: transcript.

Bishop, R. H. (2008). *Mechatronic Systems, Sensors, and Actuators: Fundamentals and Modeling.* Boca Raton, London, New York, USA: CRC Press - Taylor & Francis Group.

Bittner, P., Hügel, S., Kreowski, H.-J., Meyer-Ebrecht, D., & Schnizel, B. (. (2014). *Gesellschaftliche Verantwortung in der digital vernetzten Welt.* Berlin: Lit Verlag Dr. W. Hopf; Schnizel, Britta (Hrsg.).

Bloching, B., Leutinger, P., Oltmanns, T., Rossbach, C., Schlick, T., Remane, G., . . . Shafranyuk, O. (01. März 2015). *Die digitale Transformation der Industrie.* (R, Produzent, & ROLAND BERGER STRATEGY CONSULTANTS in Zusammenarbeit mit BUNDESVERBAND DER DEUTSCHEN INDUSTRIE) Abgerufen am 24. November

2015   von
http://bdi.eu/media/presse/publikationen/infor
mation-und-
telekommunikation/Digitale_Transformation.
pdf

Bluetooth SIG. (02. Dezember 2014). *Specification of
the Bluetooth System - Master Table of
Contents & Compliance Requirements*. (B.
SIG, Produzent) Abgerufen am 23. Januar
2016 von Specification of the Bluetooth
System:
https://www.bluetooth.org/DocMan/handlers/
DownloadDoc.ashx?doc_id=286439

Bluetooth SIG, Inc. (o. Jg.). *Bluetooth Fact or
Fiction*. Abgerufen am 23. Januar 2016 von
bluetooth.com:
https://www.bluetooth.com/what-is-bluetooth-
technology/bluetooth-fact-or-fiction

Blümlein, A. (2013). *eBooks: Von den technischen
Grundlagen ber die Vermarktung bis zur ...*
Hamburg: Diplomica Verlag.

BMI De-Mail. (o. J.). *De-Mail – einfach verschlüsselt
und jederzeit nachweisbar* . Abgerufen am 16.
März 2016 von Bundesministerium des
Innern:
http://www.cio.bund.de/Web/DE/Innovative-
Vorhaben/De-Mail/de_mail_node.html

BMWi German Mittelstand . (Mai 2014). *German Mittelstand: Motor der deutschen Wirtschaft.* (Bundesministerium für Wirtschaft und Energie) Abgerufen am 1. April 2016 von BMWI: https://www.bmwi.de/BMWi/Redaktion/PDF/ Publikationen/factbook-german-mittelstand,property=pdf,bereich=bmwi2012,s prache=de,rwb=true.pdf

BMWi, BMI, BMVI. (August 2014). *Die Digitale Agenda 2014 - 2017.* Abgerufen am 19. Januar 2016 von Bundesministerium für Verkehr und digitale Infrastruktur. Gestaltung und Produktion: http://www.digitale-agenda.de/Content/DE/_Anlagen/2014/08/201 4-08-20-digitale-agenda.pdf?__blob=publicationFile&v=6

Bock, A. (21. Oktober 2015). *Flüchtlingskrise verdeutlicht Notwendigkeit zur stärkeren Digitalisierung der Verwaltung .* (Bearing Point) Abgerufen am 16. März 2016 von BearingPoint: http://toolbox.bearingpoint.com/de/digitalisier ung/news-detail-digitalisierung/fluechtlingskrise-verdeutlicht-notwendigkeit-zur-staerkeren-digitalisierung-der-verwaltung/2825/

Boie, J. (03. März 2010). *Leere Speicher, volle Kosten .* Abgerufen am 24. Januar 2016 von

Süddeutsche   Zeitung:
http://www.sueddeutsche.de/digital/urteil-zur-
vorratsdatenspeicherung-leere-speicher-volle-
kosten-1.9796

Bonin, H., Gregory, T., & Zierahn, U. (Juni 2015).
*Übertragung der Studie von Frey/Osborne
(2013) auf Deutschland.* (ZWE) Abgerufen
am 16. März 2016 von Forschungsbericht:
http://www.bmas.de/SharedDocs/Downloads/
DE/PDF-
Publikationen/Forschungsberichte/fb-
455.pdf;jsessionid=4605AD14C24C801FEA
D3C423E3D21984?__blob=publicationFile&
v=2

Borchers, D. (25. Januar 2015). *Bill Gates: Die
nächsten 15 Jahre sind entscheidend* . (Heise)
Abgerufen am 06. Februar 2016 von Heise
Online:
http://www.heise.de/newsticker/meldung/Bill-
Gates-Die-naechsten-15-Jahre-sind-
entscheidend-2527954.html

Borges, G., & Schwenk, J. (2012). *Daten- und
Identitätsschutz in Cloud Computing, E-
Government und E-Commerce* . Heidelberg
Dordrecht London New York: Borges, Georg;
Springer-Verlag.

269

Börsenverein. (Februar 2016). *E-Books* . Abgerufen am 05. März 2016 von http://www.boersenverein.de/ebook-markt

Börsenverein des deutschen Buchhandels. (2013). *Verankert im Markt - Das E-Book in Deutschland 2013*. Abgerufen am 05. März 2016 von http://www.boersenverein.de/sixcms/media.ph p/976/Kurzversion_E-Book-Studie2014.pdf

Boyer, C. (15. Januar 2016). *ETSI Seeks Harmonization of NFV Information Modelling across Standards Bodies and Open Source* . (ETSI) Abgerufen am 22. März 2016 von ETSI: http://www.etsi.org/news-events/news/1053-2016-01-news-etsi-seeks-harmonization-of-nfv-information-modelling-across-standards-bodies-and-open-source

Boysen, G. (2012). *Mobilfunk - Datenübertragung in der Industrie.* Blomberg: PHOENIX CONTACT.

Bradley, G. (07. Mai 2015). *Big Data für grünere Städte* . (Computerwoche) Abgerufen am 26. März 2016 von Computerwoche: http://www.computerwoche.de/a/big-data-fuer-gruenere-staedte,3098136

Brandt, M. (07. August 2014). *Dramatischer Preisverfall bei Festplattenspeichern* . Abgerufen am 23. Januar 2016 von Statista:

http://de.statista.com/infografik/2544/entwickl
ung-preis-pro-gigabyte-festplattenspeicher/

Breitenreuter, D. (11. Mai 2015). *Hat der Mittelstand
Angst vor Veränderung durch IT?* . Abgerufen
am 29. Februar 2016 von cloudmagazin.com:
http://www.cloudmagazin.com/2015/05/11/hat
-der-mittelstand-angst-vor-veraenderung-
durch-it/

Brenner, W., & Hess, T. (. (2014).
*Wirtschaftsinformatik in Wissenschaft und
Praxis* . Heidelberg: Springer Gabler.

Brock, H., & Bieberstein, I. (. (2015). *Multi- und
Omnichannel-Management in Banken und
Sparkassen: Wege in eine erfolgreiche
Zukunft*. Wiesbaden: Springer Gabler; Brock,
Harald (Hrsg.).

Bröker, J. (12. Oktober 2015). *Deutsche Bildung ist
ein Exportschlager*. Abgerufen am 16. März
2016 von Die Welt:
http://www.welt.de/sonderthemen/mittelstand/
export/article147495720/Deutsche-Bildung-
ist-ein-Exportschlager.html

Brühl, J., & Fuchs, F. (12. September 2014). *Polizei-
Software zur Vorhersage von Verbrechen* .
Abgerufen am 05. März 2016 von
Süddeutsche Zeitung:
http://www.sueddeutsche.de/digital/polizei-

software-zur-vorhersage-von-verbrechen-gesucht-einbrecher-der-zukunft-1.2115086

Brühl, V. (2015). *Wirtschaft des 21. Jahrhunderts: Herausforderungen in der Hightech-Ökonomie.* Wiesbaden: Springer Fachmedien.

Bub, U., & Wolfenstetter, K.-D. (. (2014). *Beherrschbarkeit von Cyber Security, Big Data und Cloud Computing: Tagungsband zur dritten EIT ICT Labs-Konferenz zur IT-Sicherheit.* Wiesbaden: Springer Vieweg; Wolfenstetter, Klaus-Dieter (Hrsg.).

Buck, K. (30. März 2012). *M2M: Wenn Maschinen kommunizieren* . (VDI Verlag) Abgerufen am 07. März 2016 von Ingenieur: http://www.ingenieur.de/Themen/Werkzeuge-Maschinen/M2M-Wenn-Maschinen-kommunizieren

Buhr, S. (21. Dezember 2015). *Meet Knightscope's Crime-Fighting Robots* . (Tech Crunch) Abgerufen am 16. März 2016 von Tech Crunch: http://techcrunch.com/2015/12/31/meet-knightscopes-crime-fighting-robots/

Bullinger, H.-J., & Hompel, t. M. (2007). *Internet der Dinge.* Berlin, Heidelberg, New York: Springer-Verlag Berlin Heidelberg.

Bund, B. (2014). *Die Lage der IT-Sicherheit in Deutschland 2014.* Abgerufen am 15. Februar 2016 von BSI BUND: https://www.bsi.bund.de/SharedDocs/Downloads/DE/BSI/Publikationen/Lageberichte/Lagebericht2014.pdf?__blob=publicationFile

Bundesamt für Sicherheit in der Informationstechnik. (2005). *Risiken und Chancen des Einsatzes von RFID-Systemen* . (BSI.BUND) Abgerufen am 4. April 2016 von BSI.BUND: https://www.bsi.bund.de/SharedDocs/Downloads/DE/BSI/ElekAusweise/RFID/RIKCHA_b arrierefrei_pdf.pdf?__blob=publicationFile

Bundesamt für Sicherheit und Informationstechnik. (2005). *Risiken und Chancen des Einsatzes von RFID-Systemen.* Abgerufen am 19. Januar 2016 von Bundesamt für Sicherheit und Informationstechnik: https://www.bsi.bund.de/SharedDocs/Downloads/DE/BSI/ElekAusweise/RFID/RIKCHA_b arrierefrei_pdf.pdf?__blob=publicationFile

Bundesdatenschutzgesetz. (o. J.). *BDSG: Technische und organisatorische Maßnahmen* . Abgerufen am 9. April 2016 von dejure: http://dejure.org/gesetze/BDSG/9.html

Bundesministerium des Innern. (September 2014). *Digitale Verwaltung 2020.* Abgerufen am 16. März 2016 von BMI Bund:

http://www.bmi.bund.de/SharedDocs/Downlo
ads/DE/Broschueren/2014/regierungsprogram
m-digitale-verwaltung-
2020.pdf?__blob=publicationFile

Bundesnetzagentur für Elektrizität, Gas,
Telekommunikation, Post und Eisenbahnen.
(01. September 2015). (F. Wulff, Produzent)
Abgerufen am 22. Januar 2016 von
http://www.bundesnetzagentur.de/DE/Sachge
biete/Telekommunikation/Unternehmen_Instit
utionen/Frequenzen/OeffentlicheNetze/Mobilf
unknetze/Projekt2016/projekt2016-node.html

Bundesverband Carsharing. (2016). *CarSharing-
Entwicklung in Deutschland.* Abgerufen am
19. März 2016 von
http://www.carsharing.de/sites/default/files/up
loads/grafik_entwicklung_carsharing_deutschl
and_2016_gesamt_mit_logo_0.pdf

Buvat, J., & Subrahmanyam, K. (2014). *Tesla
Motors: A Silicon Valley Version of the
Automotive Business Model.* (Captemini
Consulting) Abgerufen am 16. März 2016 von
Capgemini   Consulting:
https://www.capgemini-
consulting.com/resource-file-
access/resource/pdf/tesla_motors.pdf

Buxmann, P. (18. Februar 2016). *Reality Check
Digitalisierung: Treiber, Hemmnisse &*

Zukunftsinvestitionen. (Technische Universität Darmstadt) Abgerufen am 15. März 2016 von TU Darmstadt: http://www.is.tu-darmstadt.de/media/bwl5_is/keynotes/folien_ 1/Reality_Check_Digitalisierung.pdf

Buyya, R., Vecchiola, C., & Selvi, S. T. (2013). *Mastering Cloud Computing: Foundations and Applications Programming.* Waltham, USA: Morgan Kaufmann.

Carl, M. I. (17. August 2012). *Staatliche Zugriffe auf Cloud-Daten.* (datenschutz nord GmbH) Abgerufen am 15. Februar 2016 von datenschutz nord gruppe: https://www.datenschutz-nord-gruppe.de/news/datenschutz-news/beitrag/bp/70/artikel/staatliche-zugriffe-auf-cloud-daten.html

Caspar, J. (25. Februar 2016). *Hamburgs Datenschutz ist in Gefahr.* (Die Welt) Abgerufen am 28. Februar 2016 von Die Welt: http://www.welt.de/regionales/hamburg/article 152661737/Hamburgs-Datenschutz-ist-in-Gefahr.html

CeBit2016. (2015). *Ein halbes Jahr länger leben .* (Cebit) Abgerufen am 16. März 2016 von Cebit: http://www.cebit.de/de/news-trends/trends/mobile/artikel-2015/wearables-ein-halbes-jahr-laenger-leben.xhtml

Chatfield, T. (2014). *50 Schlüsselideen: Digitale Kultur (1. Auflage)*. Berlin Heidelberg New York: Springer-Verlag.

Cisco. (03. Februar 2015). *Cisco Visual Networking Index: Global Mobile Data Traffic Forecast Update, 2014–2019*. (Cisco and/or its affiliates) Abgerufen am 20. Januar 2016 von Cisco Visual Networking Index: http://www.cisco.com/c/en/us/solutions/collat eral/service-provider/visual-networking-index-vni/white_paper_c11-520862.pdf

Cisco Global Cloud Index. (2014). *Cisco Global Cloud Index: Forecast and Methodology, 2014–2019 White Paper* . (Cisco) Abgerufen am 04. Februar 2016 von Cisco.com: http://www.cisco.com/c/en/us/solutions/collat eral/service-provider/global-cloud-index-gci/Cloud_Index_White_Paper.html

Cisco Systems. (16. Oktober 2012). *http://docwiki.cisco.com/wiki/Internetworking _Technology_Handbook#WAN_Technologies*. Abgerufen am 23. Januar 2016 von http://docwiki.cisco.com/wiki/Internetworking _Technology_Handbook#WAN_Technologies

Cisco Systems. (27. Mai 2015). *Cisco Visual Networking Index: Forecast and Methodology, 2014–2019*. (Cisco Systems) Abgerufen am 24. Januar 2016 von

Cisco.com:
http://www.cisco.com/c/en/us/solutions/collat
eral/service-provider/ip-ngn-ip-next-
generation-network/white_paper_c11-
481360.pdf

Clauß, U. (16. Februar 2016). *Der lukrative Kampf gegen die Angst vor der "Wolke".* (Die Welt) Abgerufen am 17. Februar 2016 von Die Welt:
http://www.welt.de/wirtschaft/webwelt/article
152290652/Der-lukrative-Kampf-gegen-die-
Angst-vor-der-Wolke.html

Cleve, J. (2014). *Studienbrief: SPF Wissensbasierte Systeme (Data Mining) Teil 1 (SoSe 2014).* Wismar: WINGS - Wismar International Graduation Services GmbH.

Cleve, J., & Lämmel, U. (2014). *Data Mining (De Gruyter Studium).* München: Oldenbourg Wissenschaftsverlag.

Cole, T. (2010). *Unternehmen 2020: Das Internet war erst der Anfang.* München: Carl Hanser Verlag.

Cole, T. (2015). *Digitale Transformation: Warum die deutsche Wirtschaft gerade die digitale Zukunft verschläft und was jetzt getan werden muss! (1. Auflage).* München: Vahlen.

comScore. (01. Dezember 2014). *Ingisights: Germany Top 20 October 2014* . (comScore) Abgerufen am 05. März 2016 von https://www.comscore.com/Insights/Market-Rankings/Germany-Top-20-October-2014

Connected Living. (15. Dezember 2015). *comdirect bank AG wird Connected Living-Mitglied* . Abgerufen am 15. März 2016 von Pressebox: http://www.pressebox.de/inaktiv/connected-living-ev/comdirect-bank-AG-wird-Connected-Living-Mitglied/boxid/770980

Czycholl, H. (08. Juni 2013). *Forscher nutzen Insekten als lebende Drohnen* . (Hamburger Abendblatt) Abgerufen am 19. März 2016 von Hamburger Abendblatt: WISSENSCHAFT UND TECHNIK: http://www.abendblatt.de/ratgeber/wissen/article116935849/Forscher-nutzen-Insekten-als-lebende-Drohnen.html

Dänzel, S., & Heun, T. (. (2014). *Marke und digitale Medien: Der Wandel des Markenkonzepts im 21. Jahrhundert* . Wiesbaden: Springer Gabler; Heun, Thomas (Hrsg.).

Dapp, T. F. (23. September 2014). *Fintech – Die digitale (R)evolution im Finanzsektor Algorithmenbasiertes Banking mit human touch.* (Deutsche Bank Research) Abgerufen am 06. März 2016 von Deutsche Bank

Research:
https://www.dbresearch.de/PROD/DBR_INT
ERNET_DE-
PROD/PROD0000000000342293.pdf

D'Arpizio, C. (2015 йил 29-Oktober). *Altagamma 2015 Worldwide Markets Monitor*. (Bain & Company) Retrieved 2016 йил 10-April from http://www.italy24.ilsole24ore.com/pdf2010/ Editrice/ILSOLE24ORE/QUOTIDIANO_INS IDE_ITALY/Online/_Oggetti_Correlati/Docu menti/2015/11/23/altagamma1.pdf

de Paly, S. (05. August 2015). *Die SMS ist tot – 5 Gründe, warum SMS Marketing lebt!* . Abgerufen am 26. März 2016 von kanalegal: http://www.kanal-egal.de/die-sms-ist-tot-5-gruende-warum-sms-marketing-lebt/

Deden, H. (November 2004). *Gesunde Arbeitsbedingungen - Ein Standortvorteil -*. Abgerufen am 16. März 2016 von Arbeitsschutz NRW: http://www.apug.nrw.de/pdf/vortrag-gesunde-arbeitsbedingungen.pdf

DeLisle, J.-J. (24. April 2015). *What's the Difference Between IEEE 802.11af and 802.11ah?* Abgerufen am 22. Januar 2016 von Mwrf.com: http://mwrf.com/active-components/what-s-difference-between-ieee-80211af-and-80211ah

Deloitte Studie. (2015). *Sharing Economy*. (Deloitte) Abgerufen am 07. März 2016 von http://www2.deloitte.com/content/dam/Deloitt e/ch/Documents/consumer-business/ch-de-cb-sharing-economy-teile-und-verdiene.pdf

Denner, V. (12. Dezember 2014). *Der Schlüssel zum Erfolg*. Abgerufen am 16. Februar 2016 von Handelsblatt: http://www.handelsblatt.com/technik/das-technologie-update/energie/industrie-4-0-der-schluessel-zum-erfolg/11114444.html

dertagesspiegel. (28. Januar 2008). *Telefonkundin erhält Rechnung über 63 Millionen Euro* . (dpa) Abgerufen am 13. Februar 2016 von Der Tagesspiegel: http://www.tagesspiegel.de/weltspiegel/frankr eich-telefonkundin-erhaelt-rechnung-ueber-63-millionen-euro/1152654.html

Deutsche Bahn. (2016). *HotSpot im ICE – die beste Verbindung von Mobilität und Internet*. Retrieved 2016 йил 5-April from db.de: http://www.bahn.de/p/view/service/zug/railnet _ice_bahnhof.shtml

Deutsche Bischoskonferenz. (2015). *Katholische Kirche in Deutschland: ZAHLEN UND FAKTEN* . Abgerufen am 21. Februar 2016 von http://www.dbk.de/fileadmin/redaktion/Zahlen

%20und%20Fakten/Kirchliche%20Statistik/A
llgemein_-
_Zahlen_und_Fakten/AH_275_DBK_Zahlen-
und-Fakten_final.pdf

Deutsche Lufthansa. (2016). *Deutsche Lufthansa FlyNe*. Abgerufen am 4. April 2016 von http://www.lufthansa.com/de/de/Fly-Net

Deutsche Messe AG. (2016). *CRM auf der CeBIT: Tools für eine neue Ära der Kundenbeziehungen* . Abgerufen am 13. Februar 2016 von http://www.digitalbusiness-cloud.de/crm-auf-der-cebit-top-tools-fuer-eine-neue-aera-der-kundenbeziehungen

Deutscher Ethikrat. (Juli 2015). *Die Vermessung des Menschen – Big Data und Gesundheit.* (Deutscher Ethikrat) Abgerufen am 17. März 2016 von ethikrat.org: http://www.ethikrat.org/dateien/pdf/infobrief-02-15.pdf

Devasahayam, S. R. (2013). *Signals and Systems in Biomedical Engineering: Signals Processing and Physiological Systems Modelling (Second Edition).* New York, Heidelberg, Dordrecht, London: Springer Science+Business Media.

Dewald, P. (09. August 2014). *Mittelstand Aufgepasst.* (D. Steil, Herausgeber, & FOCUS Online) Abgerufen am 19. Januar 2016 von Focus   online:

http://www.focus.de/finanzen/mittelstand-
digital/mittelstand-aufgepasst-warum-sie-die-
digitalisierung-nicht-verschlafen-
sollten_id_4047489.html

DGQ. (2016). *Deutsche Gesellschaft für Qualität.*
Abgerufen am 13. Februar 2016 von
http://www.dgq-iso-9001.de/

DHL Paketkopter. (o. J.). *DHL.* (DHL) Abgerufen am
16. März 2016 von
http://www.dhl.de/paketkopter

Dialog Consult / VATM. (2015). *17. TK-
Marktanalyse Deutschland 2015.* (Dialog
Consult / VATM) Abgerufen am 05. März
2016 von
http://www.vatm.de/uploads/media/VATM_T
K-Marktstudie_2015_211015.pdf

Dickgreber, F., Grabowski, S., Campanini, C., &
Sorensen, T. (2014). *The Future of Telecom
Operators in Europe As the
telecommunications industry faces a mixed
financial outlook and rapid change, telecom
operators have reached a strategic crossroads
.* (ATKearney) Abgerufen am 27. März 2016
von ATKearney:
https://www.google.de/url?sa=t&rct=j&q=&e
src=s&source=web&cd=3&cad=rja&uact=8&
ved=0ahUKEwjH5taDpuHLAhVrMJoKHX9j
D1sQFggmMAI&url=https%3A%2F%2Fww

w.atkearney.com%2Fdocuments%2F10192%
2F7026987%2FThe%2BFuture%2Bof%2BTe
lecom%2BOperators%2Bin%2BEurope.pdf%
2F04e78f77-ea18-43f0-9503-
5866190685e8&usg=AFQjCNG64uuvXpuG
WLcS49BykwlboMCTLw&sig2=YyxOrJejE
Vr_0WZK_mimUA&bvm=bv.117868183,d.b
Gs

Die Schweizerische Post. (02. März 2016). *Die Post
baut am Internet der Dinge* . (Schweizerische
Post) Abgerufen am 07. März 2016 von
post.ch: https://www.post.ch/de/ueber-
uns/unternehmen/medien/medienmitteilungen/
2016/die-post-baut-am-internet-der-dinge

Digital Manufacturing Magazin. (28. September
2015). *Fernwartung mit M2M: Vernetzt über
die „Cloud der Dinge"* . (H.-J. Grohmann,
Produzent, & WIN-Verlag) Abgerufen am 07.
März 2016 von DIGITAL
MANUFACTURING Magazin:
http://www.digital-manufacturing-
magazin.de/fachartikel/fernwartung-mit-m2m-
vernetzt-ueber-die-cloud-der-dinge

Digitale Gesellschaft e.V. (o. J.). *WLAN-
STÖRERHAFTUNG BESEITIGEN*. (Digitale
Gesellschaft e V.) Abgerufen am 8. April
2016 von Digitale Gesellschaft:
https://digitalegesellschaft.de/mitmachen/store
rhaftung-beseitigen/

Dimitz, U. (08. Dezember 2014). *Vier Internet-Riesen stecken 30 Dax-Firmen in die Tasche* . Abgerufen am 05. März 2016 von Das Investment.com: http://www.dasinvestment.com/nc/investment s/maerkte/news/datum/2014/12/08/vier-internet-riesen-stecken-30-dax-firmen-in-die-tasche/

Dinger, J., & Hartenstein, H. (2008). *Netzwerk- und IT-Sicherheitsmanagement: Eine Einführung.* Karlsruhe: Universitätsverlag Karlsruhe.

Dinnes, M. (3. November 2014). *Die neue ISO/IEC 27018 im Überblick* . (Computerwoche) Abgerufen am 9. April 2016 von Computerwoche: http://www.computerwoche.de/a/die-neue-iso-iec-27018-im-ueberblick,3069892

Dirlich, G., Freksa, C., Schwalto, U., & Wimmer, K. (1986). *Kognitive Aspekte der Mansch-Computer-Interaktion: Workshop, München 12.-13. April 1984.* Berlin Heidelberg New York Tokyo: Dirlich, G.; Freska, C.; Schwalto, U.; Wimmer, K.; Springer-Verlag.

Dittert, K. (Januar 2016). *Smartes Panopticon: Können Objekte moralisch handeln?* (Sigs Datacom) Abgerufen am 04. April 2016 von sigs Datacom: http://www.sigs-datacom.de/uploads/tx_dmjournals/dittert_OS_01_06_S5Bf.pdf

Dobrindt, A. (25. November 2015). *Chance auf digitales Wirtschaftswunder.* (Bundesregierung, Produzent) Abgerufen am 16. Februar 2016 von Bundesregierung: Aktuelles: https://www.bundesregierung.de/Content/DE/Namensbeitrag/2015/11/2015-11-25-dobrindt-handelsblatt.html

Dolata, U., & Schrape, J.-F. (. (2013). *Internet, Mobile Devices und die Transformation der Medien: radikaler Wandel als schrittweise Rekonfiguration.* Berlin: edition sigma.

Doll, N. (10. August 2015). *Warum selbstfahrende Autos so teuer sein werden.* (Die Welt) Abgerufen am 16. März 2016 von Die Welt: http://www.welt.de/wirtschaft/article145015200/Warum-selbstfahrende-Autos-so-teuer-sein-werden.html

Donner, A. (22. Januar 2016). *Studie: Cloud-PBX-Marktanteil steigt rasant .* (Vogel Business Media) Abgerufen am 29. Feburar 2016 von IP Insider: http://www.ip-insider.de/studie-cloud-pbx-marktanteil-steigt-rasant-a-518546/

Dorst, W. (10. April 2015). *Zwei Jahre Vorsprung – die Zwischenbilanz der Plattform Industrie 4.0 .* Abgerufen am 16. Februar 2016 von

Bitkom:
https://www.bitkom.org/Presse/Blog/Zwei-
Jahre-Vorsprung-die-Zwischenbilanz-der-
Plattform-Industrie-40.html

dpa - Spiegel Online Wirtschaft. (19. Mai 2015).
*Taxi-Konkurrenz: Uber passt sich deutschen
Regeln an* . (dpa) Abgerufen am 03. März
2016   von
http://www.spiegel.de/wirtschaft/unternehmen
/uber-startet-uberx-in-deutschland-a-
1034452.html

DPA/N24. (19. Januar 2016). *Airbus nimmt
Produktion mit 3D-Druckern auf* . (DPA)
Abgerufen am 21. März 2016 von N24:
http://www.n24.de/n24/Nachrichten/Wirtschaf
t/d/7937300/airbus-nimmt-produktion-mit-3d-
druckern-auf.html

Drilling, T. (16. Januar 2016). *Internet der Dinge
gewinnt stark an Einfluss* . Abgerufen am 14.
Februar 2016 von Big Data Insider:
http://www.bigdata-insider.de/internet-der-
dinge-gewinnt-stark-an-einfluss-a-518990/

Drucker, P. F. (1957). *Landmarks of Tomorrow.* New
York, USA: Harper & Brothers, New York.

DTAG. (15. März 2015). *Telekom will
Wirtschaftswunder 4.0* . Abgerufen am 23.
Januar 2016 von Medienmappe CeBIT 2015 :

286

https://www.telekom.com/medien/konzern/27
1960

DTAG CeBIT. (17. März 2015). *CeBIT 2015: Telekom unterstützt Digitalisierung der Industrie* . (DTAG) Abgerufen am 07. März 2016 von Telekom Proessemitteilung: https://www.telekom.com/medien/loesungen-fuer-unternehmen/271754

DTAG Medien. (2016). *Cloud ist fester Bestandteil der Sourcing-Strategie.* (Deutsche Telekom) Abgerufen am 29. Februar 2016 von Cloud Großkunden: https://www.telekom.com/medien/medienmap pen/192764

Dueck, G. (10. Februar 2016). *Was von der Arbeitswelt übrig bleibt* . (Merton Magazin) Abgerufen am 16. März 2016 von Merton Magazin: https://merton-magazin.de/was-von-der-arbeitswelt-%C3%BCbrig-bleibt

Dumm, T., & Schild, H. (2009). *Energie und Wärmelehre: Lerntext, Aufgaben mit kommentierten Lösungen und Kurztheorie.* Zürich: Compendio Bildungsmedien.

eBay International AG. (März 2015). *Mobiler Handel ist gelebte Realität* . (Innofact, Produzent, & ebay) Abgerufen am 09. März 2016 von Zukunft des Handels: http://www.zukunftdeshandels.de/technologie

Eberspächer, J., & Vögel, H.-J. (1997). *GSM - Global System for Mobile Communication: Vermittlung, Dienste und Protokolle in digitalen Mobilfunknetzen.* Stuttgart: B. G. Teubner.

Ebner, T. (02. Dezember 2014). *Was ist ein Shitstorm? Eine klare Checkliste und Definition* . Abgerufen am 12. Januar 2016 von social media facts: http://www.socialmediafacts.net/de/social-media/shitstorm-checkliste-definition

Eckert, C. (30. September 2015). *SECURITY IM ZEITALTER VON INDUSTRIE 4.0 UND INTERNET DER DINGE.* Abgerufen am 15. Februar 2016 von Frauenhofer AISEC: http://docplayer.org/storage/25/5831148/1455568326/FIvkgLeLlaW2bOlSUmKnZA/5831148.pdf

Eisner, A. (23. Februar 2016). *Zuckerbergs Mega-Projekt: Facebook startet Satelliten-Internet* . Abgerufen am 22. März 2016 von Chip: http://www.chip.de/news/Zuckerbergs-Mega-Projekt-Facebook-startet-Satelliten-Internet_90062151.html

Engelien, M. (19. April 2014). *Google Now hilft bei der Organisation des Tages.* (Die Welt) Abgerufen am 10. April 2016 von Die Welt: http://www.welt.de/wirtschaft/webwelt/article

288

127116469/Google-Now-hilft-bei-der-
Organisation-des-Tages.html

Eppinger, E. H., Hölzle, K., & Kamprath, M. (2015).
*Dienstleistungspotenziale und
Geschäftsmodelle in der Personalisierten
Medizin.* Wiesbaden: Springer Gabler.

Erdkönig, P., & Falkner, J. (2014). *DIE CLOUD
Chancen & Nutzen für den Mittelstand: Ein
Whitepaper der Comarch AG in Kooperation
mit dem Fraunhofer-Institut für
Arbeitswirtschaft und Organisation IAO.*
(Comarch) Abgerufen am 27. März 2016 von
Frauenhofer IAO:
https://www.iao.fraunhofer.de/lang-
de/images/leistungen/cloud-chancen-und-
nutzen-mittelstand.pdf

Erfanian, J., & Hattachi, R. E. (17. Februar 2015). *5G
White Paper.* (5G Initiative Team) Abgerufen
am 24. Januar 2016 von NGMN Alliance:
https://www.ngmn.org/uploads/media/NGMN
_5G_White_Paper_V1_0.pdf

Ericsson Corporate Public & Media Relations. (06.
Januar 2016). *Ericsson delivers massive IoT
with millions of connections per cell site for
AT&T.* Abgerufen am 24. Januar 2016 von
ericsson.com:
http://www.ericsson.com/news/160106_ericss
on_delivers_massive_iot_244039856_c

Eurobarometer, S. (Februar 2015). *Special Eurobarometer 423 "Cyber Security"*. Abgerufen am 13. Februar 2016 von http://ec.europa.eu/public_opinion/archives/eb s/ebs_423_en.pdf

Europäische Kommission. (21. April 2014). *From 1G to 5G Infographic*. (E. Kommission, Produzent, & Europäische Kommission) Abgerufen am 24. Januar 2016 von The Digital Agenda website: http://ec.europa.eu/digital-agenda/en/news/1g-5g-infographic

eurostat. (1. März 2016). *Januar 2016: Arbeitslosenquote im Euroraum bei 10,3% In der EU28 bei 8,9%*. (eurostat) Abgerufen am 1. April 2016 von eurostat: http://ec.europa.eu/eurostat/documents/29955 21/7197748/3-01032016-AP-DE.pdf/6e66e6c2-29f6-4184-946f-6215e4b75783

Evans, D. (April 2011). *Das Internet der Dinge So verändert die nächste Dimension des Internet die Welt*. (Cisco) Abgerufen am 8. April 2016 von Cisco Whitepaper: http://www.cisco.com/web/DE/assets/executiv es/pdf/Internet_of_Things_IoT_IBSG_0411FI NAL.pdf

Expertenkommission Forschung und Innovation (EFI). (2016). *GUTACHTEN ZU FORSCHUNG, INNOVATION UND TECHNOLOGISCHER LEISTUNGSFÄHIGKEIT DEUTSCHLANDS.* Abgerufen am 29. Februar 2016 von Gutachten 2016: http://www.e-fi.de/fileadmin/Gutachten_2016/EFI_Gutachten_2016.pdf

facebook Inc. (26. März 2015). *F8 2015: Updates on Connectivity Lab, Facebook AI Research and Oculus.* Abgerufen am 24. Januar 2016 von facebook newsroom: http://newsroom.fb.com/news/2015/03/f8-day-two-2015/

facebook Investor Relations. (27. Januar 2016). *Facebook Investor Relations.* Abgerufen am 21. Februar 2016 von Facebook: http://investor.fb.com/results.cfm

Fachschule Osnabrück. (März 2011). (RECO, c/o Science to Business GmbH) Abgerufen am 12. Januar 2016 von http://www.wt-os.de/fileadmin/user_upload/alle/reco/crm/leitfaden-crm-neg-2011-04.pdf

Fallgren, M., & Kusume, K. (30. April 2015). *Mobile and wireless communications Enablers for the Twenty-twenty Information Society (METIS).* Abgerufen am 24. Januar 2016 von Updated scenarios, requirements and KPIs for 5G mobile and wireless system with recommendations for future investigations: https://www.metis2020.com/wp-content/uploads/deliverables/METIS_D1.5_v1.pdf

Feitag, M. (18. März 2016). *Daimler offenbar vor Megaauftrag von Uber.* Abgerufen am 19. März 2016 von http://www.manager-magazin.de/unternehmen/autoindustrie/daimle r-uber-soll-autonom-steuernde-s-klassen-bestellt-haben-a-1082886.html

Felser, R. (02. März 2016). *IT-Verantwortliche haben Mühe beim Übergang zu digitalen Geschäftsmodellen* . Abgerufen am 03. März 2016 von Computerwelt: http://www.computerwelt.at/news/wirtschaft-politik/unternehmen/detail/artikel/114808-it-verantwortliche-haben-muehe-beim-uebergang-zu-digitalen-geschaeftsmodellen/

Finger, S. (12. Februar 2016). *NEUE VERANSTALTUNGSREIHE "INDUSTRIE 4.0 @ MITTELSTAND"* . (Verlag moderne industrie) Abgerufen am 16. Februar 2016 von Plattform Industrie 4.0 : http://www.ke-next.de/news/neue-veranstaltungsreihe-industrie-4-0-mittelstand-309.html

Fleig, J. (26. Oktober 2015). *Disruptive Innivationen.* (J. Fleig, Herausgeber, & Business Wissen Information Service, Karlsruhe) Abgerufen am 19. Januar 2016 von Business Wissen Information Service: http://www.business-wissen.de/artikel/disruptive-innovationen-die-regeln-der-branche-radikal-veraendern

Fleisch, E., & Mattern, F. (2005). *Das Internet der Dinge - Ubiquitous Computing und RFID in der Praxis: Visionen,Technologien,Anwendungen,Handlu ngsanleitungen* . Berlin, Heidelberg: Mattern, Friedemann; Springer Verlag.

focusonline. (04. November 2015). *ARD schreibt Brief an „Hans Werner": Feuersalamander soll GEZ-Gebühren zahlen* . Abgerufen am 13. Februar 2016 von Focus Money: http://www.focus.de/finanzen/steuern/behoerd en-verstehen-keinen-spass-ard-schreibt-brief-an-hans-werner-feuersalamander-soll-gez-gebuehren-zahlen_id_5061346.html

Frank, M. (2011). *Deer Iran und die Atombombe.* Berlin: Lulu Inc.

Frankfurter Allgemeine Zeitung Nr. 82. (07. April 2014). Handelsszenario 2020. *FAZ*, 26.

Franz, C. (März 2002). *Die Computer für das 21. Jahrhundert* . Abgerufen am 11. April 2016 von Universität Potsdam: http://ddi.cs.uni-

potsdam.de/Lehre/UbiComp/Vortragsausarbei
tung/Die_Computer_fuer_das_2021_Jahrhund
ert.htm

Franz-Rudolf, E. (04. Februar 2016). *Franz-Rudolf Esch: „Potenziale der Digitalisierung werden nicht ausgeschöpft"* . (Fachmedien & Mittelstand) Abgerufen am 28. März 2017 von Absatzwitschaft: http://www.absatzwirtschaft.de/potenziale-der-digitalisierung-werden-nicht-ausgeschoepft-74519/

Frey, C. B., & Osborne, A. M. (17. September 2013). *THE FUTURE OF EMPLOYMENT: HOW SUSCEPTIBLE ARE JOBS TO COMPUTERISATION?* (Oxford University Engineering Sciences Department) Abgerufen am 09. März 2016 von Oxford University Engineering Sciences Department: http://www.oxfordmartin.ox.ac.uk/downloads/academic/The_Future_of_Employment.pdf

Fröhlich, C. (12. August 2015). *Apple Pay: Jetzt auch in Europa* . Abgerufen am 28. März 2016 von Internetworld.de: http://www.internetworld.de/technik/apple/apple-pay-jetzt-in-europa-997884.html

Fuchs, M. (2011). *Kampf um Sinn: Kulturmächte der Moderne im Widerstreit* . München: Herbert Utz Verlag.

294

Funk, D., Buettner, R., Süss, C., Henning, N., & Tulzer, A. (2012). *Vergleich von Geschäftsmodellen sozialer Netzwerke.* Abgerufen am 05. März 2016 von FOM Hochschule für Oekonomie und Management: http://www.prof-buettner.com/downloads/funk2012a.pdf

Gabriel, S. (18. Februar 2016). *Gabriel: "Europa braucht wieder mehr Industrie" - Bündnis "Zukunft der Industrie" legt Handlungsempfehlungen für europäische Industriepolitik vor* . (BMWI) Abgerufen am 21. Februar 2016 von Bundesministerium für Wirtschaft und Energie: GEMEINSAME PRESSEMITTEILUNG : http://www.bmwi.de/DE/Presse/pressemitteilu ngen,did=752408.html

Gador, K. (2015). *BITKOM: Kognitive Maschinen – Meilenstein in der Wissensarbeit.* (BITKOM) Abgerufen am 26. Januar 2016 von https://www.bitkom.org/Publikationen/2015/L eitfaden/Kognitive-Maschinen/150213-Kognitive-Maschinen-11Febr2015.pdf

Galitz, R., Görlich, R., Grünewald, H., Hagenhoff, S., Huck, H., Reinerth, L., . . . Weiß, M. (2012). *Erfolgreich publizieren im Zeitalter des E-Books: Ein pragmatischer und zielorientierter Leitfaden für die Zukunft des digitalen Buches.* Wiesbaden: Springer Vieweg.

Gates, B. (19. Mai 2005). *The New World of Work.* (Microsoft) Abgerufen am 24. Januar 2016 von Microsoft.com: https://www.microsoft.com/mscorp/execmail/2005/05-19newworldofwork.mspx

Gates, M. a. (2015). *Out Big Bet for the Future.* (Melinda and Bill Gates Foundation) Abgerufen am 06. März 2016 von gatesnotes: https://www.gatesnotes.com/2015-Annual-Letter?page=3&lang=en

Gazin, G. (21. Juni 2011). *A QR Code tells a much bigger story than a barcode.* (Troy Media) Abgerufen am 23. Januar 2016 von Troy Media: http://www.troymedia.com/2011/06/21/a-qr-code-tells-a-much-bigger-story-than-a-barcode/

Geisberger, E., Cengarle, M., Keil, P., Niehaus, J., & Thiel, C. T.-F.-J. (Dezember 2011). *Cyber-Physical Systems Innovationsmotor für Mobilität, Gesundheit, Energie und Produktion.* (acatech) Abgerufen am 16. Februar 2016 von acatech : http://www.acatech.de/fileadmin/user_upload/Baumstruktur_nach_Website/Acatech/root/de/Publikationen/Stellungnahmen/POSITION_CPS_NEU_WEB_120130_final.pdf

Geisler, F. (2014). *Datenbanken: Grundlagen und Design (5. aktualisierte und erweiterte Auflage)*. Frechen: mitp Verlag.

Gershgorn, D. (2016). *Human-Like: Facebook Is Using Our Data To Build The 'World's Best' Artificial Intelligence Lab* . Abgerufen am 10. Januar 2016 von http://www.popsci.com/: http://www.popsci.com/facebook-ai

Gfk Verein Compact. (2015). *Sharing Economy*. Abgerufen am 07. März 2016 von gfk-verein.org: http://www.gfk-verein.org/sites/default/files/medien/1289/dok umente/1513_sharing_download_final.pdf

Gibbs, S. (26. Februar 2016). *Mercedes-Benz swaps robots for people on its assembly lines* . Abgerufen am 07. März 2016 von the guardian: http://www.theguardian.com/technology/2016 /feb/26/mercedes-benz-robots-people-assembly-lines

Gillberg, F. (12. Januar 2015). *Großbritannien möchte wirksame Verschlüsselung verbieten: WhatsApp & Co. in England bald geblockt?* Abgerufen am 15. Februar 2016 von netzpolitik.org: https://netzpolitik.org/2015/whatsapp-co-in-england-bald-geblockt-cameron-kuendigt-

ueberwachungsausbau-im-fall-seiner-
wiederwahl-an/

Gitlin, S. (17. Februar 2011). *AeroVironment
Develops World's First Fully Operational
Life-Size Hummingbird-Like Unmanned
Aircraft for DARPA* . (AeroVironment,
Produzent) Abgerufen am 19. März 2016 von
http://www.avinc.com/resources/press_release
/aerovironment_develops_worlds_first_fully_
operational_life-size_hummingbird

Google AlphaGo. (2016). *MASTERING THE GAME
OF GO WITH DEEP NEURAL NETWORKS
AND TREE SEARCH* . Abgerufen am 10.
Januar 2016 von AlphaGo:
http://deepmind.com/alpha-go.html

Google Loon. (2013). *BALLOON-POWERED
INTERNET FOR EVERYONE* . (Google)
Abgerufen am 22. März 2016 von Loon For
All: https://www.google.com/loon/

Google Official Blog. (27. Januar 2016). *AlphaGo:
using machine learning to master the ancient
game of Go*. Abgerufen am 15. März 2016
von Google:
https://googleblog.blogspot.de/2016/01/alphag
o-machine-learning-game-go.html

Gould, E. (22. Februar 2016). *Why Africa's banks are
racing to embrace fintech* . (WEF) Abgerufen
am 06. März 2016 von World Economic

Forum:
https://www.weforum.org/agenda/2016/02/wh
y-africas-banks-are-racing-to-embrace-
fintech?utm_content=buffer4700e&utm_medi
um=social&utm_source=facebook.com&utm_
campaign=buffer

Granig, P., Hartlieb, E., & Lingelhel, D. (2016).
*Geschäftsmodellinnovationen: Vom Trend
zum Geschäftsmodell.* Wiesbaden: Springer
Fachmedien; Granig, Peter.

Gray, A. (19. Januar 2016). *The 10 skills you need to
thrive in the Fourth Industrial Revolution* .
(WEF) Abgerufen am 16. März 2016 von
WEF:
http://www.weforum.org/agenda/2016/01/the-
10-skills-you-need-to-thrive-in-the-fourth-
industrial-revolution

Greif, B. (16. März 2016). *EuGH-Generalanwalt
verneint Störerhaftung bei offenen WLAN-
Netzen* . Abgerufen am 22. März 2016 von
ZDNet: http://www.zdnet.de/88263502/eugh-
generalanwalt-verneint-stoererhaftung-bei-
offenen-wlan-netzen/

Greiner, F., Schlaak, H., Tschulena, G., & Korb, W.
(2011). *Hessisches Ministerium für
Wirtschaft, Verkehr und Landesentwicklung.*
(S. Hummel, R. Waldschmidt, A. Bracht, M.
Lämmer, Herausgeber, H. H. GmbH,

Produzent, & HA) Abgerufen am 19. Januar 2016 von Hessisches Ministerium für Wirtschaft, Verkehr und Landesentwicklung: http://www.hessen-nanotech.de/mm/Broschuere_Mikro-Nano-Integration_web.pdf

Greis, F. (06. März 2016). *BMW will das "intelligenteste Auto" bauen* . (golem) Abgerufen am 16. März 2016 von golem.de: http://www.golem.de/news/autonomes-fahren-bmw-will-das-intelligenteste-auto-bauen-1603-119588.html

Grieß, A. (06. Juni 2014). *Drohnen werden zunehmend für zivile Zwecke gebaut* . (Statista) Abgerufen am 19. März 2016 von Statista: https://de.statista.com/infografik/2336/bekannt e-aktive-drohnentypen-laut-rpas-jahrbuch-nach-art-der-nutzung/

Grieß, A. (2016 йил 12-April). *Jeder Dritte 14-35 Jähriger in Deutschland sieht sich in der Meinungsfreiheit eingeschränkt*. Retrieved 2016 йил 13-April from statista: https://de.statista.com/infografik/4636/befragu ng-zur-meinungsfreiheit/

Gropp, M. (16. März 2016). *Von intelligenten Weinbergen und Äckern* . (FAZ) Abgerufen am 21. März 2016 von Frankfurter

Allgemeine:
http://www.faz.net/aktuell/wirtschaft/cebit/int
ernet-der-dinge-in-der-landwirtschaft-auf-
cebit-2016-14128380.html

Grosser, D. (16. Ferbruar 2016). *Internet in
Thüringen zu langsam* . (Thüringer
Allgemeine) Abgerufen am 17. Februar 2016
von Thüringer Allgemeine:
http://www.thueringer-
allgemeine.de/startseite/detail/-
/specific/Internet-in-Thueringen-zu-langsam-
687026406

GSM Association. (2015). *Global growth of cellular
M2M.* (GSM Association) Abgerufen am 22.
Januar 2016 von The Mobile Economy 2015:
http://www.gsmamobileeconomy.com/GSMA
_Global_Mobile_Economy_Report_2015.pdf

GSMA Press Release. (22. Februar 2016). *GLOBAL
OPERATORS, GOOGLE AND THE GSMA
ALIGN BEHIND ADOPTION OF RICH
COMMUNICATIONS SERVICES.* (GSMA)
Abgerufen am 26. März 2016 von GSMA:
http://www.gsma.com/newsroom/press-
release/global-operators-google-and-the-
gsma-align-behind-adoption-of-rcs/

Günther, W., & Hompel, t. M. (2010). *Internet der
Dinge in der Intralogistik* . Heidelberg

Dordrecht London New York: Günther, Willibald; Springer Verlag.

Gurlow, L., & Jordans, A. (30. Oktober 2015). *Cisco-Studie: Viermal mehr Daten in der Cloud bis 2019* . (Cisco) Abgerufen am 4. April 2016 von Cisco Pressemeldungen: http://globalnewsroom.cisco.com/de/de/press-releases/cisco-studie-viermal-mehr-daten-in-der-cloud-bis--nasdaq-csco-1225784

Haag, C. N. (12. Juni 2014). *Internationaler Datenschutz*. (intersoft consulting services AG) Abgerufen am 04. Februar 2016 von intersoft consulting services AG: https://www.datenschutzbeauftragter-info.de/internationaler-datenschutz/

Hackmann, F. (09. Juni 2014). *18-Milliarden-Dollar-Startup: Wie Uber Taxiverbänden davonfährt* . Abgerufen am 03. März 2016 von förderland: Wissen für Gründer und Unternehmer: http://www.foerderland.de/digitale-wirtschaft/netzwertig/news/artikel/18-milliarden-dollar-startup-wie-uber-taxiverbaenden-davonfaehrt/

Hackmann, J. (14. Mai 2013). *Industrie 4.0 ist das Internet der Ingenieure* . Abgerufen am 21. Februar 2016 von Computerwoche:

http://www.computerwoche.de/a/industrie-4-0-ist-das-internet-der-ingenieure,2538117

Hagenhoff, S. (2006). *Internetökonomie der Medienbranche.* Göttingen: Hagenhoff, Svenja (Hrsg.).

Hajkowicz, S., Reeson, A., Rudd, L., Bratanova, A., Leonie, H., Mason, C., & Boughen, N. (Januar 2016). *Tomorrow's Digitally Enabled Workforce: Megatrends and Scenarios for jobs and employment in Australia over the next twenty years [pdf · 7mb].* (CSIRO, Produzent) Abgerufen am 16. März 2016 von Megatrends and scenarios for jobs and employment in Australia over the coming twenty years: http://www.csiro.au/~/media/D61/Files/16-0026_DATA61_REPORT_TomorrowsDigiallyEnabledWorkforce_WEB_160204.pdf?la=en

Hamann, G., & Soboczynski, A. (10. September 2014). *Der Angriff der Intelligenz .* Abgerufen am 20. Februar 2016 von Zeit Online: http://www.zeit.de/kultur/2014-09/yvonne-hofstetter-kuenstliche-intelligenz

Hammermann, A. (März 2016). *Qualifikationsbedarf und Qualifizierung Anforderungen im Zeichen der Digitalisierung.* (Institut der deutschen Wirtschaft Köln) Abgerufen am 16. März 2016 von Unternehmen wollen mehr als IT-

Nerds   :
http://www.iwkoeln.de/presse/pressemitteilun
gen/beitrag/digitalisierung-unternehmen-
wollen-mehr-als-it-nerds-252008

Handelsblatt / dpa. (06. Februar 2014). *Banken
    verlieren Vertrauen der Privatanleger* .
    Abgerufen am 06. März 2016 von
    Handelsblatt:
    http://www.handelsblatt.com/finanzen/steuern
    -recht/recht/studie-banken-verlieren-
    vertrauen-der-privatanleger/9471030.html

Handelsblatt / dpa. (20. Februar 2016). *Telekom will
    neues Branchen-Modell bei Firmenkunden
    etablieren* . Abgerufen am 22. März 2016 von
    Handelsblatt:
    http://www.handelsblatt.com/unternehmen/it-
    medien/ngena-telekom-will-neues-branchen-
    modell-bei-firmenkunden-
    etablieren/12991898.html

Handelszeitung CH. (11. März 2016). *Mensch vs.
    Maschine: Siegt der Mega-Computer?* .
    Abgerufen am 15. März 2016 von
    Handelszeitung   Schweiz:
    http://www.handelszeitung.ch/vermischtes/me
    nsch-vs-maschine-siegt-der-mega-computer-
    1016762

Handesblatt. (02. März 2015). *Sicherheitsrisiko
    Smartphone-Apps*. (Handelsblatt) Abgerufen

am 14. Februar 2016 von Handelsblatt: http://www.handelsblatt.com/technik/gadgets/hackerangriffe-sicherheitsrisiko-smartphone-apps/11446036.html

Hänisch, T., & Volker, A. P. (2016). *eHealth: Wie Smartphones, Apps und Wearables die Gesundheitsversorgung verändern werden.* Wiesbaden: Springer Fachmedien.

Harrach, S. (2014). *Neugierige Strukturvorschläge im maschinellen Lernen: Eine technikphilosophische Verortung.* Bielefeld: transcript Verlag.

Harris, M. (29. Januar 2016). *Project Skybender: Google's secretive 5G internet drone tests revealed* . (The Guardian) Abgerufen am 03. Februar 2016 von The Guardian UK: http://www.theguardian.com/technology/2016/jan/29/project-skybender-google-drone-tests-internet-spaceport-virgin-galactic

Härting, N. (17. Februar 2016). *CRonline: Portal zum IT-Recht.* Abgerufen am 1. April 2016 von http://www.cr-online.de/blog/2016/02/17/acht-thesen-zum-dateneigentum/

Härting, R.-C. (2014). *Big Data - Daten strategisch nutzen!* Norderstedt: Härting, Ralf-Christian (Hrsg); BoD - Books on Demand.

Harvard College. (o. J.). *RoboBees: Practical Applications*. (Harvard College) Abgerufen am 19. März 2016 von http://robobees.seas.harvard.edu/

Hase, T. (29. Dezember 2015). *Telekom-Chef Höttges für bedingungsloses Grundeinkommen* . (Zeit Online) Abgerufen am 17. März 2016 von Zeit Online: http://www.zeit.de/wirtschaft/2015-12/digitale-revolution-telekom-timotheus-hoettges-interview

Hatton, M., & Chua, G. (4. Dezember 2015). *Service Provider Opportunities & Strategies in the Internet of Things*. Abgerufen am 27. März 2016 von Machina Research: https://www.cisco.com/c/dam/en/us/solutions/collateral/service-provider/mobile-internet/service-provider.pdf

Haufe Online / Mindbreeze. (21. Dezember 2015). *Mit diesen Big-Data-Trends sollten Sie sich beschäftigen* . (Haufe) Abgerufen am 21. Februar 2016 von acpuisa: https://www.haufe.de/marketing-vertrieb/crm/diese-big-data-trends-sind-wichtig_124_333316.html

Haun, M. (2014). *Cognitive Computing: Steigerung des systemischen Intelligenzprofils*. Berlin, Heidelberg: Springer Vieweg.

Hecht, B. (12. Januar 2016). *Nano-Drohnen mit Lichtantrieb* . (Universität Würzburg) Abgerufen am 19. März 2016 von Universität Würzburg: http://www.presse.uni-wuerzburg.de/einblick/single/artikel/nano-drohnen-mit-lichtantrieb/

Hecking, M. (26. Januar 2016). *Warum Daimler sein Taxi-Geschäft aufs Spiel setzt* . Abgerufen am 07. März 2016 von Manager Magatin: http://www.manager-magazin.de/unternehmen/autoindustrie/mytaxi-app-daimlers-aerger-mit-der-taxibranche-a-1074009.html

Heiden, M. (2014). *Arbeitskonflikte: Verborgene Auseinandersetzungen um Arbeit, Überlastung und Prekarität.* Berlin: edition sigma.

Heinze, R., Schleupner, L., & Manzei, C. (2016). *Industrie 4.0 im internationalen Kontext Kernkonzepte, Ergebnisse, Trends.* Berlin, Offenbach: Heinze, Ronald (Hrsg.); VDE VERLAG.

Heller, G. (18. Juli 2013). *Warum der "German Mittelstand" nicht kopierbar ist.* Abgerufen am 29. Februar 2016 von Die Welt: http://www.welt.de/wirtschaft/article118171834/Warum-der-German-Mittelstand-nicht-kopierbar-ist.html

Heller, P. (07. Juni 2015). *Energy Harvesting: Maschinen nabeln sich ab*. (Deutschlandfunk) Abgerufen am 23. Januar 2016 von Deutschlandfunk: http://www.deutschlandfunk.de/endlich-ernten-energy-harvesting-maschinen-nabeln-sich-ab.740.de.html?dram:article_id=321169

Hemmerich, L. (08. Mai 2012). *Fahrerloses Google-Auto erhält erste Lizenz* . Abgerufen am 11. Januar 2016 von netzwelt.de: http://www.netzwelt.de/news/92168-fahrerloses-google-auto-erhaelt-erste-lizenz.html

Henkes, H., & Praxmarer, L. (2015). *Technologie-Trends & CIO Prioritäten 2016*. Abgerufen am 27. März 2016 von ExpertON Group: http://www.experton-group.de/fileadmin/experton/mailings/2015/pdf_21835467865/Experton_Technologie-Trends__CIO_Prioritaeten_2016.pdf

Henry, C. (22. Oktober 2015). *EightyLEO Details Vision for IoT SmallSat Constellation*. (Access Intelligence) Abgerufen am 07. März 2016 von ViaSatellite: Integrating SatelliteToday.com: http://www.satellitetoday.com/telecom/2015/10/22/eightyleo-details-vision-for-iot-smallsat-constellation/

Hesseling, C. (25. August 2015). *Google-Dienste datensparsam verwenden* . Abgerufen am 29. Februar 2016 von mobilsicher.de: https://mobilsicher.de/2015/08/25/android-ohne-google-google-dienste-datensparsam-verwenden/

Heun, S.-E., & Assion, S. (2015). *Internet(recht) der Dinge Zum Aufeinandertreffen von Sachen- und Informationsrecht.* Abgerufen am 14. Februar 2016 von Recherchieren und juris / Das Rechtsportal: http://www.degruyter.com/view/j/cr.2015.31.issue-12/cr-2015-1212/cr-2015-1212.xml

High, R. (28. September 2015). *Watson Uses Cognitive Computing To Improve People's Lives.* Abgerufen am 27. Januar 2018 von Forbes Magazin: http://www.forbes.com/sites/ibm/2015/09/28/watson-uses-cognitive-computing-to-improve-peoples-lives/#7abb955e4c0b

Hildebrand, K. (10. Juli 2015). *Wenn Google in die Wolken starrt.* Abgerufen am 10. Januar 2016 von Süddeutsche Zeitung - Kunst von Computern: http://www.sueddeutsche.de/kultur/kunst-von-computern-wenn-google-in-die-wolken-starrt-1.2559161

Hildebrand, K., Gebauer, M., Hinrichs, H., & Mielke, M. (. (2015). *Daten- und Informationsqualität: Auf dem Weg zur Information Excellence (3.,erweiterte Auflage).* Wiesbaden: Springer Vieweg; Mielke, Michel (Hrsg.).

Hiller, M. (12. Februar 2016). *Die Produktion der Zukunft* . (KPMG AG Wirtschaftsprüfungsgesellschaft) Abgerufen am 23. Februar 2016 von KPMG AG Wirtschaftsprüfungsgesellschaft: http://news.kpmg.de/industrie-4-0-die-produktion-der-zukunft/

Hintringer, M. (2014). *Einsatz von Cisco Unified Computing im Klinischen Rechenzentrum.* Hamburg: disserta Verlag.

Hof, H.-J. (o. J.). *IT-Security für Cyber-Physical Systems.* Abgerufen am 15. Februar 2016 von Munich IT Security Research Group: https://w3-mediapool.hm.edu/mediapool/media/fk07/fk0 7_lokal/diefakultt_4/ansprechpartner_2/profes soren_1/hof/downloads_4/itsecurityforcyberp hysicalsystemscpssecurity.pdf

Hohensee, M. (26. Januar 2016). *Wie Mark Zuckerberg einen Mediengiganten schmiedet* . Abgerufen am 03. März 2016 von Wirtschaftswoche:

http://www.wiwo.de/unternehmen/it/facebook
-wie-mark-zuckerberg-einen-mediengiganten-
schmiedet/12859012.html

Holger, F. (16. Mai 2010). *QR-Code - was ist das?*
Abgerufen am 24. Januar 2016 von Computer
& Technik - Info: http://www.comptech-
info.de/component/content/article?id=355:qr-
code

Holland, H. (2014). *Digitales Dialogmarketing:
Grundlagen, Strategien, Instrumente.*
Wiesbaden: Holland, Heinrich (Hrsg);
Springer Fachmedien.

Höller, J., Tsiatsis, V., Mulligan, C., Karnouskos, S.,
Avesand, S., & Boyle, D. (1. Auflage (2014)).
*From Machine-to-Machine to the Internet of
Things - Introduction to a New Age of
Intelligence.* Amsterdam, Boston, NL, USA:
Academic Press.

Holtel, S. (2015). *Kognitive Maschinen – Meilenstein
in der Wissensarbeit: Leitfaden.* (BITKOM,
Produzent) Abgerufen am 24. Januar 2016
von   BITKOM:
https://www.bitkom.org/Publikationen/2015/L
eitfaden/Kognitive-Maschinen/150213-
Kognitive-Maschinen-11Febr2015.pdf

Horden, W. (28. April 2013). *Reaching for the Heart
of Spring .* Abgerufen am 14. April 2016 von
Huffpost   Healthy   Living:

http://www.huffingtonpost.com/william-horden/spring_b_2713013.html

Huawai Technologies. (März 2015). *Connections and Data Management in the IoT Era.* Abgerufen am 23. 01 2016 von Mobile World Congress 2015: http://www.huawei.com/minisite/mwc2015/en/articles/connections-and-data-management-in-the-iot-era.html

Hulick, K. (2016). *Artificial Intelligence.* Minneapolis, Minnesota, USA: Abdo Publishing.

Hundt, S. (2015). *Informationsgehalt von Credit Ratings: Eine empirische Analyse europäischer Aktien- und Anleihenmärkte.* Wiesbaden: Springer Gabler.

IBM Institute for Business Value. (04. November 2015). *IBM Studie: die Angst vor der „Uberisierung".* Abgerufen am 03. März 2016 von IBM Pressemitteilung: http://www-03.ibm.com/press/de/de/pressrelease/48021.wss

IBM Press. (15. Dezember 2015). *IBM macht München zur Watson IoT-Hauptstadt.* Abgerufen am 23. Januar 2016 von IBM Pressemitteilungen: http://www-03.ibm.com/press/de/de/pressrelease/48484.wss

IBM Whitepaper. (April 2015). *Was kann Industrie 4.0? Und können Sie das auch? - Potenzial für die deutsche Industrie.* Abgerufen am 18. Februar 2016 von IBM Whitepaper: http://www-935.ibm.com/services/multimedia/Whitepaper _Industrie_4.0_screen.pdf

IDATE DigiWorld. (Mai 2015). *NFV and SDN market size worldwide by region from 2014 to 2018 (in million euros)* . (IDATE) Abgerufen am 22. März 2016 von Statista: http://www.statista.com/statistics/461573/sdn-and-nfv-markets-worldwide-by-region/

IDC/SAP. (Februar 2016). *Thriving in the Digital Economy: How small and midsize enterprises are adapting to digital transformation.* Abgerufen am 29. Februar 2016 von http://3ltddlexn3z1jo9ym15ce9rc.wpengine.ne tdna-cdn.com/wp-content/blogs.dir/1/files/IDC-Thriving-in-the-Digital-Economy.pdf

IKT.NRW. (08. August 2014). *Augmented Reality für die Smart Factory* . Abgerufen am 07. März 2016 von Cluster Informations- und Kommunikationstechnologie: http://ikt.nrw.de/einzelmeldung/article/augme nted-reality-fuer-die-smart-factory/

Infosys. (18. Januar 2016). *Young Workers Optimistic about Careers, Positive about Technology* . (Infosys) Abgerufen am 9. April 2016 von Infosys Newsroom: https://www.infosys.com/newsroom/press-releases/Pages/human-potential-education-industrial.aspx

Intel. (Juni 2012). *Einführung in Big Data: Die Analyse unstrukturierter Daten.* Abgerufen am 24. Januar 2016 von Intel IT Center: http://www.intel.de/content/dam/www/public/emea/de/de/pdf/unstructured-data-analytics-paper.pdf

Isikdag, U. (2015). *Enhanced Building Information Models: Using IoT Services and Integration Patterns.* Heidelberg, New York, Dordrecht, London: Springer Verlag.

IT-Finanzmagazin. (18. Februar 2016). *girocard kommt ins Smartphone: Deutsche Telekom, Telefonica und Vodafone ermöglichen mobiles Bezahlen.* Abgerufen am 23. März 2016 von IT Finanzmagazin: http://www.it-finanzmagazin.de/girocard-kommt-ins-smartphone-deutsche-telekom-telefonica-und-vodafone-ermoeglichen-mobiles-bezahlen-26957/

Jähnichen, S. (August 2015). *Von Big Data zu Smart Data – Herausforderungen für die Wirtschaf.*

(Smart Data Begleitforschung) Abgerufen am 13. Februar 2016 von http://www.digitale-technologien.de/DT/Redaktion/DE/Download s/Publikation/SmartData_NL1.pdf?__blob=pu blicationFile&v=5

Jain, E. (2015). *Verlust der Seele: Eine kulturkritische Studie zum Menschenbild der Gegenwart.* Norderstedt: BoD - Books on Demand.

Janocha, H. (2013). *Unkonventionelle Aktoren - Eine Einführung; 2. ergänzte und aktualisierte Auflage.* Berlin: Walter de Gruyter.

Jimenez, F. (09. März 2016). *So funktioniert das schwierigste Brettspiel der Welt.* Abgerufen am 15. März 2016 von http://www.welt.de/wissenschaft/article15307 0800/So-funktioniert-das-schwierigste-Brettspiel-der-Welt.html

Jiw, I. K. (15. Juli 2015). *So entscheidet Facebook in einer Auktion, welche Anzeigen ausgeliefert werden .* Abgerufen am 05. März 2016 von allfacebook: http://allfacebook.de/fbmarketing/anzeigen-auktion

Johnson, R. (28. Oktober 2012). *Micro-Drones Combined With DNA Hacking Could Create A Very Scary Future .* (Business Insider) Abgerufen am 19. Mär 2016 von Business Insider:

315

http://www.businessinsider.com/government-collected-dna-and-future-micro-drones-are-downright-scary-2012-10?IR=T

Jones, N. (14. Januar 2014). *Wie Maschinen lernen lernen* . Abgerufen am 10. Januar 2016 von Spektrum Verlag: http://www.spektrum.de/news/maschinenlernen-deep-learning-macht-kuenstliche-intelligenz-praxistauglich-spektrum-de/1220451

Kaelin, M. (17. Juni 2015). *Windows 10 supports AllJoyn making the Internet of Things possible.* Abgerufen am 28. Januar 2016 von TechRepublic: http://www.techrepublic.com/article/windows-10-supports-alljoyn-making-the-internet-of-things-possible/

Kaeser, E. (Juni 2019). *Deepfakes: Eeine Gefahr fuer den gesellschaftlichen Zusammenhalt.* Von Neue Züricher Zeitung: https://www.nzz.ch/meinung/deepfakes-eine-gefahr-fuer-den-gesellschaftlichen-zusammenhalt-ld.1500353 abgerufen

Kahle, C. (18. Februar 2016). *Telekom testet 70-Gbit-Technik als Ergänzung zum 5G-Mobilfunknetz* . Abgerufen am 23. Februar 2016 von WinFuture: http://winfuture.de/news,91118.html

Kalyvas, J. R., & Overly, R. M. (2015). *Big Data: A Business and Legal Guide.* Boca Raton, Fla: CRC Press (Boca Raton, Fla).

Kammerer, S. C. (1999). *Rating von Volkswirtschaften mit künstlich-neuronalen Netzen.* Wiesbaden: Springer Fachmedien.

Kanning, T. (08. Dezember 2015). *Auch die Deutsche Bank setzt jetzt auf Roboter .* Abgerufen am 07. März 2016 von Frankfurter Allgemeine: http://www.faz.net/aktuell/finanzen/geldanlag e-trotz-niedrigzinsen/deutsche-bank-startet-mit-robo-advisor-anlageberatung-online-13953517.html

Karcher, H. (20. Mai 2015). *just 4 business GmbH.* (just 4 business GmbH) Abgerufen am 19. Januar 2016 von MittelstandsWiki: Themen für Unternehmen: http://www.mittelstandswiki.de/wissen/5G_f %C3%BCrs_Internet_der_Dinge

Karlstetter, F. (28. November 2012). *DriveNow setzt bei der Lokalisierung von Fahrzeugen auf Google Maps .* (Vogel Business Media) Abgerufen am 07. März 2016 von Cloud Computing Insider: http://www.cloudcomputing-insider.de/drivenow-setzt-bei-der-lokalisierung-von-fahrzeugen-auf-google-maps-a-386878/

Karpovich, B., Sanders, L., Peranandam, C., & Hipfer, S. (Februar 2016). *Growing up hybrid: Accelerating digital transformation* . (IBM Center for Applied Insights) Abgerufen am 09. März 2016 von IBM Center for Applied Insights: http://www-01.ibm.com/common/ssi/cgi-bin/ssialias?subtype=WH&infotype=SA&htmlfid=GMW14087USEN&attachment=GMW14087USEN.PDF

Kashyap, M., Garfinkel, H., Shipman, J., Davies, S., & Nicolacakis, D. (März 2016). *Blurred lines: How FinTech is shaping Financial Services.* (PwC) Abgerufen am 21. März 2016 von Global FinTech Report: http://www.pwc.com/gx/en/advisory-services/FinTech/PwC%20FinTech%20Global%20Report.pdf

Katzer, M., & Crawford, D. (2014). *Office 365: Migrating and Managing Your Business in the Cloud.* New York, USA: Apress.

Kaufmann, T. (2015). *Geschäftsmodelle in Industrie 4.0 und dem Internet der Dinge: Der Weg vom Anspruch in die Wirklichkeit* . Wiesbaden: Springer Vieweg.

Keil-Slawik, R., & Kerres, M. (2005). *Hochschulen im digitalen Zeitalter: Innovationspotenziale und Strukturwandel.* Münster: Waxmann.

Kemper, H.-G., Pedell, B., & Schäfer, H. (. (2012). *Management vernetzter Produktionssysteme: Innovation, Nachhaltigkeit und Risikomanagement.* München: Franz Vahlen; Henry Schäfer (Hrsg.).

Kennedy, J. (25. November 2015). *How digital disruption changed 8 industries forever .* Abgerufen am 05. März 2016 von Silicon Republic: https://www.siliconrepublic.com/companies/2015/11/25/digital-disruption-changed-8-industries-forever

Kerkmann, C., & Karabasz, I. (11. November 2015). *Microsoft will die Cloud deutsch machen.* (Handelsblatt) Abgerufen am 05. Februar 2016 von Handelsblatt: http://www.handelsblatt.com/unternehmen/it-medien/kooperation-mit-telekom-microsoft-will-die-cloud-deutsch-machen/12570888.html

Kern, J. (15. Juli 2015). *Von M2M zum IoT.* (R. Ladner, Herausgeber, & WEKA FACHMEDIEN) Abgerufen am 20. Januar 2016 von funkschau - Fachmedien für Profis: http://www.funkschau.de/mobile-solutions/artikel/111011/1/

Keuper, F., Hamidian, K., Verwaayen, E., Kalinowski, T., & Kraijo, C. (. (2013).

Digitalisierung und Innovation: Planung, Entstehung, Enwicklungsperspektiven. Wiesbaden: Springer Gabler; Christian Kraijo (Hrsg.).

Kief, H. B., Roschiwal, H. A., & Schwarz, K. (2015). *CNC-Handbuch 2015/2016.* München: Kief, Hans B.; Roschiwal, Helmut A.; Schwarz, Karsten; Carl Hanser Verlag.

King, S. (2014). *Big Data: Potential und Barrieren der Nutzung im Unternehmenskontext (1. Auflage).* Berlin, Heidelberg, New York: Springer Verlag.

Kirk, M. (2015). *Thoughtful Machine Learning.* Sebastopol: O'Reilly Media.

Kleine, J., Venzin, M., Ludwig, F., & Krautbauer, M. (April 2012). *Mobile Payment – wohin geht die Reise? Chancen und Risiken für Marktteilnehmer in Europa.* (RESEARCH CENTER FOR FINANCIAL SERVICES STEINBEIS-HOCHSCHULE BERLIN) Abgerufen am 28. März 2016 von RESEARCH CENTER FOR FINANCIAL SERVICES STEINBEIS-HOCHSCHULE BERLIN: http://www.steinbeis-research.de/pdf/Zusammenfassung_Mobile_Payment-wohin_geht_die_Reise.pdf

Kleingers, D. (24. März 2014). *Sci-Fi-Romanze "Her" mit Joaquin Phoenix: Computer sind die besseren Liebhaber* . Abgerufen am 14. Januar 2016 von Spiegel Online: Kultur: http://www.spiegel.de/kultur/kino/her-von-spike-jonze-mit-joaquin-phoenix-scarlett-johansson-a-960028.html

Kleinz, T. (14. März 2016). *Die zweite Halbzeit der Telekom* . (Zeit Online) Abgerufen am 22. März 2016 von Zeit Online: http://www.zeit.de/digital/internet/2016-03/cebit-telekom-open-cloud-fort-knox

Klemm, T. (8. März 2016). *Warum überhaupt noch bar bezahlen?* . (FAZ) Abgerufen am 8. April 2016 von Frankfurter Allgemeine: Finanzen: http://www.faz.net/aktuell/finanzen/digital-bezahlen/warum-ueberhaupt-noch-bar-bezahlen-14108069.html

Klier, D. (05. Januar 2016). *Die Wi-Fi Alliance will ins Internet der Dinge.* Abgerufen am 19. Januar 2016 von IT-Markt: http://www.it-markt.ch/de-CH/News/2016/01/05/Die-Wi-Fi-Alliance-will-ins-Smarthome.aspx

Klimonczyk, & Sebastian. (2010). *RFID und Barcode im Kommissionierprozess.* Hamburg: Diplomica Verlag.

Klinger, D., Androile, S., Militello, L., Adelmann, L., & Klein, G. (März 1993). *DESIGNING FOR PERFORMANCE: R A COGNITIVE SYSTEMS ENGINEERING M APPROACH*

TO MODIFYING AN AWACS S HUMAN COMPUTER INTERFACE. (Armstrong Laboratory) Abgerufen am 17. März 2016 von DTIC.MIL: http://www.dtic.mil/dtic/tr/fulltext/u2/a275187 .pdf

Klotz, M. (20. 12 2015). *Mobile Payment in Deutschland: Warum Apple und Google den Markt unter sich aufteilen werden* . (t3n) Abgerufen am 28. März 2016 von t3n: digital pioneers: http://t3n.de/news/mobile-payment-deutschland-apple-666313/

Klotz, M. (28. Juli 2015). *Warum du auch in Deutschland schon bald mit Apple Pay bezahlst* . Abgerufen am 23. März 2016 von t3n: http://t3n.de/news/apple-pay-deutschland-626404/

Klotz, M. (21. März 2016). *Mobilfunkunternehmen stellen die Weichen für mobile Payment - schon wieder.* Abgerufen am 23. März 2016 von Mobilebranche.de: http://mobilbranche.de/2016/03/mobilfunkunt ernehmen-weichen-mobile?xing_share=news

Klug, H.-G. (22. Januar 2016). *WhatsApp: So will der Messaging-Dienst Geld verdienen* . Abgerufen am 05. März 2016 von teltarif: http://www.teltarif.de/whatsapp-

geschaeftsmodell-
unternehmen/news/62548.html

Knab, S., Pezzei, M., & Dancu, S. (September 2014). *Social Trends Luxus und Lifestyle 2014.* (TOMORROW FOCUS Media) Abgerufen am 05. März 2016 von omorrow-focus-media.de: http://download.tomorrow-focus-media.de/TFM_Social_Trends_Luxus_Lifesty le.pdf

Knauer, D. (2015). *Act Big - Neue Ansätze für das Informationsmanagement: Informationsstrategie im Zeitalter von Big Data und digitaler Transformation.* Wiesbaden: Springer Fachmedien.

Kneussel, J. (26. Februar 2016). *WhatsApp-Erfinder: Wer hat die Firma gegründet? .* Abgerufen am 05. März 2016 von http://www.giga.de/apps/whatsapp-fuer-android/specials/whatsapp-erfinder-wer-hat-die-firma-eigentlich-gegruendet/

Knierim-Moser, A. (2014). *Vorratsdatenspeicherung: Zwischen Überwachungsstaat und Terrorabwehr.* Wiesbaden: Springer Fachmedien.

Knöchelmann, M. (04. Februar 2014). *Disruptive Innovation als Erfolgsfaktor am Beispiel Amazon.* Abgerufen am 05. März 2016 von lepublikateur:

http://www.lepublikateur.de/wp-
content/uploads/2014/03/Disruptive-
Innovation-Amazon-Erfolgsfaktor.pdf

Knöpke, H., & Gerstner, H. (Oktober 2015).
*Marktanalyse: Wachstumschancen für
Unternehmen im Smart Home-Markt.*
(Qivicon) Abgerufen am 26. März 2016 von
qivicon:
https://www.qivicon.com/assets/PDF/Deutsch
e-Telekom-QIVICON-Marktanalyse-Smart-
Home.pdf

Koeppen, J. (12. Dezember 2013). *Wie Smart GPRS
M2M- und Telemetrie-Anwendungen
vereinfacht.* Abgerufen am 24. Januar 2016
von Elektronik Praxis:
http://www.elektronikpraxis.vogel.de/messen-
und-testen/articles/428104/

Kogler, U. (08. Februar 2016). *Aufholbedarf in Zeiten
von Industrie 4.0* . (mindbreeze GmbH)
Abgerufen am 13. Februar 2016 von it daily:
http://www.it-daily.net/it-management/big-
data-analytics/12056-aufholbedarf-in-zeiten-
von-industrie-4-0

Kölnische Rundschau. (03. Dezember 2012). *Geht ihr
die Puste aus? Die SMS wird 20 Jahre alt* .
(Kölnische Rundschau) Abgerufen am 05.
März 2016 von Kölnische Rundschau:
http://www.rundschau-

online.de/wirtschaft/geht-ihr-die-puste-aus--
die-sms-wird-20-jahre-alt-3810746

Koninklike Philips N.V. (2015). *Philips Hue tap.*
(Philips) Abgerufen am 23. Januar 2016 von
Philips: http://www2.meethue.com/de-
de/productdetail/philips-hue-tap-switch

Kontio, C. (02. Dezember 2013). *Achtung, da kommt
ein Amazon-Paket geflogen!* . (Handelsblatt)
Abgerufen   am   16.   März   2016   von
Handelsblatt:
http://www.handelsblatt.com/unternehmen/ha
ndel-konsumgueter/prime-air-mit-mini-
drohnen-achtung-da-kommt-ein-amazon-
paket-geflogen/9155732.html

Körner, R. (03. Dezember 2015). *A.T. Kearney: 45
Prozent der heutigen Jobs durch Roboter
bedroht.* (AT Kearney) Abgerufen am 16.
März 2016 von AT Kearney Pressemitteilung:
https://www.atkearney.de/documents/856314/
5503477/PM+45+Prozent+der+Jobs+durch+R
oboter+bedroht.pdf/68b88f7e-d59c-4bef-816f-
318a4732e566

Kornstädt, C. (10. Juli 2015). *FINTECH – EINE
DISRUPTIVE   (R)EVOLUTION   DES
FINANZSEKTORS?* . Abgerufen am 06. März
2016   von   Financial   Disruption   Lab:
http://www.financial-disruption.de/fintech-
eine-disruptive-revolution-des-finanzsektors/

Kraemer, K., & Nessel, S. (. (2015). *Geld und Krise: Die sozialen Grundlagen moderner Geldordnungen.* Campus Verlag; Nessel, Sebastian (Hrsg.).

Kranawetter, M. (2015). *Die Dinge sind da – und die Sicherheit?* . Abgerufen am 14. Februar 2016 von Zeitschrift für Informations-Sicherheit: https://www.kes.info/archiv/leseproben/2015/ die-dinge-sind-da-und-die-sicherheit

Kraus, W. (04. April 2014). *Industry Group Launches Li-Fi Consortium, to Promote Optical Wireless Communications.* Abgerufen am 22. Januar 2016 von Free Press Release: http://www.free-press-release.com/news-industry-group-launches-li-fi-consortium-to-promote-optical-wireless-communications-1318939124.html

Krause, M. (12. Juni 2015). *Mehr Bankfilialen als Tankstellen* . Abgerufen am 06. März 2016 von Neue Westfälische: http://www.nw.de/lokal/bielefeld/mitte/mitte/2 0484686_Mehr-Bankfilialen-als-Tankstellen.html

Krauße, M., & Konrad, R. (2014). *Drahtlose ZigBee-Netzwerke: Ein Kompendium.* Wiesbaden: Springer Fachmedien.

Krempl, S. (28. Dezember 2015). *32C3: Hardware-Trojaner als unterschätzte Gefahr.* Abgerufen am 14. Februar 2016 von http://www.heise.de/newsticker/meldung/32C 3-Hardware-Trojaner-als-unterschaetzte-Gefahr-3056452.html

Kreutzer, R., & Land, K.-H. (2013). *Digitaler Darwinismus - Der stille Angriff auf Ihr Geschäftsmodell und Ihre Marke.* Wiesbaden: Springer Fachmedien.

Kroker, M. (02. Juni 2014). *60 Sekunden im Internet: Twitter, YouTube, Facebook, Google, Snapchat & Co.* Abgerufen am 06. Januar 2016 von Krokers Look @ IT: Neues aus Hightech- und Medienwelt: http://blog.wiwo.de/look-at-it/2014/06/02/60-sekunden-im-internet-twitter-youtube-facebook-google-snapchat-co/

Kroker, M. (29. Juni 2015). *Darum drängen alle IT-Giganten in die deutsche Wolke* . (Wirtschaftswoche) Abgerufen am 9. April 2016 von http://www.wiwo.de/technologie/cebit-spezial/cloud-computing-darum-draengen-alle-it-giganten-in-die-deutsche-wolke/11950460.html

Kroker, M. (25. November 2015). *Internet of Things: 24 Milliarden vernetzte Dinge und 6 Billionen Dollar Investitionen bis 2020* . Abgerufen am 14. Januar 2016 von http://blog.wiwo.de/look-

at-it/2015/11/25/internet-of-things-24-
milliarden-vernetzte-dinge-und-6-billionen-
dollar-investitionen-bis-2020/

Kröll, M., & Schnauber, H. (1997). *Lernen der
Organisation durch Gruppen- und
Teamarbeit: Wettbewerbsvorteile durch
umfassende Unternehmensplanung.* Berlin,
Heidelberg: Springer-Verlag. Abgerufen am
62 von Miniaturisierung der Informations-
und Kommunikationstechnik:
http://www.bfdi.bund.de/DE/Service/Impressu
m/impressum_node.html;jsessionid=6E8C982
F132C7BFE7635C6265B9915C8.1_cid319

Kühl, E. (25. Januar 2016). *Deine Webcam ist meine
Webcam.* Abgerufen am 14. Februar 2016 von
Zeit Online:
http://www.zeit.de/digital/datenschutz/2016-
01/shodan-suchmaschine-internet-der-dinge-
webcam-unsicher

Kunze, B. (2007). *Überwachung operationeller
Risiken bei Banken: Interne und externe
Akteure im Rahmen qualitätiver und
quantitativer Überwachung.* Wiesbaden:
Deutscher Universitäts-Verlag.

Kuo, L. (23. Februar 2016). *Could blockchain
technology revolutionize the music industry? .*
(WEF, Produzent) Abgerufen am 06. März
2016 von World Economic Forum:

https://www.weforum.org/agenda/2016/02/co
uld-blockchain-technology-revolutionize-the-
music-
industry?utm_content=bufferffa8e&utm_medi
um=social&utm_source=facebook.com&utm_
campaign=buffer

Kurp, M., Hauschild, C., & Wiese, K. (2002). *Musikfernsehen in Deutschland: Politische, soziologische und medienökonomische Aspekte (1. Auflage August 2002)*. Wiesbaden: Westdeutscher Verlag.

Kurz, C. (2014). *Arbeit in der Industrie 4.0: „Besser statt billiger" als zukunftsfähige Gestaltungsperspektive*. Abgerufen am 07. März 2016 von Information Management und Consulting: http://scheer-management.com/wp-content/uploads/2014/10/IM_3_I.4.0_Seiten_5 6-59_Arbeit-i.d.-Industrie-4.0.pdf

Kurz, C. (10. November 2014). *Industrie 4.0 – Chancen und Risiken für die Industriearbeit der Zukunft aus Sicht der IG Metall* . (IG Metall) Abgerufen am 29. Februar 2016 von IG Metall: http://www.forum-fuer-politik-und-kultur.de/uploads/1/2/0/7/12076347/_hannove r_2014_11_10.pdf

Kurzweil, R. (19. Dezember 2014). *Don't Fear Artificial Intelligence* . (Time) Abgerufen am 16. März 2016 von Time: http://time.com/3641921/dont-fear-artificial-intelligence/

Landefeld, K. (November 2014). *Verbreitung und Nutzbarkeit von WLAN, WLAN-Zugangspunkten - Sowie öffentlicher Hotspots in Deutschland.* (K. Landefeld, Produzent, & eco - Verband der deutschen Internetwirtschaft) Abgerufen am 24. Januar 2016 von https://www.eco.de/wp-content/blogs.dir/eco-microresearch_verbreitung-und-nutzung-von-wlan1.pdf

Langer, J., & Roland, M. (2010). *Anwendungen und Technik von Near Field Communication (NFC).* Berlin Heidelberg New York: Springer Verlag.

Langheinrich, M., & Mattern, F. (Januar 2002). *Wenn der Computer verschwindet: Was Datenschutz und Sicherheit in einer Welt intelligenter Alltagsdinge bedeuten* . (ETH Zürich, Department Informatik) Abgerufen am 14. Februar 2016 von Researchgate: https://www.researchgate.net/publication/2422 54001_Wenn_der_Computer_verschwindet_ Was_Datenschutz_und_Sicherheit_in_einer_ Welt_intelligenter_Alltagsdinge_bedeuten

Laucker, E. (1996). *Stand der Anwendung und Entwicklungsperspektiven der Kreditwürdigkeit mit Neuronalen Netzen und Expertensystemen (Universität Rostock).* Hamburg: Diplomarbeiten Agentur .

Lechner, J. (Februar 2008). *INTERNATIONAL ARTICLE NUMBER & EAN-BARCODE.* (P. D. Ziegenbalg, Produzent, & PH Karlsruhe Institut für Mathematik und Informatik) Abgerufen am 19. Januar 2016 von http://www.ziegenbalg.ph-karlsruhe.de: http://www.ziegenbalg.ph-karlsruhe.de/materialien-homepage-jzbg/cc-interaktiv/EAN/EAN-Internationale-Artikel-Nummer.pdf

Lemke, A. (14. Juli 2014). *Revolutioniert NFV das Geschäftsmodell der Netzbetreiber?* . Abgerufen am 30. Januar 2016 von ZDNet: http://www.zdnet.de/88198152/revolutioniert-nfv-das-geschaeftsmodell-der-netzbetreiber/

Lenz, H.-J., & Müller, M. R. (2013). *Business Intelligence.* Berlin Heidelberg: Springer Vieweg.

Levine, B. (22. Januar 2015). *Persado scores $21M to become the Moneyball of marketing.* Abgerufen am 26. Januar 2016 von VentureBeat: http://venturebeat.com/2015/01/22/persado-scores-21m-to-become-the-moneyball-of-marketing/

Lewinski, K. v. (2013). *Datenflut und Recht - Informationsrecht als Deich, Kanal, Wasserhahn oder Rettungsring?* (Bd. 3). Karlsruhe: Karlsruher Insititut für Technologie (KIT).

Likamwa, R., Liu, Y., Lane, N., & Zong, L. (2013). *oodScope: Building a Mood Sensor from Smartphone Usage Patterns.* Abgerufen am 24. Januar 2016 von http://www.ruf.rice.edu/: http://www.ruf.rice.edu/~mobile/publications/likamwa2013mobisys2.pdf

Lindlar, H., & Schweinsberg, K. (2015). *Sicherheitsreport 2015: Ergebnisse einer repräsentativen Bevölkerungsumfrage.* (Deutsche Telekom; Institut für Demoskopie Allensbach) Abgerufen am 15. Februar 2016 von https://www.telekom.com/static/-/282168/1/150723-sicherheitsreport-2015-si

Linsenbarth, R. (15. Dezember 2015). *IT Finanzmagazin.* Abgerufen am 23. Januar 2016 von T Finanzmagazin - Das Fachmagazin für IT und Organisation bei Banken, Sparkassen und Versicherungen: http://www.it-finanzmagazin.de/aldi-und-lidl-le-sans-contcat-der-ohne-kontakt-24073/

Liu, C. (August 2015). *WORLDWIDE INTERNET AND MOBILE USERS*. Abgerufen am 15. Februar 2016 von eMarketer: https://insights.ap.org/uploads/images/eMarke ter_Estimates_2015.pdf

Lobo, S. (22. April 2015). *Die Mensch-Maschine: Automatischer Mord*. Abgerufen am 05. März 2016 von Spiegel Online: Netzwelt: http://www.spiegel.de/netzwelt/web/sascha-lobo-die-voelkerrechtswidrige-praxis-des-drohnenkrieges-a-1029935.html

Lomas, C. (21. Oktober 2014). *Dr. Watson – Mensch und Maschine im Kampf gegen die Tuberkulose-Epidemie*. Abgerufen am 24. Januar 2016 von Wired: https://www.wired.de/artikel/dr-watson-mensch-und-maschine-im-kampf-gegen-die-epidemie

Loozen, T., Murdoch, R., & Orr, S. (2013). *Mobile Web Watch 2013: The New Persuaders*. Abgerufen am 28. März 2016 von Accenture: https://www.accenture.com/t00010101T00000 0_w_/ch-de/_acnmedia/Accenture/Conversion-Assets/DotCom/Documents/Global/PDF/Tech nology_5/Accenture-Mobile-Web-Watch-2013-Survey-New-Persuaders.ashx

Lorenz, P., & Heumann, S. (26. Oktober 2015). *Bedroht Software die Jobs unserer Azubis?* . Abgerufen am 09. März 2016 von Cicero: Magazin für politische Kultur: http://www.cicero.de/kapital/computerisierung -bedrohen-maschinen-die-jobs-unserer- azubis/60027

Ludwig, W. (23. Februar 2016). *Weltweite Interoperabilität im Internet of Things erstmals mit konkreten Geräten präsentiert - Wichtiger Schritt hin zu einer einheitlichen Standardisierung.* Abgerufen am 29. Februar 2016 von finanzen.net: http://www.finanzen.net/nachricht/aktien/Welt weite-Interoperabilitaet-im-Internet-of- Things-erstmals-mit-konkreten-Geraeten- praesentiert-Wichtiger-Schritt-hin-zu-einer- einheitlichen-Standardisieru-4747500

Luttmer, N. (23. November 2014). *Banken: Das Sterben der Bankfiliale* . Abgerufen am 06. März 2016 von Frankfurter Rundschau: http://www.fr-online.de/wirtschaft/banken- das-sterben-der- bankfiliale,1472780,29129402.html

Mack, D., & Vilberger, D. (2016). *Social Media für KMU: Der Leitfaden mit allen Grundlagen, Strategien und Instrumenten.* Wiesbaden: Springer Gabler.

MacMillan, D. (31. Juli 2015). *Uber Valued at More Than $50 Billion* . Abgerufen am 03. März 2016 von Wall Street Journal: http://www.wsj.com/articles/uber-valued-at-more-than-50-billion-1438367457

Mamertino, M. (28. Januar 2016). *10 Job-Trends der Zukunft* . Abgerufen am 16. März 2016 von Berufebilder: http://berufebilder.de/2016/automatisierung-arbeitsmarkt-veraendert-10-trends-zukunft/#text

Mana, J. (2013). *Data Mining Mobile Devices* . Boca Raton, USA: CRC Press.

Manhart, K. (02. August 2011). *Cloud Computing - SaaS, PaaS, IaaS, Public und Private* . Abgerufen am 25. Januar 2016 von tecchannel - IT im Mittelstand: http://www.tecchannel.de/server/cloud_compu ting/2030180/cloud_computing_das_muessen _sie_wissen_saas_paas_iaas/index6.html

Marwan, P. (28. August 2014). *Deutsche Telekom umwirbt Mittelstand mit Rabattaktion für TK-Anlagen* . Abgerufen am 29. Februar 2016 von IT Espresso: http://www.itespresso.de/2014/08/28/deutsche -telekom-umwirbt-mittelstand-mit-rabattaktion-fuer-tk-anlagen/

Mattern, F., & Floerkemeier, C. (April 2010). *Publications of the Distributed Systems Group.* (Informatik-Spektrum, Vol. 33, No. 2, pp. 107-121) Abgerufen am 19. Januar 2016 von ETH Zurich: http://www.vs.inf.ethz.ch/publ/papers/Internet -der-Dinge.pdf

Mauerer, J. (14. Juli 2015). *Predictive Analytics in der Praxis* . (Computerwoche) Abgerufen am 21. Februar 2016 von Computerwoche: http://www.computerwoche.de/a/predictive-analytics-in-der-praxis,3212192

McCarthy, J. (29. Januar 1999). *The PageRank Citation Ranking: Bringing Order to the Web.* Abgerufen am 16. Februar 2016 von Stanford: http://ilpubs.stanford.edu:8090/422/1/1999-66.pdf

Merkle, W., & Kreutzer, R. T. (2008). *Die neue Macht des Marketing: Wie Sie Ihr Unternehmen mit Emotion, Innovation und Präzision profilieren.* Wiesbaden: Betriebswirtschaftlicher Verlag Dr. Th. Gabler / GWV Facherlage.

Merz, A. (17. Februar 2016). *Mittelstand: Studie zeigt Zusammenhang zwischen Wachstum und digitaler Transformation.* (SAP) Abgerufen am 12. April 2016 von SAP News: http://news.sap.com/germany/2016/02/17/mitt

elstand-studie-zeigt-zusammenhang-zwischen-wachstum-und-digitaler-transformation/

Meulen, R. v. (27. Januar 2016). *Gartner Estimates That 90 Percent of Large Organizations Will Have a Chief Data Officer by 2019* . (Gartner) Abgerufen am 16. März 2016 von Gartner Newsroom: http://www.gartner.com/newsroom/id/319011 7

Meusers, R. (26. November 2015). *Lifi als WLAN-Ersatz: Superschnelles Internet aus der Deckenlampe.* Abgerufen am 23. Januar 2016 von Spiegel.de: http://www.spiegel.de/netzwelt/web/lifi-superschnelle-datenuebertragung-per-licht-a-1064718.html

MilwardBrown. (2015). *Brand Value rises 14 percent year-on-year, 126 percent over a turbulent decade.* Abgerufen am 6. April 2016 von millwardbrown.com: http://www.millwardbrown.com/BrandZ/2015/Global/2015_BrandZ_Top100_Report.pdf

Moesch, J. (05. März 2012). *the institute - The IEEE news source.* Abgerufen am 23. Januar 2016 von theinstitute.ieee.org: http://theinstitute.ieee.org/briefings/business/membership-tops-415-000

337

Monck, A. (04. März 2016). *19 must-read stories for the weekend* . Abgerufen am 09. März 2016 von World Economic Forum: http://www.weforum.org/agenda/2016/03/19-must-read-stories-for-the-weekend-3cc247f1-1a00-4377-a819-795791538570?utm_content=buffer6d2c9&utm_medium=social&utm_source=facebook.com&utm_campaign=buffer

Mörer-Funk, A. (07. März 2014). *Zahnersatz kommt künftig aus dem 3-D-Drucker* . (VDI Verlag) Abgerufen am 21. März 2016 von ingenieur.de: http://www.ingenieur.de/Themen/Werkzeuge-Maschinen/Zahnersatz-kommt-kuenftig-3-D-Drucker

Morris, I. (03. Februar 2015). *Deutsche Telekom Turns On Pan-European IP* . Abgerufen am 30. Januar 2016 von Light Reading: Networking the Communcation Industry: http://www.lightreading.com/ethernet-ip/ip-protocols-software/deutsche-telekom-turns-on-pan-european-ip/d/d-id/714107

Mosig, S., & Sommer, M. (2014). *Auflage), Mobile Payment & Mobile Marketing Der Weg weg vom Bargeld. Von der Idee bis zur kundenfreundlichen Umsetzung. (1.* Hamburg: tredition.

Mosler, D. (26. Januar 2016). *Taxifahrer protestieren gegen Uber* . Abgerufen am 03. März 2016 von   Tagesspiegel: http://www.tagesspiegel.de/wirtschaft/streiks-in-frankreich-taxifahrer-protestieren-gegen-uber/12879950.html

Mukhopadhyay, S. C. (2014). *Internet of Things: Challenges and Opportunities.* Heidelberg, New York, Dordrecht, London: Springer International Publishing Switzerland.

Müller, T. (2016). *eco Umfrage IT-Sicherheit 2016.* (eco – Verband der Internetwirtschaft e. V) Abgerufen am 16. Februar 2016 von eco – Verband der Internetwirtschaft e. V: https://www.eco.de/wp-content/blogs.dir/eco-report-it-sicherheit-2016.pdf

Münzl, G., Pauly, M., & Reti, M. (2015). *Cloud Computing als neue Herausforderung für Management und IT.* Berlin Heidelberg: Springer Vieweg.

Murtz, B. (2015). *AppAgile: Dank Platform-as-a-Service schnell am Markt* . Abgerufen am 27. Januar 2016 von T-Systems Cloud Lösungen: http://cloud.t-systems.de/loesungen/enterprise-appagile

Myers, D. G. (2014). *Psychologie (3. Auflage).* Berlin Heidelberg: Springer-Verlag.

Myers, J. (19. Oktober 2015). *The Most Endangered Jobs in 2015*. (WEF) Abgerufen am 21. März 2016 von World Economic Forum: Technology: https://www.weforum.org/agenda/2015/10/these-are-the-most-endangered-jobs-in-2015/

Myers, J. (29. Februar 2016). *What new jobs will exist in 2035?* . (World Economic Forum) Abgerufen am 09. März 2016 von World Economic Forum: http://www.weforum.org/agenda/2016/02/these-scientists-have-predicted-which-jobs-will-be-human-only-in-2035?utm_content=bufferbd34c&utm_medium=social&utm_source=facebook.com&utm_campaign=buffer

Nagel, P. (07. März 2016). *Monsees wird Digitalisierungs-Chef von BMW* . (Media Manufaktur) Abgerufen am 16. März 2016 von automotiveIT: http://www.automotiveit.eu/monsees-wird-digitalisierungs-chef-von-bmw/news/id-0052339

Naumann, H. (2015). *Studienbrief: SWPF Informatik/Organisation: EDV-gestütztes Controlling (Semester IX; Auflage WiSe 2015/2016))*. Wismar: WINGS GmbH.

nbc chicago. (25. November 2015). *NBC Chicago*. (NBC) Abgerufen am 14. Januar 2016 von NBC Chicago: http://www.nbcchicago.com/investigations/W EB-10p-pkg-Surveillance-Toy_Leitner_Chicago-353434911.html

Nemat, C. (16. Februar 2016). *Dinge, die das Netz von morgen ausmachen* . (Deutsche Telekom) Abgerufen am 28. März 2016 von Telekom Pressestelle: https://www.telekom.com/301106

Nemat, C., Jacobfeuerborn, B., Menzel, G., & Orth, B. (26. Februar 2015). *DT Superior Production Model.* (Deutsche Telekom) Abgerufen am 30. Januar 2016 von DEUTSCHE TELEKOM CAPITAL MARKETS DAY 2015: https://www.telekom.com/static/-/268010/6/4-presentation-cn-si

Netflix. (29. September 2015). *Netflix*. Abgerufen am 19. Januar 2016 von https://pr.netflix.com/WebClient/getNewsSum mary.do?newsId=2632

Neuhetzki, T. /. (29. Februar 2016). *Innenstadt gegen Internet: Was tun gegen Amazon & Co.?* . (Teltarif) Abgerufen am 09. März 2016 von Teltarif:

http://mobil.teltarif.de/onlineshopping-
amazon-now-gegenwehr/news/63019.html

Neuhetzki, T. (12. 02 2015). *300 MBit/s per Telekom-
LTE: Praxis-Erfahrungen aus Berlin.*
Abgerufen am 20. 01 2016 von teltarif.de:
rundum   gut   informiert:
http://www.teltarif.de/lte-cat6-300-mbit-wie-
schnell-telekom/news/58632.html

Neuhetzki, T. (12. Februar 2016). *Deutsche Telekom
beliebteste   Telekommunikationsanbieter-
Marke* . Abgerufen am 12. Februar 2016 von
teltarif.de: rundum   gut   informiert:
http://www.teltarif.de/deutsche-telekom-
marke-beliebt-beliebtheit-
umfrage/news/62793.html

Neunteufel, H. (2014). *SPF Wissensbasierte Systeme
/ Wissensmanagement, Teil 2: IT: Sicherheit
(Semester VII, WiSe 2014/2015).* Wismar:
WINGS Wismar.

Nier, H. (04. März 2016). *Apps in Echtzeit* . (statista)
Abgerufen am 05. März 2016 von statista:
https://de.statista.com/infografik/4382/app-
nutzung-pro-minute-im-mobilen-internet/

n-tv.de. (2. April 2016). *Mittelständler bedroht:
Jedem dritten Autozulieferer droht das Aus* .
(n-tv) Abgerufen am 4. April 2016 von n-tv:
http://www.n-tv.de/wirtschaft/Jedem-dritten-

Autozulieferer-droht-das-Aus-article17373941.html

Nußbaum, S. (2016). *Mittelstand 4.0-Kompetenzzentren* . Abgerufen am 29. Februar 2016 von Bundesministerium für Wirtschaft und Energie: http://www.mittelstand-digital.de/DE/Foerderinitiativen/Mittelstand-4-0/kompetenzzentren.html

Oakes, Z. (03. März 2015). *Für junge Konsumenten hat das Auto als Statussymbol ausgedient: Das Smartphone wird zur Mobilitätslösung der Generation Y.* (Prophet Germany) Abgerufen am 05. März 2016 von presseportal: http://www.presseportal.de/pm/112455/2963008

Oberkogler, F. (1981). *Faust von Johann Wolfgang von Goethe: II. Teil* . Novalis Verlag.

Oberlandesgericht Hamm. (02. Juli 2015). *Justiz NRW*. Abgerufen am 1. April 2016 von https://www.justiz.nrw.de/nrwe/olgs/hamm/j2015/28_U_46_15_Beschluss_20150702.html

Ohland, G. (2013). *Smart-Living: Vom Luxusspielzeug zum gesellschaftlichen Pflichtprogramm.* Norderstedt: BoD - Books on Demand.

OIC. (Juli 2015). *The Open Interconnect Consortium and IoTivity Setting Standards for Device Interoperability.* Abgerufen am 24. Januar 2016 von http://openinterconnect.org/: http://openinterconnect.org/wp-content/uploads/2015/07/OIC-IoTivity_White-Paper_Final1.pdf

O'Mathúna, D. (2009). *Nanoethics: Big Ethical Issues with Small Technology.* London New York: Continuum International Publishing Group.

Open Interconnect Consortium. (2015). *Open Interconnect Consortium: MEMBERS.* Abgerufen am 23. 01 2016 von Open Interconnect Consortium: http://openinterconnect.org/members/

Orebaugh, A. (Januar 2015). *Internet der Dinge: Was zu tun ist, um IoT-Security Realität werden zu lassen .* (TechTarget Search Security) Abgerufen am 13. Februar 2016 von TechTarget Search Security: http://www.searchsecurity.de/meinung/Internet-der-Dinge-Was-zu-tun-ist-um-IoT-Security-Realitaet-werden-zu-lassen

Osman, I., Anouze, A. L., & Emrouzejad. (2013). *Handbook of Research on Strategic Performance Management and Measurement Using Data Envelopment Analysis.* Hershey, USA: IGI Global.

Oster, S. (03. März 2016). *China Tries Its Hand at Pre-Crime* . (Bloomberg) Abgerufen am 16. März 2016 von Bloomberg Business: http://www.bloomberg.com/news/articles/201 6-03-03/china-tries-its-hand-at-pre-crime

Osterwalder, A., & Pigneur, Y. (2011). *Business Model Generation.* Frankfurt/Main: Campus Verlag.

Otis, B., & Parviz, B. (2014 йил 16-Januar). *Introducing our smart contact lens project.* (Google) Retrieved 2016 йил 10-April from https://googleblog.blogspot.de/2014/01/introd ucing-our-smart-contact-lens.html

Ottenheimer, D., & Wallace, M. (2012). *Securing the Virtual Environment: How to Defend the Enterprise Against Attack.* Indianapolis, USA: John Wiley & Sons.

Özbicerler, B. (16. Januar 2016). *Schluss mit Datenkraken: Schritt für Schritt erklärt: So verhindern Sie, dass Ihr Smartphone Sie ausspäht* . Abgerufen am 14. Februar 2016 von Focus Online: http://www.focus.de/digital/handy/schluss-mit-datenkraken-so-verhindern-sie-dass-ihr-smartphone-sie-ausspaeht_id_5228212.html

Pablo Iacopino, D. N.-C. (2017). *The 5G era in the US.* Retrieved from https://www.gsmaintelligence.com/research/?f

345

ile=4cbbdb475f24b3c5f5a93a2796a4aa28&do
wnload

Pallas, F., & Spors, A. (Februar 2016). *eSIM: Simlos in die Zukunft?* (Iskander Business Partner) Abgerufen am 28. März 2016 von Iskander Business Partner: http://i-b-partner.com/wp-content/uploads/2016/02/20160229_eSIM-Studie.pdf

panorama, s. (01. August 2013). *Neuseeland: Stromfirma schickt Mahnung an Straßenlaterne* . (Spiegel Online) Abgerufen am 13. Februar 2016 von http://www.spiegel.de/panorama/stromfirma-schickt-mahnung-an-strassenlaterne-in-neuseeland-a-914214.html

Papmehl, A., & Tümmers, H. (. (2013). *Die Arbeitswelt im 21. Jahrhundert: Herausforderungen, Perspektiven, Lösungsansätze.* Wiesbaden: Springer Fachmedien; Tümmers, Hans (Hrsg.).

Parsad, R., & Muñoz, L. (2003). *WLANs and WPANs towards 4G Wireless.* Boston, London: Artech House (Norwood).

Pasqua, E. (2015). *Industrie 4.0 Reloaded.* (A. research, Produzent, & ABI research) Abgerufen am 21. Februar 2016 von https://www.abiresearch.com/market-research/product/1022262-industrie-40-reloaded/

Paukner, P. (20. Februar 2014). *Zuckerberg hat verstanden* . Abgerufen am 05. März 2016 von Süddeutsche Zeitung: http://www.sueddeutsche.de/digital/whatsapp-uebernahme-durch-facebook-zuckerberg-hat-verstanden-1.1893836

Payman, A., Nilufar, F., Rossmann, A., Steimel, B., & Wichmann, K. (2014). *Digital Transformation Report 2014*. (B. Steimel, Produzent, & neuland) Abgerufen am 19. Januar 2016 von http://www.wiwo.de/downloads/10773004/1/d ta_report_neu.pdf

paypal. (2016). *Über Paypal*. (Paypal) Abgerufen am 06. März 2016 von paypal.de: https://www.paypal.com/de/webapps/mpp/abo ut

Pentsi, A., & Miosga, J. (29. Dezember 2015). *Teilen liegt weiter im Trend* . Abgerufen am 06. März 2016 von Bitkom: https://www.bitkom.org/Presse/Presseinformat ion/Teilen-liegt-weiter-im-Trend.html

Peterson, H. (02. November 2015). *The 12 jobs most at risk of being replaced by robots* . (WEF) Abgerufen am 07. März 2016 von World Economic Forum:

347

https://www.weforum.org/agenda/2015/11/the
-12-jobs-most-at-risk-of-being-replaced-by-
robots?utm_content=buffer0c4f3&utm_mediu
m=social&utm_source=facebook.com&utm_c
ampaign=buffer

Petry, D. (16. März 2016). *Siemens eröffnet Cyber
Security Operation Center zum Schutz von
Industrieanlagen* . (Siemens) Abgerufen am
21. März 2016 von Siemens Pressestelle:
http://www.siemens.com/press/de/pressemittei
lungen/2016/digitalfactory/pr2016030210dfde
.htm?content[]=DF

Petschar, S. (14. Juli 2014). *Innovation für das CV
Parsing - die Deep Learning Technologie* .
(Textkernel, Produzent) Abgerufen am 11.
Januar   2016   von   Textkernel:
http://www.hrm.de/fachartikel/innovation-
f%C3%BCr-das-cv-parsing-die-deep-
learning-technologie-11793

Pfeifer, R. (13. Mai 2015). *Nutzt Facebook
Bilderkennung für Werbung?* . (Computer
Service Robin Pfeifer) Abgerufen am 05.
März   2016   von   http://computer-service-
remscheid.de/nutzt-facebook-bilderkennung-
fuer-werbung/

Plass, C., Rehmann, F. J., Zimmermann, A., Janssen,
H., & Wibbing, P. (2013). *Chefsache IT: Wie
Sie Cloud Computing und Social Media zum*

Treiber Ihres Geschäfts machen. Heidelberg: Springer Gabler.

Pols, A., & Heidkamp, P. (2015). *Cloud Monitor 2015: Cloud-Computing in Deutschland - Status quo und Perspektiven.* (KPMG) Abgerufen am 04. Januar 2016 von KPMG: cutting through complexity: https://www.bitkom.org/Publikationen/2015/S tudien/Cloud-Monitor-2015/Cloud-Monitor-2015-KPMG-Bitkom-Research.pdf

Portal, J., Ali, S., Moral, E., Sparks, K., Valencia-Hernandez, E., Prakash, S., & Raman, N. (2015). *Reshaping the future with NFV and SDN: The impact of new technologies on carriers and their networks* . (Arthur D. Little) Abgerufen am 21. März 2016 von Bell Labs: http://www2.alcatel-lucent.com/landing/bell-labs/adl/

Portio Research. (2014). *Worldwide A2P SMS Markets 2014-2017 Understanding and analysis of application-to-person text messaging markets worldwide.* (Portio Research) Abgerufen am 26. März 2016 von strikerion: http://www.strikeiron.com/wp-content/uploads/2014/12/whitepaper-sms-2014-2017-portio-research.pdf

Press, G. (6. Juni 2006). *Google Announces limited test on Google Labs: Google Spreadsheets.*

Abgerufen am 25. Januar 2016 von
http://googlepress.blogspot.de/2006/06/google
-announces-limited-test-on-google_06.html

Prising, J. (19. Januar 2016). *Four changes shaping
the labour market* . Abgerufen am 09. März
2016 von World Economic Forum:
http://www.weforum.org/agenda/2016/01/four
-changes-shaping-the-labour-market

Probst, M., & Trotier, K. (2012 йил 23-August).
Gigant ohne Geist. (Zeit Online) Retrieved
2016 йил 9-April from Zeit Online:
http://www.zeit.de/2012/35/Verlag-
Buchhaendler-Amazon

Radke, J. (13. März 2016). *CeBIT Deutsche Telekom
will mit IoT die Lebensmittelproduktion
verbessern* . (heise) Abgerufen am 27. März
2016 von heise.de:
http://www.heise.de/newsticker/meldung/Deut
sche-Telekom-will-mit-IoT-die-
Lebensmittelproduktion-verbessern-
3133554.html

Rahmann, T. (27. September 2011). *Krisengewinner
Deutschland* . Abgerufen am 16. März 2016
von Wirtschaftswoche:
http://www.wiwo.de/politik/konjunktur/finanz
krise-krisengewinner-
deutschland/5224066.html

Rajaraman, V. (2010). *ESSENTIALS OF E-COMMERCE TECHNOLOGY*. New Delhi, Indien: PHI Learning Private.

Rath, M. (28. Januar 2016). *Daten-Treuhand als Abwehrmittel gegen Überwachung?* . Abgerufen am 05. März 2016 von Computerwoche: http://www.computerwoche.de/a/daten-treuhand-als-abwehrmittel-gegen-ueberwachung,3222181

Rauner, M. (04. Januar 2016). *Industrie 4.0: Wenn ich mit euch fertig bin, seid ihr ein Joghurt* . Abgerufen am 16. Februar 2016 von Zeit Online: http://www.zeit.de/zeit-wissen/2016/01/industrie-4-0-kuenstliche-intelligenz-maschinen/seite-2

Rauschner, M. (2004). *Künstliche neuronale Netze zur Risikomessung bei Aktien und Renten: Am Beispiel deutscher Lebensversicherungsunternehmen.* Wiesbaden: Deutscher Universitäts-Verlag.

Rebbeck, T. (12. Mai 2015). *TELECOMS OPERATORS' APPROACHES TO M2M AND IOT Operators should consider providing a platform of capabilities to support the M2M/IoT opportunity.* (Analysys Mason) Abgerufen am 27. März 2016 von Analysys Mason:

http://www.analysysmason.com/Research/Con
tent/Reports/M2M-IoT-operators-approaches-
May2015/Report-PDF/

Rebiger, S. (02. November 2015). *Spiegel-Bericht: 70 Prozent der EU-Datenschutz-Grundverordnung in trockenen Tüchern.* Abgerufen am 15. Februar 2016 von netzpolitik.org: https://netzpolitik.org/2015/spiegel-bericht-70-prozent-der-eu-datenschutz-grundverordnung-in-trockenen-tuechern/

Reek, F. (16. Oktober 2014). *Druckfrisch auf die Straße .* (Süddeutsche Zeitung) Abgerufen am 21. März 2016 von Süddeutsche Zeitung: http://www.faz.net/aktuell/technik-motor/auto-verkehr/freie-modellwahl-das-auto-aus-dem-3d-drucker-13401965.html

Reichert, R. (2014). *Big Data: Analysen zum digitalen Wandel von Wissen, Macht und Ökonomie (1. Auflage).* Bielefeld: Reichert, Ramón (Hrsg.); transcript Verlag.

Research, A. (Mai 2014). *IoE VS. IoT VS. M2M WHAT'S THE DIFFERENCE?* Abgerufen am 11. April 2016 von http://www.rfid24-7.com/wp-content/uploads/2014/05/Internet-of-Things-ABI.pdf

Reuters. (02. März 2016). *Germany to cooperate with US on IT standards to reboot industry .*

Abgerufen am 02. März 2016 von The Economic Times: http://economictimes.indiatimes.com/news/international/business/germany-to-cooperate-with-us-on-it-standards-to-reboot-industry/articleshow/51227539.cms

Riedel, K. (15. Dezember 2015). *IBM zieht mit Supercomputer Watson nach München.* Abgerufen am 23. Januar 2016 von Süddeutsche Zeitung: http://www.sueddeutsche.de/muenchen/softwarekonzern-ibm-siedelt-neue-entwicklungszentrale-im-muenchner-norden-an-1.2784035

Rifkin, J. (2004). *Das Ende der Arbeit und ihre Zukunft: Neue Konzepte für das 21. Jahrhundert.* Frankfurt New York: Campus Verlag.

Rittinghouse, J., & Ransome, J. (2010). *Cloud Computing: Implementation, Management, and Security.* Boca Raton London New York: CRC Press.

Rivera, J., & Meulen, R. v. (14. November 2014). *Gartner Says 4.9 Billion Connected "Things" Will Be in Use in 2015.* (Gartner Inc.) Abgerufen am 20. Januar 2016 von Press Release:

http://www.gartner.com/newsroom/id/290571
7

Roebers, F., & Leisenberg, M. (2010). *Web 2.0 im Unternehmen: Theorie & Praxis - Ein Kursbuch für Führungskräfte.* COMPUTERWOCHE.

Rohleder, B. (22. September 2015). *Datenschutz in der digitalen Welt.* (Bitkom) Abgerufen am 13. Februar 2016 von https://www.bitkom.org/Presse/Anhaenge-an-PIs/2015/09-September/Bitkom-Charts-PK-Datenschutz-22092015-final.pdf

Roßnagel, A., Jandt, S., Skistims, H., & Zirfas, J. (2012). *Datenschutz bei: Eine juristische Analyse am Beispiel.* Wiesbaden: Springer Fachmedien.

Roth, A. (2016). *Einführung und Umsetzung von Industrie 4.0: Grundlagen, Vorgehensmodell und Use Cases aus der Praxis.* Berlin Heidelberg: Springer Gabler; Armin Roth (Hrsg.).

Rottinger, D. (03. März 2016). *DeutschlandLAN NFON: Telekom zeigt IP-Alternative zur klassischen Telefonanlage* . (teltarif) Abgerufen am 03. März 2016 von teltarif.de: http://mobil.teltarif.de/telekom-ip-telefonie-cebit/news/63063.html

Rungg, A. (21. November 2014). *Eine Umsatz-Enthüllung zur rechten Zeit* . Abgerufen am 03. März 2016 von manager magazin: http://www.manager-magazin.de/unternehmen/it/umsatz-von-uber-soll-2015-auf-zwei-milliarden-us-dollar-anschwellen-a-1004327.html

Russel, S. (28. Mai 2015). *Take a stand on AI weapons.* (Macmillan Publishers) Abgerufen am 17. März 2016 von Nature: http://www.nature.com/news/robotics-ethics-of-artificial-intelligence-1.17611

Sauter, M. (2006). *Grundkurs Mobile Kommunikationssysteme - Von UMTS, GSM und GPRS zu Wireless LAN und Bluetooth Piconetzen (2. Auflage).* Wiesbaden: Friedr. Vieweg & Sohn.

Sawall, A. (14. März 2016). *Huawei entwickelt Industrieroboter mit deutscher Kuka* . Abgerufen am 15. März 2016 von Golem: http://www.golem.de/news/internet-der-dinge-huawei-entwickelt-industrieroboter-mit-deutscher-kuka-1603-119751.html

Schaar, P. (o. J.). *BFDI BUND.* Abgerufen am 27. Februar 2016 von Beitrag des Bundesbeauftragten für den Datenschutz und die Informationsfreiheit, Peter Schaar, in der Fachzeitschrift „Identity in the Information

Society"(Informatorische Übersetzung): http://www.bfdi.bund.de/SharedDocs/Publikat ionen/%22PrivacyByDesign%22.pdf?__blob= publicationFile

Schamberg, J. (22. Februar 2016). *Ngena als globale Plattform: Telekom will Firmenkunden-Geschäft der Branche revolutionieren* . Abgerufen am 22. März 2016 von Onlinekosten.de: http://www.onlinekosten.de/news/ngena-als-globale-plattform-telekom-will-firmenkunden-geschaeft-der-branche-revolutionieren_203590.html

Schelewsky, M., Jonuschat, H., Bock, B., & Stephan, K. (2014). *Smartphones unterstützen die Mobilitätsforschung: Neue Einblicke in das ...* Wiesbaden: Springer Fachmedien. Von Smartphones unterstützen die Mobilitätsforschung: Neue Einblicke in das abgerufen

Schermann, M., Siller, H., & Volcic, K. (2013). *Strategische Managementpraxis in Fallstudien: Umsetzung einer erfolgreichen Strategie in vier Schritten.* Wien: Linde Verlag.

Schickler Media Index. (September 2015). *Online- und Offline-Volumen des Werbemarktes in Deutschland im Jahr 2014 und Prognose bis*

2016 (in Milliarden Euro) . Abgerufen am 05. März 2016 von Statista: http://de.statista.com/statistik/daten/studie/459 107/umfrage/online-und-offline-volumen-des-werbemarktes-in-deutschland/

Schindelar, V. (19. Juni 2015). *Ralf Nejedl: Schritt für Schritt zum Internet der Dinge [Interview]* . (T-Mobile Austria) Abgerufen am 21. März 2016 von T-Mobile Austria: http://businessblog.t-mobile.at/ralf-nejedl-internet-der-dinge-interview/

Schindler, M. (22. Februar 2016). *Intel, Samsung und Microsoft gründen IoT-Allianz* . (NetMediaEurope) Abgerufen am 23. Februar 2016 von silicon: http://www.silicon.de/41621240/intel-samsung-und-microsoft-gruenden-iot-allianz/

Schindler, M. (18. März 2016). *Open Telekom Cloud rechnet für das CERN* . (NetMediaEurope) Abgerufen am 20. März 2016 von silicon: http://www.silicon.de/41622028/open-telekom-cloud-rechnet-fuer-das-cern/

Schindler, R. (04. August 2015). *Verdrängen neue Geschäftsmodelle die Provider?* . (Medienhaus) Abgerufen am 28. März 2016 von IT-Zoom: http://www.it-zoom.de/mobile-business/e/verdraengen-neue-geschaeftsmodelle-die-provider-10386/

Schlaak, H., Lotz, P., & Matysek, M. (2006). *Muskeln unter Hochspannung – Antriebe mit elektroaktiven Polymeren*. (H. F. Schlaak, Produzent, & thema FORSCHUNG 2/2006, Technische Universität Darmstadt) Abgerufen am 21. Januar 2016 von Technische Universität Darmstatdt: http://www.tu-darmstadt.de/media/illustrationen/referat_kom munikation/publikationen_km/themaforschun g/2006_2/06_02_gesamt.pdf

Schlatt, A. (2014). *Predictive Maintenance: Maschinenfehler und -ausfälle im Vorfeld erkennen (1. Auflage)*. GBI Genios Wirtschaftsdatenbank.

Schlick, C. (. (2015). *Arbeit in der digitalisierten Welt: Beiträge der Fachtagung des BMBF 2015*. Frankfurt Main: Campus Verlag; Schlick, Christopher (Hrsg.).

Schmidt, J. (14. März 2016). *Forscher finden reihenweise Sicherheitslücken in Embedded-Linux-Systemen* . (heise) Abgerufen am 15. März 2016 von heise security: http://m.heise.de/security/meldung/Forscher-finden-reihenweise-Sicherheitsluecken-in-Embedded-Linux-Systemen-3133112.html

Schmidt-Wiedemann, S. (September 2012). *Home sweet Home: Nutzwert für die Kunden Management* . (energiespektrum) Abgerufen

am 26. März 2016 von energiespektrum:
http://www.energiespektrum.de/index.cfm?pid
=1461&pk=125177&p=1

Schnabel, P. (2015). *Elektronik Kompendium*. (P.
Schnabel, Produzent) Abgerufen am 19.
Januar 2016 von http://www.elektronik-
kompendium.de/sites/kom/1502031.htm

Schnitter, S., & Markova, V. (14. Dezember 2015).
*SDN und NFV unterstützen die
Transformation von
Telekommunikationsunternehmen*. (DeTeCon)
Abgerufen am 21. März 2016 von detecon:
https://www.detecon.com/sites/default/files/S
DN_und_NFV.pdf

Schoenebeck, G. v. (05. November 2015). *Facebook:
Künstliche Intelligenz erkennt, was auf Fotos
zu sehen ist* . (V. V. GmbH, Produzent)
Abgerufen am 10. Januar 2016 von
Ingenieur.de:
http://www.ingenieur.de/Themen/Forschung/F
acebook-Kuenstliche-Intelligenz-erkennt-
Fotos-zu-sehen

Schoentahler, J. (18. Dezember 2000). *12 Mio. Euro
für E-Loft*. Abgerufen am 16. Februar 2016
von   Pressrelations:
http://presseservice.pressrelations.de/pressemi
tteilung/12-mio-euro-fuer-eloft-46361.html

Schönefeld, F. (2015). *Digitale Transformation: Überleben im Zeitalter von Big Data, Industrie 4.0 und des Internets der Dinge.* Abgerufen am 06. April 2016 von Slideshare: http://de.slideshare.net/crentschufdiu/digital-tranformation-berleben-im-zeitalter-von-big-data-industrie-40-und-des-internet-der-dinge

Schröder, B., & Bukowski, C. (2015). *Die No-Bank-Strategie: Wie Sie den Einfluss der Banken auf Ihr Leben reduzieren.* Norderstedt: Books on Demand.

Schroeck, M., Shockley, R., Smart, J., Romero-Morales, D., & Tufano, P. (2012). *Analytics: Big Data in der Praxis - Wie innovative Unternehmen ihre Datenbestände effektiv nutzen.* (I. I. Value, Produzent, & IBM) Abgerufen am 23. Januar 2016 von Cebit.de: http://www.cebit.de/files/007-fs5/media/downloads/besucher/datability-studie-ibm.pdf

Schroeder, P. (29. Februar 2016). *Überraschung: Mercedes ersetzt Roboter durch neue Arbeitskräfte* . Abgerufen am 29. Februar 2016 von ingenieur.de: http://www.ingenieur.de/Fachbereiche/Robotik/Ueberraschung-Mercedes-ersetzt-Roboter-neue-Arbeitskraefte

Schulenberg, N. (2016). *Führung einer neuen Generation: Wie die Generation Y führen und geführt werden sollte.* Wiesbaden: Springer Gabler.

Schulte-Zurhausen, M. (2014). *Organisation (6. Auflage).* München: Vahlen.

Schütte, S. (23. Oktober 2014). *Die vierte industrielle Revolution – Wie verändert sie Deutschland Rede von Herrn Staatssekretär Dr. Schütte anlässlich des SAP Executive Summit 2014 Fellbach, 23.10.2014.* Abgerufen am 16. Februar 2016 von Bundesministerium für Bildung und Forschung: https://www.bmbf.de/pub/reden/Rede_StS_S AP_Summit_Industrie_23_10_2014.pdf

Schwarz, T. (2015). *Big Data im Marketing: Chancen und Möglichkeiten für eine effektive Kundenansprache (1. Auflage).* Freiburg: Torsten Schwarz (Hrsg.), Haufe-Lexware.

Seemann, M. (11. Oktober 2013). *Die Privatsphären-Falle.* (Zeit Online) Abgerufen am 13. Februar 2016 von Zeit Pnline: http://www.zeit.de/digital/datenschutz/2013-10/privatsphaere-ueberwachung-nsa-seemann

Segal, B. (April 1995). *A Short History of Internet Protocols at CERN .* Abgerufen am 26. Januar 2016 von CERN IT-PDP-TE : http://ben.web.cern.ch/ben/TCPHIST.html

Segaran, T. (2008). *Kollektive Intelligenz analysieren, programmieren und nutzen (1. Auflage 2008)*. Köln: O'Reilly Verlag.

Seidler, C. (22. November 2008). *Künstliche Insekten: US-Militär will Mini-Drohnen ausschwärmen lassen* . (Spiegel Wissenschaft) Abgerufen am 19. März 2016 von Spiegel Wissenschaft: http://www.spiegel.de/wissenschaft/mensch/k uenstliche-insekten-us-militaer-will-mini-drohnen-ausschwaermen-lassen-a-592115.html

Seitz, J. (April 2014). *Dem Verbrechen auf der Datenspur* . Abgerufen am 05. März 2016 von Zukunftsinstitut: https://www.zukunftsinstitut.de/artikel/big-data/predictive-policing/

Shad, M., & Grimm, F. (07. März 2016). *Chief Digital Officer – das unbekannte Wesen* . (bikom) Abgerufen am 16. März 2016 von bitkom: https://www.bitkom.org/Presse/Presseinformat ion/Chief-Digital-Officer-das-unbekannte-Wesen.html

Shafranyuk, O., Quick, P., Remane, G., Schlick, T., Rossbach, C., Oltmanns, T., . . . Bloching, B. (17. März 2015). *Die digitale Transformation der Industrie: Detailbetrachtung von Roland*

362

Berger Strategy Consultants im Auftrag des Bundesverbandes der Deutschen Industrie e. V. . Abgerufen am 7. April 2016 von Roland Berger: https://www.rolandberger.de/media/pdf/Roland_Berger_Analysen_zur_Studie_Digitale_Transformation_20150317.pdf

Siebenpfeiffer, W. (. (2014). *Vernetztes Automobil: Sicherheit - Car-IT - Konzepte.* Wiesbaden: Wolfgang Siebenpfeiffer; Springer Fachmedien.

Siebert, J. (o. J.). *Arbeit digital – Chancen und Risiken* . (Online Akademie) Abgerufen am 07. März 2016 von bildungsexperten: http://www.bildungsxperten.net/job-karriere/arbeit-im-digitalen-wandel-chancen-und-risiken/

Simonite, T. (17. März 2014). *Facebook's new AI research group reports a major improvement in face-processing software.* Abgerufen am 11. Januar 2016 von MIT Technology Review: https://www.technologyreview.com/s/525586/facebook-creates-software-that-matches-faces-almost-as-well-as-you-do/

Sokolov, D. A. (21. November 2015). *Deepsec: ZigBee macht Smart Home zum offenen Haus.* Abgerufen am 19. Januar 2016 von heise security: http://www.heise.de/newsticker/meldung/Dee psec-ZigBee-macht-Smart-Home-zum-offenen-Haus-3010287.html

Sonderegger, T., & Hartmann, S. (2015). *Akzeptanz von Telematik in der Motorfahrzeugvericherung: Eine Bedürfnisanalyse bei motorfahrzeughaltenden Privatpersonen in der Schweiz.* Wiesbaden: Fichter, Christian (Hrsg.); Springer Fachmedien. Von http://www.presseportal.de/pm/112681/305691 6 abgerufen

Sonntag, N. (2001). *Wissensbasierte Konzernsteuerrechnung: Ein modulares Instrument des Steuermanagements für EU-Konzerne.* Berlin: Erich Schmidt Verlag.

Soper, T. (11. Juni 2015). *The Uber effect: Seattle taxi industry revenue dipped 28% in past 2 years* . Abgerufen am 03. März 2016 von GeekWire: http://www.geekwire.com/2015/the-uber-effect-seattle-taxi-industry-revenue-dipped-28-in-past-two-years/

Spector, D. (07. Juli 2014). *Tiny Flying Robots Are Being Built To Pollinate Crops Instead Of Real Bees* . (Business Insider) Abgerufen am 19. März 2016 von Business Insider:

http://www.businessinsider.com/harvard-
robobees-closer-to-pollinating-crops-2014-
6?IR=T

Spektrum Akademischer Verlag, Heidelberg. (1998).
Lexikon der Physik. Abgerufen am 20. Januar
2016 von IEEE:
http://www.spektrum.de/lexikon/physik/ieee/7
109

Spiegel Karriere. (04. Februar 2016). *US-Angestellte
wünschen sich deutsche Sozialleistungen* .
(Spiegel) Abgerufen am 21. März 2016 von
Karriere Spiegel:
http://www.spiegel.de/karriere/ausland/arbeite
n-in-usa-us-angestellte-wuenschen-sich-
deutsche-sozialleistungen-a-1075623.html

Spiegel Online / cis. (15. März 2016). *Brettspiel-
Turnier: Software schlägt Go-Genie mit 4 zu 1*
. Abgerufen am 15. März 2016 von Spiegel
Online Netzwelt:
http://www.spiegel.de/netzwelt/gadgets/alpha
go-besiegt-lee-sedol-mit-4-zu-1-a-
1082388.html

Spiegel Online: mbö/dpa. (24. Februar 2016). *RCS:
Google unterstützt SMS-Nachfolger* . (Spiegel
Online) Abgerufen am 26. März 2016 von
Spiegel Online Netzwelt:
http://www.spiegel.de/netzwelt/web/sms-

nachfolger-google-unterstuetzt-rcs-a-
1079061.html

Spiegel Online: Wissenschaft. (12. April 2011).
*Justiz-Studie: Müde Richter entscheiden
gegen Angeklagte* . Abgerufen am 16. März
2016 von Spiegel Online:
http://www.spiegel.de/wissenschaft/mensch/ju
stiz-studie-muede-richter-entscheiden-gegen-
angeklagte-a-756452.html

StatCounter . (05. März 2016). *Marktanteile von
Social Media Seiten nach Seitenabrufen
weltweit im Februar 2016* . (StatCounter)
Abgerufen am 05. März 2016 von
http://gs.statcounter.com/#all-social_media-
ww-monthly-201602-201602-bar

Statista / ABI Research. (2012). *Prognose zum
Marktvolumen von Mobile Payment über
NFC-Technologie 2012, 2016 und 2017 (in
Mrd. US-Dollar)* . Abgerufen am 8. April
2016 von statista:
http://de.statista.com/statistik/daten/studie/244
800/umfrage/prognose-zum-mobile-payment-
umsatz-weltweit/

statista. (April 2011). *Welche der folgenden
persönlichen Daten und Infos haben Sie in
mindestens einem sozialen Netzwerk
angegeben?* . (Bitkom) Abgerufen am 13.
Februar 2016 von Statista:

http://de.statista.com/statistik/daten/studie/183
092/umfrage/angabe-persoenlicher-daten-in-
sozialen-netzwerken-in-deutschland/

statista. (2015). *Smart Home*. (statista) Abgerufen am
26. März 2016 von statista:
https://de.statista.com/outlook/279/102/smart-
home/europa#

statista DMO. (2015). *Digitale Werbung*. Retrieved
2016 йил 7-April from statista:
https://de.statista.com/outlook/216/100/digital
e-werbung/weltweit#market-revenue

Statista-Research.com. (2015). *An welche Art von
Anbieter würden Sie sich wenden, um Ihre
Smart-Home-Anwendungen zu kaufen?* .
(Statista-Research.com) Abgerufen am 26.
März 2016 von
http://de.statista.com/statistik/daten/studie/217
771/umfrage/bevorzugter-anbietergruppen-
von-kunden-fuer-smart-home-loesungen/

Statistisches Bundesamt. (o. J.).
Gesamtwirtschaftliche Bedeutung . Abgerufen
am 8. April 2016 von BMWI:
http://www.bmwi.de/BMWi/Redaktion/PDF/I
/industrie-gesamtwirtschaftliche-bedeutung-
bis-
2012,property=pdf,bereich=bmwi2012,sprach
e=de,rwb=true.pdf

Stoller, D. (04. April 2016). *Intelligenter Gabelstapler gehorcht aufs Wort* . Abgerufen am 04. April 2016 von ingenieur.de: http://www.ingenieur.de/Branchen/Verkehr-Logistik-Transport/Intelligenter-Gabelstapler-gehorcht-aufs-Wort

Stoycheff, E. (25. Februar 2016). *Under Surveillance: Examining Facebook's Spiral of Silence Effects in the Wake of NSA Internet Monitoring.* (Wayne State University, Detroit, MI, USA) Abgerufen am 29. März 2016 von Wayne State University: http://m.jmq.sagepub.com/content/early/2016/02/25/1077699016630255.full.pdf?ijkey=1jxr Yu4cQPtA6&keytype=ref&siteid=spjmq

Strawe, C. (Dezember 1994). *Arbeitszeit - Sozialzeit - Freizeit Ein Beitrag zur Überwindung der Arbeitslosigkeit.* (Strawe) Abgerufen am 17. März 2016 von dreigliederung.de: http://www.dreigliederung.de/download/1994-12-001.pdf

Strobel, C. (2015 йил 30-November). *Der Effekt der Sharing Economy auf den Umweltschutz.* Retrieved 2016 йил 10-April from Techtag: http://www.techtag.de/it-und-hightech/share-economy/der-effekt-der-sharing-economy-auf-den-umweltschutz/

Strudthoff, M. (3. November 2014). *Mobile Payment in Deutschland (8): Mobilfunkanbieter am Rand der Klippe?* . Abgerufen am 23. März 2016 von Mobile Zeitgeist: http://www.mobile-zeitgeist.com/2014/11/03/mobile-payment-deutschland-8-mobilfunkanbieter-rand-der-klippe/

Stückler, M. (07. Juni 2014). *18,4 Milliarden Dollar: Uber bricht Finanzierungs- und Bewertungsrekorde* . (t3n digital pioneers) Abgerufen am 03. März 2016 von t3n.de: http://t3n.de/news/uber-18-milliarden-dollar-finanzierung-rekord-550091/

Süddeutsche Zeitung. (06. April 2013). *Wie die Hersteller tricksen.* (Süddeutsche Zeitung) Abgerufen am 21. Januar 2016 von Süddeutsche Zeitung: http://www.sueddeutsche.de/digital/technische-tricks-drucker-hersteller-zocken-kunden-ab-1.1641097-2

Süße, H., & Rodner, E. (2014). *Bildverarbeitung und Objekterkennung: Computer Vision in Industrie und Medizin.* Wiesbaden: Springer Fachmedien.

sz.de. (08. April 2015). *Frau soll mehr als vier Billiarden an Minijob-Zentrale zahlen* . (Süddeutsche Zeitung) Abgerufen am 13.

Februar 2016 von http://www.sueddeutsche.de/wirtschaft/essen-frau-soll-mehr-als-vier-billiarden-an-minijob-zentrale-zahlen-1.2426297

Tafazolli, R. (2006). *Technologies for the Wireless Future: Wireless World Research Forum (Volume 2)*. Chichester, England: John Wiley & Sons.

TagesAnzeiger CH. (23. April 2013). *Die Terrorfahnder und der Schreibfehler* . Abgerufen am 13. Februar 2016 von Tages Anzeiger Schweiz: http://www.tagesanzeiger.ch/ausland/amerika/Die-Terrorfahnder-und-der-Schreibfehler/story/12648172?track

Taglinger, H. (2003). *Jetzt lerne ich HTML: Der einfache Einstieg in die eigene Webseite*. München: Markt+Technik Verlag.

Telekom Deutschland. (2015). *DeutschlandLAN: Telefonanlage aus dem Netz auf Basis von Swyx*. Abgerufen am 25. Januar 2016 von https://geschaeftskunden.telekom.de/blobCache/umn/uti/115406_1437567330000/blobBinary/broschuere-deutschlandlan-swyx-ps.pdf

Telekom.com. (2016). *Wie sicher ist die Cloud? Datenschutz und -sicherheit*. (Deutsche Telekom AG) Abgerufen am 14. Februar 2016 von telekom.de:

https://www.telekom.com/medien/medienmap
pen/cloud-computing/135566

Tesla Motors. (2016). *Tesla Motors Support*.
Abgerufen am 11. Januar 2016 von Tesla
Softwareupdates:
https://www.teslamotors.com/de_DE/support/
software-updates

Thierse, W. (Dezember 2003). *Traditionswahrung
und Modernisierung - Sozialdemokratie in der
Entscheidung*. (B. Friedrich-Ebert-Stiftung,
Produzent) Abgerufen am 19. Januar 2016
von
http://library.fes.de/fulltext/historiker/01705-
03.htm

Thomas, J. (02. Dezember 2014). *Berlin will mit
Software Einbrüche vorhersagen*. Abgerufen
am 05. März 2016 von golem.de:
http://www.golem.de/news/precobs-berlin-
will-mit-software-einbrueche-vorhersagen-
1412-110918.html

thüringer allgemeine. (13. Februar 2016). *Kritik an
Forderung nach knackbarer Verschlüsselung*.
Abgerufen am 15. Februar 2016 von
Thüringer Allgemeine: Großbritannien
möchte wirksame Verschlüsselung verbieten:
WhatsApp & Co. in England bald geblockt?

Todesco, R. (o. J.). *Lexikon der
Hyperkommunikation*. Abgerufen am 10.

Februar 2016 von Hyperkommunikation: http://www.hyperkommunikation.ch/lexikon/i nformationsgehalt.htm

Tolentino, J. (16. Februar 2015). *Why are people still using SMS in 2015?* . (Nexmo) Abgerufen am 26. März 2016 von thenextweb: http://thenextweb.com/future-of-communications/2015/02/16/people-still-using-sms-2015/#gref

travelnews. (09. Februar 2016). *US-HOTELS MÜSSEN SICH WARM ANZIEHEN — AIRBNB IST AUF DEM VORMARSCH* . (travelnews) Abgerufen am 05. März 2016 von travelnews: http://www.travelnews.ch/hotellerie/1576-us-hotels-muessen-sich-warm-anziehen-airbnb-ist-auf-dem-vormarsch.html

Tremp, H., & Bruderer, T. H. (2016). *Mobile Computing und Business: Überblick zu mobilen Netzwerken, Endgeräten ... (1. Auflage)*. Norderstedt: BoD - Books on Demand.

Trick, U., & Weber, F. (2015). *SIP und Telekommunikationsnetze: Next Generation Networks und Multimedia (5. überarbeitete und erweiterte Auflage)*. Berlin Boston: Walter de Gruyter.

Tripathi, B. K. (2015). *High Dimensional Neurocomputing: Growth, Appraisal and Applications*. New Dehli Heidelberg New York Dordrecht London: Springer India.

T-Systems. (12. Dezember 2013). *USE CASE TELEMAtik auf dem feld – INDUSTRie 4.0* . (T-Systems) Abgerufen am 21. März 2016 von T-Systems: Ein Netz im Kornfeld : https://www.telekom.com/static/-/250910/1/140911-uc-claas-pdf-si

TÜV Hessen. (o. J.). *Untersuchungen für Fahrgastbeförderer und LKW-Fahrer* . Abgerufen am 07. März 2016 von TÜV Hessen: https://www.tuev-hessen.de/content/know_how__services/life_s ervice/untersuchungen_fuer_fahrgastbefoerder er_und_lkw_fahrer/index_ger.html

Twenga Solutions. (27. April 2015). *Wie funktionieren Facebook Ads?* . (Twenga Solutions) Abgerufen am 05. März 2016 von https://www.twenga-solutions.com/de/insights/wie-funktionieren-facebook-ads/

Uhlig, C. (. (2008). *Reformpädagogik und Schulreform: Diskurse in der sozialistischen Presse der Weimarer Republik*. Frankfurt Main: Peter Lang.

Uhlmann, B. (27. März 2010). *Ein banaler Zahlendreher.* (Süddeutsche Zeitung) Abgerufen am 23. Februar 2016 von http://www.sueddeutsche.de/wissen/rhein-kuerzer-als-gedacht-ein-banaler-zahlendreher-1.2166

Ulfers, H. A. (2004). *Der Consultance-Berater: Basiswissen für Manager, Berater und deren Auftraggeber.* Erlangen: Publicis Corporate Publishing.

Umweltbundesamt. (15. Februar 2016). *Elektrogeräte werden immer kürzer genutzt Gründe für den frühzeitigen Austausch sind vielfältig – UBA empfiehlt Mindesthaltbarkeit.* Abgerufen am 15. Februar 2016 von Umweltbundesamt.de: https://www.umweltbundesamt.de/presse/pres seinformationen/elektrogeraete-werden-immer-kuerzer-genutzt

Unispiegel. (01. Dezember 2000). *BEGEGNUNG IM OFFENEN RAUM* . (Der Spiegel) Abgerufen am 16. Februar 2016 von http://www.spiegel.de/spiegel/unispiegel/d-17993053.html

University of Southampton. (2016). *Eternal 5D data storage could record the history of humankind* . Abgerufen am 17. Februar 2016 von University of Southampton - Optoelectronics

Research   Center:
http://www.orc.soton.ac.uk/962.html

Upbin, B. (08. Februar 2013). *IBM's Watson Gets Its
First Piece Of Business In Healthcare.* (F.
Magazin, Produzent) Abgerufen am 24.
Januar 2016 von Forbes Tech:
http://www.forbes.com/sites/bruceupbin/2013/
02/08/ibms-watson-gets-its-first-piece-of-
business-in-healthcare/#1db6d13d44b1

Usländer, T., Pfrommer, J., & Schleipen, M. (2014).
*Das Internet der Dinge in der Automation –
Anforderungen und Technologien.*
(Fraunhofer IOSB) Abgerufen am 25. Januar
2016 von fraunhofer.de:
Informationsmanagement und Leittechnik :
http://akme-
a2.iosb.fraunhofer.de/EatThisGoogleScholar/d
/2014_Das%20Internet%20der%20Dinge%20
in%20der%20Automation%20-
%20Anforderungen%20und%20Technologien
.pdf

Vallancey, S. (14. September 2015). *Elon Musk plans
launch of 4000 satellites to bring Wi-Fi to
most remote locations on Earth* .
(Independent) Abgerufen am 07. März 2016
von Independent:
http://www.independent.co.uk/life-
style/gadgets-and-tech/news/elon-musk-plans-
launch-of-4000-satellites-to-bring-wi-fi-to-

most-remote-locations-on-earth-
10499886.html

VATM / Dialog Consult. (21. 10 2015). *17. TK-Marktanalyse Deutschland 2015: Ergebnisse einer Befragung der Mitgliedsunternehmen im Verband der Anbieter von Telekommunikations- und Mehrwertdiensten e. V. im dritten Quartal 2015* . (Dialog Consult / VATM) Abgerufen am 28. März 2016 von VATM: http://vatm.de/fileadmin/pdf/pressemitteilunge n/TK-Marktstudie_2015_211015.pdf

Vehlow, M., & Golkowsky, C. (März 2013). *Cloud Computing: Evolution in der Wolke.* (PricewaterhouseCoopers AG Wirtschaftsprüfungsgesellschaft) Abgerufen am 04. Januar 2016 von PricewaterhouseCoopers AG Wirtschaftsprüfungsgesellschaft: https://www.pwc.de/de/prozessoptimierung/as sets/evolution-in-der-wolke-reifegrad-der-cloud-services-steigt2.pdf

Vehlow, M., Resetko, A., Regener, I., Opfermann, E., Helios, O., Herter, R., . . . Thier, K.-F. (Juni 2015). *Cloud Governance in Deutschland - eine Standortbestimmung.* Abgerufen am 07. Januar 2016 von PricewaterhouseCoopers: http://www.pwc.de/de/prozessoptimierung/ass

376

ets/cloud-governance-eine-
standortbestimmung-2015.pdf

Venkataraman Krishnamurthy, T., & Shetty, R.
(2014). *4G: Deployment Strategies and
Operational Implications*. New York, USA:
Apress.

Verge, J. (23. Juli 2015). *The IoT Standards Wars* .
Abgerufen am 29. Januar 2016 von Data
Center   Knowledge:
http://www.datacenterknowledge.com/archive
s/2015/07/23/the-iot-standards-war/

Voß, O. (10. Februar 2016). *Dropbox will deutsche
Kundendaten nicht mehr in den USA
speichern* . Abgerufen am 10. Februar 2016
von andelsblatt GmbH - ein Unternehmen der
Verlagsgruppe Handelsblatt GmbH & Co.
KG:
http://www.wiwo.de/unternehmen/it/datensch
utz-dropbox-will-deutsche-kundendaten-nicht-
mehr-in-den-usa-speichern/12942732.html

Wächter, M. (17. November 2016). *Mobile Strategy:
Marken- und Unternehmensführung im
Angesicht des Mobile Tsunami*. Wiesbaden:
Springer Gabler. Abgerufen am 28. März
2016   von   Stern:
http://www.stern.de/digital/smartphones/esim-
-so-wollen-telekom--apple-und-samsung-die-
sim-karte-abschaffen-6560790.html

Walters, M. (25. September 2015). *Big-Data-Projekte effizient umsetzen.* (Vogel Business Media) Abgerufen am 13. Februar 2016 von Big Data Insider: http://www.bigdata-insider.de/big-data-projekte-effizient-umsetzen-a-502903/

Warislohner, F. (23. März 2016). *Die Digitalisierung der Verwaltung: Vom Online-Formular zu staatlichem Big Data?* Abgerufen am 23. März 2016 von Netzpolitik.org: https://netzpolitik.org/2016/die-digitalisierung-der-verwaltung-vom-online-formular-zu-staatlichem-big-data/

Warnecke, H. J., Bullinger, H.-J., & Westkämpfer, E. (1996 und 2003). *Neue Organisationsformen im Unternehmen: Ein Handbuch für das moderne Management (2., neu bearbeitete und erweiterte Auflage).* (J. Nieman, P. Balve, & S. Bauer, Hrsg.) Heidelberg: Westkämpfer, Engelbert (Hrsg.); Springer-Verlag.

Warren, D., & Dewar, C. (Dezember 2014). *Understanding 5G: Perspectives on future technological advancements in mobile.* (GSMA Intelligence) Abgerufen am 24. Januar 2016 von GSMA Intelligence: https://gsmaintelligence.com/research/?file=1 41208-5g.pdf&download

Weber, M. (2010). *Cloud Computing – Was Entscheider wissen müssen: Ein ganzheitlicher Blick über die Technik hinaus Positionierung, Vertragsrecht, Datenschutz, Informationssicherheit, Compliance.* (Bitkom) Abgerufen am 8. April 2016 von Bitkom: https://www.bitkom.org/Publikationen/2010/L eitfaden/Leitfaden-Cloud-Computing-Was-Entscheider-wissen-muessen/BITKOM-Leitfaden-Cloud-Computing-Was-Entscheider-wissen-muessen.pdf

Weber, T. (o. J.). *Industrie 4.0 - große Chancen für neue Arbeitsplätze .* (VDMA) Abgerufen am 16. Februar 2016 von VDMA: http://industrie40.vdma.org/article/-/articleview/7701840

Weberschläger, M. (2013). *Mobile Payment am Point of Sale: Maßnahmen und Erfolgsfaktoren für eine erfolgreiche Markteinführung.* Hamburg: Diplomica Verlag.

Weckbrodt, H. (5. Oktober 2015). *Was ist Industrie 4.0?* Abgerufen am 16. Februar 2016 von Oiger - Neues aus der Wirtschaft und Forschung: http://oiger.de/2015/10/05/was-ist-industrie-4-0/155895

Weicksel, J., Kriegeskotte, N., & Pentsi, A. (21. Mai 2015). *Starker Schub für Breitbandausbau.* (bitkom) Abgerufen am 20. Januar 2016 von bitkom.org:

https://www.bitkom.org/Presse/Presseinformat
ion/Starker-Schub-fuer-Breitbandausbau.html

Weis, B. X. (2014). *Praxishandbuch Innovation: Leitfaden für Erfinder, Entscheider und Unternehmen (2. Auflage)*. Wiesbaden: Springer Fachmedien.

Weiser, M. (September 1991). *The Computer for the 21st Century*. Abgerufen am 11. April 2016 von Universtität Paris Sud: https://www.lri.fr/~mbl/Stanford/CS477/paper s/Weiser-SciAm.pdf

Weiss, H. (03. Februar 2012). *"Predictive Maintenance": Vorhersagemodelle krempeln die Wartung um* . (VDI Verlag) Abgerufen am 21. Februar 2016 von ingenieur.de: http://www.ingenieur.de/Themen/Forschung/P redictive-Maintenance-Vorhersagemodelle-krempeln-Wartung-um

Weiß, M., & Zilch, A. (2014). *Status und Zukunft von Industrie 4.0 aus Unternehmenssicht*. (Experton) Abgerufen am 18. Februar 2016 von Experton Group: http://www.experton-group.de/index.php?eID=dumpFile&t=f&f=7 61&token=68c24c9a22ad64275153219bbc00 403833db851d

Wendehorst, T. (26. März 2013). *Hohe Datenqualität schafft Mehrwert für Unternehmen* . Abgerufen am 13. Februar 2016 von http://www.computerwoche.de/a/hohe-datenqualitaet-schafft-mehrwert-fuer-unternehmen,2515711

Wi-Fi Alliance. (04. Januar 2016). *Wi-Fi Alliance® introduces low power, long range Wi-Fi HaLow*. (E. Suthers, Produzent, & Wi-Fi Alliance) Abgerufen am 21. Januar 2016 von Wi-Fi Alliance: The worldwide network of companies that brings you Wi-Fi: http://www.wi-fi.org/news-events/newsroom/wi-fi-alliance-introduces-low-power-long-range-wi-fi-halow

Wilde, D. K., & Hippner, H. (2004). *Grundlagen des CRM: Konzepte und Gestaltung (1. Auflage)*. Wiesbaden: Betriebswirtschaftlicher Verlag Dr. Th. Gabler/GWV Fachverlage.

Wilde, D. K., & Hippner, H. (2006). *Grundlagen des CRM: Konzepte und Gestaltung (2., überarbeitete und erweiterte Auflage)*. Wiesbaden: Betriebswirtschaftlicher Verlag Dr. Th. Gabler/GWV Fachverlage.

Williams, R. (2014 йил 15-April). *Google embeds cameras in contact lenses to aid the blind*. (Telegraph) Retrieved 2016 йил 10-April from http://www.telegraph.co.uk/technology/google/10766925/Google-embeds-cameras-in-contact-lenses-to-aid-the-blind.html

Williams, R. (2016 йил 7-April). *Samsung's smart contact lens could communicate with smartphones through your eyes*. Retrieved 2016 йил 10-April from The Telegraph: Technology: http://www.telegraph.co.uk/technology/2016/04/07/samsungs-smart-contact-lens-communicates-with-smartphone-through/

Willmroth, J. (18. März 2015). *Wer Taxi spielt, muss Taxi sein* . Abgerufen am 03. März 2016 von Süddeutsche Zeitung: http://www.sueddeutsche.de/wirtschaft/uber-verboten-wer-taxi-spielt-muss-taxi-sein-1.2398887

Wimmer, B. (18. Februar 2016). *BMW verunsichert Kunden mit fragwürdigem Datensammeln* . Abgerufen am 23. Februar 2016 von futurezone: Technology News: http://futurezone.at/digital-life/bmw-verunsichert-kunden-mit-fragwuerdigem-datensammeln/181.609.334

Withnall, A. (11. Juni 2014). *Uber registrations 'increase 850%' as black cab drivers stage London protest* . Abgerufen am 03. März 2016 von Independent: http://www.independent.co.uk/news/uk/home-news/uber-sign-ups-increase-850-as-black-cab-drivers-stage-london-taxi-protest-9530061.html

Wocher, M. (26. Februar 2014). *INTERNET DER DINGE: Ein Versprechen für die Zukunft.* Abgerufen am 20. Januar 2016 von Handelsblatt: http://www.handelsblatt.com/unternehmen/it-medien/internet-der-dinge-ueber-allem-schweben-ungeloeste-rechtsfragen/9636674-2.html

Wolfenstetter, K.-D., Bub, U., & Deleski, V. (2015). *Sicherheit im Wandel von Technologien und Märkten: Tagungsband zur vierten EIT ICT Labs-Konferenz zur IT-Sicherheit.* Wiesbaden: Springer Vieweg, Dr. Udo Bub (Hrsg.).

WSTS. (01. Dezember 2015). *WSTS Semiconductor Market Forcast Autumn 2015.* (WSTS) Abgerufen am 19. Januar 2016 von WSTS World Semiconductor Trade Statistics: http://www.wsts.org/content/download/3909/2 6658

Wunderlich, F. (09. März 2016). *Alpha Go spielt wie eine Göttin.* (golem) Abgerufen am 09. März 2016 von golem: IT News für Profis: http://www.golem.de/news/kuenstliche-intelligenz-alpha-go-spielt-wie-eine-goettin-1603-119646.html

Zakharian, S., Ladewig-Riebler, P., & Thoer, S. (1998). *Neuronale Netze für Ingenieure: Arbeits- und Übungsbuch für*

regelungstechnische   Anwendungen.
Wiesbaden: Springer Fachmedien.

Zarnekow, R., Wulf, J., & Bornstaedt, F. v. (2013).
*Internetwirtschaft: Das Geschäft des
Datentransports im Internet.* Heidelberg:
Springer Gabler.

ZDF. (06. August 2015). *Wie Taubblinde sich
mitteilen: Die Lorm-Hand für eine bessere
Zukunft.* (ZDF) Abgerufen am 28. März 2016
von   ZDF.de: http://www.zdf.de/volle-
kanne/praxis-taeglich-die-lorm-hand-
kommunikationsmittel-fuer-taubblinde-
39231930.html

ZEIT Online / rtr, pb. (16. März 2016). *EuGH-Anwalt
stellt die Störerhaftung infrage .* (Zeit Online)
Abgerufen am 8. April 2016 von Zeit Online:
Digital:
http://www.zeit.de/digital/internet/2016-
03/urheberrecht-wlan-stoererhaftung-eugh-
gutachten

ZeitOnline. (19. April 2015). *Ein Grundsatz, der die
IT-Branche seit 50 Jahren antreibt .*
Abgerufen am 10. Januar 2016 von
http://www.zeit.de/digital/2015-
04/moorsches-gesetz-computerchip-50-jahre

Zheng, Y. (2015). *Encyclopedia of Mobile Phone
Behavior.* Hershey, USA: IGI Global.

Zhou, H. (2013). *The Internet of Things in the Cloud: A Middleware Perspective*. Boca Raton, USA: CRC Press Taylor & Francis Group.

Zimmer, T. (17. April 2007). *Verbesserung der Kontexterkennung in Ubiquitären Informationsumgebungen*. Abgerufen am 16. März 2016 von http://digisrv-1.biblio.etc.tu-bs.de:8080/docportal/servlets/MCRFileNodeS ervlet/DocPortal_derivate_00004189/Ediss.pd f?hosts=local

Zivadinovic, D. (18. Februar 2016). *5G-Mobilfunkforschung: Telekom und Huawei erreichen 70 GBit/s im 73-GHz-Band*. (Heise Medien) Abgerufen am 23. Februar 2016 von Heise.de: http://www.heise.de/newsticker/meldung/5G-Mobilfunkforschung-Telekom-und-Huawei-erreichen-70-GBit-s-im-73-GHz-Band-3109841.html

Zonenberg, A. (17. Februar 2016). *Remotely Disabling a Wireless Burglar Alarm* . Abgerufen am 18. Februar 2016 von IO Active: SECURITY SERVICES: http://blog.ioactive.com/2016/02/remotely-disabling-wireless-burglar.html

Zühlke, K. (05. Februar 2016). *Von der Produktdenke zu »Outcome based Services«* . Abgerufen am 05. März 2016 von

http://www.elektroniknet.de/elektronikfertigu
ng/strategien-trends/artikel/127252/